Social Mobilization and Liberal Democracy

Social Mobilization and Liberal Democracy

A Macroquantitative Analysis of Global and Regional Models

Philip Coulter
University of Massachusetts
and Center for Population
Research and Services,
Research Triangle Institute

Lexington Books
D.C. Heath and Company
Lexington, Massachusetts
Toronto London

Library of Congress Cataloging in Publication Data

Coulter, Philip B.
Social mobilization and liberal democracy.

Includes index.
1. Comparative government. 2. Democracy. 3. Social history—1945-
I. Title.
JF31.C68 321.8 74-28972
ISBN 0-669-98053-6

Published simultaneously in Canada.

Printed in the United States of America.

International Standard Book Number: 0-669-98053-6

Library of Congress Catalog Card Number: 74-28972

For Mignon

Contents

List of Figures

List of Tables

Preface

Only recently has it become possible to revive the Aristotelean tradition of cross-national, macroquantitative political analysis. Political scientists have access to data from well over one-hundred nation states, colonies, and territories, which they can draw upon to test and retest old, and generate new, cross-national hypotheses about the important questions of political life. Such material is available thanks to the yeoman service of United Nation's agencies in their data compendia,[1] and the highly skillful and imaginative data collections in *A Cross-Polity Survey*[2] and the *World Handbook of Political and Social Indicators*, volumes one[3] and two.[4] The publication of these data compendia and their accompanying analyses has produced a small but rapidly growing volume of political science literature in cross-national analysis that is clearly in the Aristotelean tradition.

In my view, *The Politics* of Aristotle stands as the first and probably the best of all cross-national empirical political analyses. From 335 to 322 B.C., Aristotle collected a large amount of empirical social, economic, and political data on each of the constitutions or political systems of 158 Greek city-states, including both colonial and metropolitan Greece.[5] The records suggest that he sent his (graduate) students out into the field to gather most of the data, but that he himself collected the data and wrote up the case study of the Athenian political system, obviously the most important of the cases included in his analyses.[6] Not only did Aristotle obtain empirical data from 158 Greek city-states, but he also gathered data on the social institutions, constitutions, political practices, habits or culture, and geography from many non-Greek states in the Mediterranean area. These ranged from Etruria and Rome to Caria and Lybia, and included Marseilles (a Greek colony going back to 600 B.C.), Crete, Rhodes, and Cyprus. Aristotle's data collection, on the basis of which he wrote several books of *The Politics,*[7] covered the entire range of the Greek "Dispersion" and embraced states on the Aegean, Ionian, and Tyrrhenian Seas and in the three continents of Europe, Asia, and Africa.[8] His work can legitimately and accurately be described as empirical, macroquantitative, cross-polity, cross-societal, and cross-continental or cross-cultural.

Aristotle undertook this massive data collection and analysis in order to supply answers to what he considered to be four primary questions that political science must ask—the four main purposes of inquiry:

First, it has to consider which is the best constitution, and what qualities a constitution must have to come closest to the ideal when there are no external factors (e.g., want of means, or unequal distribution of means) to hinder it doing so. Secondly, politics has to consider which sort of constitution suits which sort of civic body. The attainment of the best constitution is likely to be impossible for the general run of states; and the good law-giver and the true statesman must therefore have their eyes open not only to what is the absolute best, but also to what is the best in relation to actual conditions. Thirdly . . . the student of politics must also be able to study a given constitution, just as it stands and simply with a view to explaining how it may have arisen and how it may be made to enjoy the longest possible life. The sort of case which we have in mind is one where a state has neither the ideally best constitution (or even the elementary conditions needed for it) nor the best constitution possible under the actual conditions, but has only a constitution of an inferior type. Fourthly, and in addition to all these functions, politics has also to provide a knowledge of the type of constitution which is best suited to states in general.[9]

Particularly relevant for this study is Aristotle's second purpose of political science, the empirical and practical determination of which kind of polity is best suited to which kinds of societal (social, economic, cultural, geographic, and other) conditions. In *The Politics*, Aristotle focused his philosophical and scientific skills on the empirical data in order to answer all four questions. The result is a classical and timeless masterpiece of political analysis. We know that Aristotle was, as a political scientist, responsible for the organization and use of a large cross-national data archive. One wonders what he would do as a political scientist if he were practicing his craft today. Or what would he have done or done differently around the period 335 to 422 B.C. if the Lyceum had had a modern computer system and if the disciplines of applied mathematics and statistics had been as practical and applicable to social analysis as they are today?

There are some rather important contemporary social scientists and philosophers who strongly maintain that both quantification and comparison in political analysis are either impossible or foolhardy or both. It seems to me that to argue such a position in the face of the analyses in Aristotle's *The Politics* is to engage in winchful thinking.[10] The cross-polity analyses in *The Politics* stand as a constant and impressive reminder of the possibility and the usefulness of cross-national political investigation. It was partially in an effort to demonstrate that point that this present investigation was undertaken. The Aristotelean tradition of political research (cross-national and empirical) has many devotees in contemporary political science.

Chapter 1 of this study sets out both conceptual and operational definitions of the two major phenomena of concern—democracy and social mobilization. In addition, certain justifications for considering these definitions and phenomena to be important are underscored. In this context, the theoretical framework and central hypotheses are discussed. Also, considerable attention is given to a description of many of the 85 nation-states with respect to their liberal democratic practices (political competitiveness, mass participation, and public liberties) and social-mobilization characteristics. Finally, the empirical connections among liberal-democratic variables and among social-mobilization variables are explored, and some of the problems of analysis are introduced.

In Chapter 2, the global empirical analysis is presented, that is, the relationships between social-mobilization and liberal-democracy variables for all 85 nations are examined in an effort to test the basic hypotheses. The purpose is to determine if social mobilization seems to be related to liberal democracy, and if so, which aspects of these two variables seem to be most closely associated. The model employed to this end is a multiple correlation and regression model, with its array of simple, partial, and multiple regression coefficients. Basically, the analysis shows that there is a fairly close association between social mobilization and liberal democracy. Yet there is deviation and there are deviant cases; these latter phenomena are investigated in detail. Finally, at the end of Chapter 3, the numerous findings are summarized in the form of 26 hypotheses that are supported or suggested by the data in the global-model analyses.

Chapter 4 serves as an introduction to the four subsequent chapters, each of whic treats the relationship between social mobilization and liberal democracy in the nations of a particular geocultural region of the world. This introduction defines and discusses the concepts of geocultural regionalism and political tradition, describes the four regions in terms of the relevant variables, and presents some arguments in support of the prima facie logical importance of geocultural regionalism in an analysis of this kind. Basically, it is hypothesized that the distinctive political tradition of a geocultural region determines the nature of the relationship between social mobilization and liberal democracy and makes this relationship similar to or different from that same relationship at the global level of analysis. The next four chapters examine the theory in the Anglo-European, Iberic-Latin, African, and Near and Far Eastern geocultural regions respectively. The relevant similarities and differences of each regional model with the global model are described. In addition, the principal characteristics of the political tradition of each region are discussed and related to the kind of association between social mobilization and liberal democracy found there. Without trying to anticipate the actual findings of these four chapters, the evidence strongly suggests that geocultural regionalism and the political traditions of regions do provide the relevant context in which social mobilization does or does not produce liberal democracy. Essentially, the results of the analyses suggest that the influence of secular liberalism in Anglo-Europa, corporatism in the Iberic-Latin region, communalism in Africa, and a unique cultural bifurcation of political traditions in the Near and Far East are largely responsible for conditioning the relationship between social-mobilization and liberal-democratic practices. That is to say, social mobilization produces or fails to produce the anticipated political consequences, in this case liberal democracy, because of the political traditions in each of the major geocultural regions of the world.

Chapter 8 presents a summary of the global and regional models and further explores the utility of geocultural regionalism and political tradition as concepts in cross-national political analysis. In addition, Chapter 8 presents the theory or strategy of political development that emerges from the analysis of global and geocultural regional models. Essentially, the strategy by which primitive communal politics begin to develop and modernize is the corporatization of communalism. The strategy through which traditional corporatist polities can develop and modernize is the adoption of what I call tutelary liberalist-socialist democracy. To support the logic of the theory, I present considerable empirical evidence from two countries—Tanzania and Peru—whose political development and modernization are following the strategies. Common elements of the two strategies are identified and suggested as essential to the manifestation of liberal democracy as a consequence of social mobilization. In the end, we are left with more questions than answers, but hopefully the results of this analysis suggest where some of the answers may lie.

The following people gave generously of their time and skill either in critically discussing various ideas in this book with me and/or reading and reacting to earlier parts of the manuscript: Martin Doornbos, Frits Wils, E.V.W. Vercruijsse, and J.F. Glastra von Loon, all of the Institute of Social Studies, The Hague, The Netherlands; Harvey Kline, Howard Wiarda, and Michael Ford, all of the University of Massachusetts; and Jorgan Rasmussen of Iowa State University. Walter Smolensky of the University of Massachusetts Computing Center provided valuable assistance in programming and computation. I deeply appreciate the insightful contributions of each of these friends and colleagues to the completion of the book; however, full and final responsibility remains with me.

1 Framework for Analysis: Theory and Research Design

The purpose of this chapter is to introduce the theoretical and conceptual framework for analysis. The substantive and operational definitions of democracy and social mobilization are established; the theory relating these two phenomena is discussed; and the major hypotheses to be examined empirically are listed and their implications described.

Liberal Democracy

The term liberal democracy is conceptually defined in terms of three separate but related continuua—political competitiveness, mass political participation, and public liberties.[1] Liberal democracy is the political organization of a nation-state[2] characterized by comparatively greater levels of competitiveness, participation, and liberties; that is, a liberal democracy is pluralistic with regard to competitiveness, inclusive with regard to participation, and libertarian with regard to liberties.[3] On the opposite end of each of these three continuua are polities which are monopolistic, exclusive, and coercive with respect to competitiveness, participation, and liberties. Admittedly, there are other important dimensions of liberal democracy, but these three are offered as crucial and necessary.[4] So when we examine liberal democracy, we are actually examining the variation of nations on each of these three dimensions and in terms of the three dimensions combined. The purpose is to attempt to explain such variation cross-nationally with respect to patterns of social mobilization.[5] Although there is a priori presumption of some degree of empirical coherence or association among the three conceptually distinct dimensions, it is possible for a nation to rank high on two of the dimensions and considerably lower on the third, and so forth, with other inconsistent combinations among the three. The following operationalization of the concepts will help to clarify their meaning and later use.

Political Competitiveness is operationally defined in the manner suggested by Phillips Cutright.[6] Each nation is allocated a number of points for each year (of a 21 year period) on the basis of whether it has politically manifested certain characteristics of competitiveness. If the nation had a legislature in which the lower or only house had representatives of more than one party and the minor party or parties had at least 30 percent of the vote, it was given two points. If the 30 percent criterion was not met, it was given one point. Any other condition was assigned no points. Secondly, if a nation had a chief political executive who was in office by virtue either of a direct vote in an open election in which he faced competition, or through selection by a party in a two- or more-party system, it received one point. Any other condition received no points. Thus the maximum total for any given year is three points, and the maximum total for the 21 year period is 63 points. This dimension is based on the degree to which nations create and sustain over time a pluralistic competitive political party system with open elections, as reflected in the composition of the national legislature and the selection of the national chief executive. Three examples illustrate the range of variation: Denmark received a maximum score of 63 points; Turkey received 38 points; and Afghanistan received zero points on the liberal-democratic dimension of competitiveness.

Participation is measured simply as the percentage of the voting age population that voted in the national elections held nearest to the year 1960.[7] In some cases, there were no elections held during the 20 year period, so the percentage for those cases is zero.

Public liberties, the third dimension of liberal democracy, is defined in terms of four separate criteria developed by Arthur S. Banks and Robert B. Textor in *A Cross Polity Survey:*[8] degree of freedom of the press, degree of freedom of group opposition, political participation by the military, and the political role of the police.

With regard to freedom of the press, if a nation was classified by Banks and Textor as having complete freedom of the press, that is, no censorship or government control of either the domestic press or foreign correspondents, four points were awarded to it. If a country's press freedom was categorized as intermittent, with occasional or selective censorship of either domestic press or foreign correspondents, it was given three points. Two points were given to a nation in which press freedom was internally absent, where there was strict domestic censorship with no restraint on foreign newsgathering, or selective cable-head censorship. One point was allocated to nations where freedom of the press was internally and externally absent, with strict direct or indirect censorship or control, domestic and foreign.

Degree of freedom of group opposition is similarly used to award points to each nation. Four points were given to nations where autonomous groups are free to enter politics and are able to oppose government (save for extremist groups, where banned); three points were awarded where autonomous groups are free to organize in politics, but are limited in capacity to oppose the government (which includes absorption of actual or potential opposition leadership into the government); two points were given where autonomous groups are tolerated informally and outside politics; and one point was allocated where no genuinely autonomous groups are tolerated.

With regard to political participation by the military, whenever Banks and Textor classified a nation as having an "interventive" military, that is, one which presently exercises or had recently exercised direct power, three points were awarded. Two points were given to nations with "supportive" military participation, where the military performs a parapolitical role in support of a traditionalist, authoritarian, totalitarian, or modernizing regime. One point was given to national militaries that are neutral—that are apolitical or of minor political importance.

When the role of the police is characterized as politically significant, with important continuing or intermittent political functions in addition to law enforcement, two points were awarded; one point was given to each police role that was not politically significant, such as that confined to law enforcement only. Thus, scores on the public-liberties dimension range from a maximum of 13 to a minimum of four.

Finally, the concept of liberal democracy is defined as the combination of high levels of political competitiveness, popular participation, and public liberties. The raw scores of each nation on each of the three dimensions were *T*-scored,[9] and these *T*-scores were used in all statistical computations. To compute the liberal democracy score for the 85 nations, each nation's scores on the three separate dimensions was summed, and the sums for all nations were *T*-scored. This procedure permits the final index of liberal democracy to reflect the relative but unweighted strengths of each of its three separate dimensions. Table 1-1 presents the scores received by each of the nations on each of the three dimensions and for the composite index of liberal democracy. The ranking from one through 85 is based on scores received on the composite index of liberal democracy.

Each of the dimensions of liberal democracy is conceptualized as a continuum along which a group of political systems can be arrayed. With regard to the dimension of political competitiveness, the continuum varies from pluralistic to monopolistic. Polities in which there was no national legislature or in which there was a legislature completely dominated by a single party and with an executive who ruled by virtue of means other than popular or legislative election, exemplify the monopolistic polity. Portugal is an example of the monopolistic polity, while Canada might be cited as a competitive-political system. The continuum of mass participation is at one end highly exclusive—a polity in which only a small select minority (or perhaps none of the public at large, in the case of a nation that holds neither elections nor plebecites) of the total adult population actually votes in national elections. There may be a variety of reasons why such a small percentage of the age-eligible adults does not participate in the national election: formal legal denial of the right to vote, informal threats or suppression, apathy, satisfaction with the status quo, inadequate factual knowledge or cultural norms on the basis of which to make and execute an electoral decision, and so forth.

At the other end of the pole of mass participation is the polity whose electoral processes are inclusive of virtually all citizens or subjects of age to vote. South Africa (blacks) and Switzerland (women until 1971) provide examples of

Table 1-1
National Scores on Competitiveness, Participation, Liberties, and Liberal Democracy

	Liberal Democracy	Competitiveness	Participation	Liberties
1. Netherlands	65.3	63.5	60.7	60.7
2. Belgium	64.7	63.5	59.3	60.7
3.5. Federal Republic of Germany	64.6	63.5	59.0	60.7
3.5. Iceland	64.6	63.5	59.0	60.7
5. New Zealand	64.5	63.5	58.7	60.7
6. Australia	64.3	63.5	58.3	60.7
7. Denmark	64.2	63.5	58.0	60.7
8.5. Austria	64.0	61.2	60.0	60.7
8.5. Sweden	64.0	63.5	57.7	60.7
10. Norway	63.4	63.5	56.3	60.7
11. United Kingdom	63.3	63.5	56.0	60.7
12. Israel	62.9	57.7	61.0	60.7
13. Canada	62.7	63.5	54.6	60.7
14. Finland	62.5	63.5	54.3	60.7
15. Ireland	62.3	63.5	53.9	60.7
16.5. Jamaica	62.2	63.5	53.6	60.7
16.5. Luxemburg	62.2	63.5	53.6	60.7
18.5. Italy	61.2	55.4	59.3	60.7
18.5. U.S.	61.2	63.5	51.2	60.7
20. Japan	60.7	60.0	53.6	60.7
21. Switzerland	60.0	63.5	48.5	60.7
22. Philippines	59.8	63.5	48.2	60.7
23. Greece	58.8	55.0	54.3	60.7
24. France	57.3	55.4	59.7	51.6
25. Nicaragua	57.0	62.4	61.0	42.5
26. Costa Rica	56.2	63.5	51.9	48.6
27. India	56.0	55.4	47.5	60.7
28. Chile	55.8	53.6	51.6	57.7
29. Ceylon	55.6	55.4	49.6	57.7
30. Colombia	55.3	53.1	51.2	57.7
31. Malaysia	55.0	55.4	48.2	57.7
32. Venezuela	54.9	54.6	58.0	48.6
33. Malagasy Republic	54.4	47.6	51.6	60.7
34. Turkey	52.8	53.8	53.9	48.6

Table 1-1 (cont.)

	Liberal Democracy	Competitiveness	Participation	Liberties
35. Mexico	52.2	55.4	41.5	57.7
36. Uganda	51.4	55.4	40.1	57.7
37. Panama	51.1	55.4	48.5	48.6
38. Bolivia	50.6	49.9	46.9	54.6
39. Uruguay	49.6	39.1	49.2	60.7
40. Gabon	49.4	39.1	61.0	48.6
41. Indonesia	49.3	42.2	60.7	45.5
42. Dominican Republic	49.1	39.1	51.2	57.7
43. Cameroun	49.0	39.1	53.9	54.6
44. Brazil	48.9	57.7	41.1	48.6
45. Ecuador	48.2	49.2	39.1	57.7
46. Trinidad-Tobago	48.1	55.4	29.6	60.7
47. Nigeria	47.8	47.2	43.1	54.6
48. Ivory Coast	47.4	39.1	62.4	42.5
49. South Africa	47.0	61.6	33.0	48.6
50. Poland	46.8	39.1	61.0	42.5
51. Yugoslavia	46.5	39.1	60.4	42.5
52. USSR	46.4	39.1	63.1	39.5
53. Hungary	45.4	39.1	61.0	39.5
54. Liberia	45.3	39.1	57.7	42.5
55. Honduras	45.1	48.4	41.8	48.6
56.5. Argentina	45.0	39.1	50.9	48.6
56.5. Bulgaria	45.0	39.1	63.1	36.4
58.5. Czechoslovakia	44.8	39.1	62.7	36.4
58.5. Rumania	44.8	39.1	62.7	36.4
60.5. German Democratic Republic	44.7	39.1	62.4	36.4
60.5. Guinea	44.7	39.1	59.3	39.5
62. Albania	44.4	39.1	61.7	36.4
63.5. Peru	43.5	46.8	42.8	45.5
63.5. Sierra Leone	43.5	39.1	35.4	60.7
65. Tunisia	43.1	39.1	46.5	48.6
66. Dahomey	42.5	39.1	51.2	42.5
67.5. Guatemala	41.3	48.8	38.8	42.5
67.5. Haiti	41.3	39.1	54.6	36.4

Table 1-1 (cont.)

	Liberal Democracy	Competitiveness	Participation	Liberties
69.5. Burma	41.0	39.1	47.9	42.5
69.5. El Salvador	41.0	47.6	39.4	42.5
71.5. Ghana	40.7	44.9	44.5	39.5
71.5. South Korea	40.7	49.2	40.1	39.5
73. Cuba	40.2	41.4	52.9	33.4
74. Paraguay	39.3	46.8	39.4	39.5
75. Syria	38.5	39.1	39.1	45.5
76. Malawi	37.0	39.1	29.6	51.6
77. Tanganyika	36.7	39.1	41.1	39.5
78. Laos	36.3	39.1	40.1	39.5
79. Portugal	35.6	39.1	35.7	42.5
80. Spain	33.0	39.1	29.6	42.5
81. Pakistan	32.3	43.7	29.6	36.4
82. Kenya	31.5	47.2	39.4	21.2
83. Sudan	30.8	40.2	29.6	36.4
84. Iraq	30.3	39.1	29.6	36.4
85. UAR	29.0	39.1	29.6	33.4

exclusive polities; polities such as Poland, the Ivory Coast, and Israel, quite different from each other in other respects, are quite inclusive.

Finally, the dimension of public liberties arrays polities on a continuum in terms of the extent to which they tend to be libertarian or coercive. A libertarian polity, such as Sweden, is one in which the freedoms of press and group opposition and both an apolitical military and police are routine practices. Nations in which these four freedoms are consistently violated and their opposites prevail are coercive. Examples of coercive politics from the sample of 85 nations include the Soviet Union, Kenya, and Cuba.

If each of the three continua of democracy is trichotomized into equal-sized categories of high, moderate, and low, competitiveness then becomes pluralistic, moderate, and coercive; participation is divided into inclusive, moderate, and exclusive; and public liberties is libertarian, moderate, and coercive. Then, since there are three continuua (one for each component of liberal democracy) and three sub-types on each continuua—high, moderate, and low—there are 27 theoretically possible types of political regimes. The 27 possible types are constructed through the various combinations of three dimensions of democracy and three subtypes for each dimension.[10] The empirical data indicate that only 19 of the regime types are exemplified by one or more of our 85 countries. Of these 19, only 10 regime types are exemplified by at least three nations. The four prominent categories deserve further elaboration, since they will be used in a later analysis of the relationship of social mobilization to liberal democracy. Table 1-2 lists the liberal-democratic regimes.[11]

These 17 nations rank in the upper one-third of the 85 nations on all three dimensions of democracy and are, therefore, classified as liberal-democratic regimes. Conspicuous by its absence is the United States, whose presidential electoral turnout is proportionally too low to place it in the top one-third of the participation dimension. With the exception of Jamaica, Japan, and Israel, all the nations are Anglo-European.

The second largest group, in Table 1-3; consists of nations that rank in the lower third of competitiveness and liberties, but in the top third on the dimension of participation. They are modern-hegemonic regimes.

Nine of the 13 nations listed in Table 1-3 are in the Soviet orbit of eastern Europe, including the Soviet Union itself, and four are not. These nations might be called highly politically mobilized in that relatively large proportions of their citizens turn out to vote in elections in which only one party is involved.

The third largest grouping consists of the 11 nations that rank in the lower third on all three dimensions, traditional-hegemonic regimes. (See Table 1-4.)

Asian and African nations are predominant in this list of traditional-hegemonic regimes; the other three fall into the Latin-Iberic tradition (Spain, Portugal, and Paraguay).

The fourth largest grouping is composed of seven nations (Table 1-5) that are moderate in competitiveness and participation, but highly libertarian. As such, they display liberal-democratic tendencies.

Table 1-2
Liberal-Democratic Regimes: Pluralistic, Inclusive, and Libertarian

1. Australia	10. Jamaica
2. Austria	11. Japan
3. Belgium	12. Luxembourg
4. Canada	13. Netherlands
5. Denmark	14. Norway
6. Finland	15. Sweden
7. Iceland	16. United Kingdom
8. Ireland	17. West Germany
9. Israel	

Table 1-3
Modern-Hegemonic Regimes: Monopolistic, Coercive, but Inclusive

1. Albania	7. Hungary
2. Bulgaria	8. Ivory Coast
3. Czechoslovakia	9. Liberia
4. East Germany	10. Poland
5. Guinea	11. Rumania
6. Haiti	12. USSR
	13. Yugoslavia

Table 1-4
Traditional-Hegemonic Regimes: Monopolistic, Exclusive, and Suppressive

1. Ghana	7. Portugal
2. Iraq	8. Korea
3. Kenya	9. Spain
4. Laos	10. Sudan
5. Pakistan	11. United Arab Republic
6. Paraguay	

Table 1-5
Putative-Liberal Democracies: Moderately Competitive and Participatory, Highly Libertarian

1. Bolivia	4. Colombia
2. Ceylon	5. India
3. Chile	6. Malaysia
	7. Mexico

All other theoretically possible subtypes contain four or fewer empirical examples, e.g., the moderately participatory but pluralistic and libertarian Philippines, Switzerland, and United States; or the moderately competitive and libertarian but highly inclusive Turkey, France, and Venezuela.

Although it might logically be expected that at least under certain conditions the three separate dimensions of liberal democracy cluster together—that is, nations that tend to be high on one dimension tend to be high on the other two—this is certainly not always the case. The causes and correlates of cross-national coherence of these three dimensions is explored in Chapter 3.

For the moment, the degree of coherence is simply documented in the form of the matrix of intercorrelations among four measures of liberal democracy, the three separate indices, and the composite index. (See Table 1-6.)

Competitiveness and public liberties are strongly related in Table 1-6, with a simple correlation coefficient of 0.71. However, neither competitiveness nor liberties is closely associated with popular participation, the weak correlations being 0.20 and 0.19 respectively. They are, however, positive even though weak. Not surprisingly, competitiveness and liberties are most strongly associated with the composite measure of liberal democracy (0.84 and 0.83 respectively), followed by participation at a fairly strong 0.61. It is easy to see that the three dimensions of liberal democracy can be considered conceptually distinct; the correlations indicate that the dimensions also tend to be more or less empirically distinct. The extent of covariance between dimensions ranges from 3.6 percent (participation and liberties, $r = 0.19$) to 50.4 percent (liberties and competitiveness, $r = 0.71$). Evidently, the conceptual dimensions of democracy postulated do have cross-national empirical manifestations that are distinct, yet interrelated, but not identical.[12]

Social Mobilization

Karl Deutsch coined the term "social mobilization" and gave it a substantive meaning, an operational definition, and political importance. *Social mobilization* is defined by Deutsch as "the process in which major clusters of old social, economic, and psychological commitments are eroded or broken and people become available for new patterns of socialization or behavior."[13] It is what happens to large numbers of people in areas that undergo the process of modernization. As a consequence of modernization, it occurs in two stages: (1) the stage of uprooting or breaking away from old habits, customs, values, settings, and commitments; and (2) the induction of the mobilized persons into new patterns of group membership, organization, and commitment. Thus groups of people are mobilized out of or from their conventional and traditional past

Table 1-6
Matrix of Intercorrelations Among Measures of Liberal Democracy for 85 Nations

	Competi-tiveness	Partici-pation	Liberties	Liberal Democracy
Competitiveness	1.00	0.20	0.71	0.84
Participation	–	1.00	0.19	0.61
Liberties	–	–	1.00	0.83
Liberal democracy	–	–	–	1.00

and into new patterns of values, socialization, and behavior. Modernization produces social mobilization, which Deutsch suggests can be measured by the following indicators: percentage of the population (1) that is exposed to important aspects of modern life, (2) that is exposed to the mass media, (3) that has changed the location of their residence, (4) that are living in towns (or cities of a certain size), (5) that are employed in nonagricultural occupations, (6) that are literate, and finally, by the net national product or per capita gross national product. With regard to indicator No. 1, Deutsch suggests such modern aspects of life as demonstrations of machinery, buildings, consumer goods, governmental or medical practices, etc.[14]

According to Deutsch, the processes of social mobilization and the indicators used to measure its extent have eight important characteristics—coherence, reinforcement, identification, thresholds, threshold correlation, positive relationships, interchangeability, and political consequences. First, the processes of social mobilization tend to have coherence, that is, they go together, in certain historical situations and stages of economic development. This is true in part because of a second feature of the process, that each of its parts tends to reinforce the effects of the other in a pattern of feedback or circular causation. Third, the process is identifiable and recurrent cross-nationally. Fourth, social mobilization is characterized both by thresholds and an association among the thresholds of individual indicators or forms or recommitment. Deutsch speaks of a *threshold of significance*, which refers to "the numerical value below which no significant departure from the customary workings of a traditional society can be detected and no significant disturbance appears to be created in its unchanged functioning."[15] There can be increases in the levels of various social indicators below the threshold of significance, and no social mobilization occurs; however, once the threshold is reached (Deutsch suggests 80 percent for literacy rate, for example), mobilization and change begin. The *threshold of criticality* is the level at which social indicators begin to produce changes in the actual or apparent side effects of social mobilization—changes in social or political side effects. In addition, for example, literacy-rate increase has no effect on birth rate until the former reaches 80 percent, at which point birth rate tends to decrease as literacy rate increases.

Fifth, although the thresholds of various indicators are not identical in quantitative terms, they do tend to be related to each other. Thresholds of significance and criticality are different but correlated. It could be that most nations that have literacy rates of 80 percent or more also tend to have urbanization levels of 40 percent or more, and that the apparent side effects of literacy at or above the 80 percent mark are observable at or above the 40 percent urbanization level. Sixth, and related to the first characteristic, all the indicators of social mobilization tend to change (increase or decrease) in the same direction but not necessarily at the same rate.

Seventh, the indicators of social mobilization are characterized, at least to a limited extent, by interchangeability; they are intercorrelated to the extent of about 0.60 to 0.80. There can, however, be lags and discrepancies between and among the indicators, for example, between the levels of exposure to mass-communication media and gross national product in per capita dollars. It is these lags and discrepancies that indicate which cases or countries can be considered variant or deviant. It is with regard to certain national political behavior that lags and discrepancies may be important explanatory tools. But more importantly, social mobilization does assume a single underlying process of which particular indicators represent only particular dimensions.

Quite important is the eighth characteristic: social mobilization is significantly correlated with major changes in the political arena. Deutsch identifies at least eight such political changes: (1) the expansion of the politically relevant strata of the population; (2) the institution of changes in the quality of politics by changing the range of human needs (as people are mobilized out of old and into new patterns); (3) the bringing about of increases in the scope of governmental services and functions as a result of increasing pressures stemming from the expansion of the politically relevant strata; (4) the generation of pressures and demands for the transformation of the nature of the political elite, such as the broadening and transformation of their functions, recruitment, and communications; (5) increased political participation, especially in electoral terms, but also in regard to voluntary social and political organization, trade-union movements, riots, uprisings, strikes, etc.; (6) a shift away from parochialism and internationalism to a supra-local but far less than worldwide preoccupation; (7) first, an expansion and then a lesser but significant reduction of the share of the international trade sector in the national economy; and (8) a tendency toward consolidation of culturally and linguistically homogeneous states that lacked unity and the strain or destruction of the unity of culturally and linguistically heterogeneous states that had unity. These and other political tendencies or changes wrought by social mobilization are likely to be more pronounced and more important in the rapid middle stages of the process, between the major lower and upper thresholds. It is in these intermediate states of social mobilization that the cumulative strain on political stability is expected to be most severe.

One final point that Deutsch makes about social mobilization concerns the way in which the indicators that comprise the operational definition are expressed. These (and presumably any other) indicators should be expressed not in terms of the total percentage of the population possessing a certain sociodemographic or ecological characteristic, (e.g., level of literacy), but in terms of the average annual percentage of the total population added to or subtracted from the total share of the population in that category over a period of years (e.g., change in literary rates). That is, the rates of change of social-mobilization indicators are presumably of more explanatory value than the actual levels of social-mobilization indicators. It is more important to know how fast a country or group of countries has been undergoing the transformations of mobilization than to know how mobilized it is, in order to explain national political characteristics as a function of social mobilization.[16]

In elaborating on Deutsch's discussion of social mobilization, S.N. Eisenstadt focuses on three consequences for political life and the reasons for them: (1) the growing extension of the territorial scope, especially through the intensification of legal, administrative, and political centralization; (2) the continual spread of political power to wider groups in society, and (3) the increasing tendency toward democratic or at least populistic political systems.[17] These results of social mobilization are certainly compatible with those of Deutsch; it is Eisenstadt's explanation of how social mobilization produces these results that is important. With increasing levels and rates of social mobilization, there is a characteristic decline of traditional legitimation of the rulers with reference to powers outside their own society (e.g., God, reason, etc.). Slowly replacing this traditional legitimation is the establishment of an ideological and/or institutional accountability of the rulers to the ruled, the latter being slowly acknowledged to be the source of political power and authority. Connected with these two basic changes are the increasing fluidity of political support, increasing degrees of functional, nonideological "interest-oriented" political allegiance, and the weakening and almost disappearance of ascriptive political commitment to any leader or group. Thus, the rulers come to believe that in order to maintain themselves in power and to guarantee support for specific goals and policies that they may pursue, they must constantly seek the political approval of the ruled, or at least the more vocal segments of the population, through elections, plebiscites, and acclamatory surrogates.[18] In short, rulers begin to see the ruled as relevant objects, beneficiaries, and legitimators of public policy. As Eisenstadt expresses the political changes accompanying social mobilization,

> The difference between modern democratic or semi-democratic and totalitarian political systems lies not necessarily in the genuineness of these beliefs, but in the extent to which they are given institutional expression in pluralistic political organizations, in public liberties, and in welfare and cultural policies.[19]

Thus Deutsch and Eisenstadt agree that among the political consequences of social mobilization are several changes which add up to "democratization" of the political system—social mobilization tends to produce democratic-political development.

Of even more direct bearing to this study is the work of Seymour Martin Lipset,[20] Daniel Lerner,[21] and others who have carried on their work;[22] they have been more concerned with the causes of democratic-political development than with the consequences of social mobilization. Nevertheless, although they start the analysis from a different perspective, they come to quite similar conclusions. Lipset originally suggested that, in general, there is a high, positive, linear relationship between socioeconomic development and democratic-political development, and he defined the former in terms of increasing levels of urbanization, education, communication, wealth, and industrialization. Lipset's linear model, and the data he used to test the hypotheses, generally confirmed that increasing levels of any and all of these measures of socioeconomic development tend to produce increasing levels of democratic development. The second, and now more popular, variant of the socioeconomic model is Lerner's consequential model, in which he poses the same socioeconomic variables as producing increasing levels of democracy, but in addition he identifies a particular developmental sequence among four such variables. Lerner's statement of the sequence, in which socioeconomic processes produce increasing levels of democratic development, deserves to be quoted in full:

> The secular evolution of a participant society appears to involve a regular sequence of three phases. Urbanization comes first, for cities alone have developed the complex of skills and resources which characterize the modern industrial economy. Within this urban matrix develop both of the attributes which distinguish the next two phases—literacy and media growth. There is a close reciprocal relationship between these, for the literate develop the media which in turn spread literacy. But, historically, literacy performs the key function in the second phase. Not until the third phase, when the elaborate technology of industrial development is fairly well advanced, does a society begin to produce newspapers, radio networks, and motion pictures on a massive scale. This, in turn, accelerates the spread of literacy. Out of this interaction develop those institutions of participation (i.e., voting) which we find in all advanced modern societies.[23]

Thus, according to the Lerner consequential model, the causal path runs from urbanization, to education, to communications development, to democratic development. Lerner finds that "increases of urbanization tend in every society to multiply national increases in literacy and media participation. By drawing people from their rural communities, cities create the demand for impersonal communications. By promoting literacy and media, cities supply this demand."[24] Urbanization creates the need and opportunity for higher levels of education and literacy, which in turn need media to produce and transmit the new goods that increasingly literate populations can consume. By supplying the demand, the media create additional demands that they seek to fulfill through increased development. And so literacy is further spread at an accelerating rate. Out of this complex interaction of urbanization, literacy, and media emerge institutionalized participation in politics and thus, according to Lerner, the advanced, modern society.[25]

Whether the social-mobilization-democratic-development relationship is viewed from the perspective of what effects social mobilization has or from the perspective of what causes democratic-political development, the basic processes and variables and their relationships are approximately the same, and both sets of researchers are in basic agreement on several key points.

Social mobilization and its resultant political processes can be viewed as a consequence of what Lucian W. Pye calls the diffusion of a "world culture."[26] Pye concludes that social mobilization is a result of modernization: the diffusion of a world culture, the content of which is based on "advanced technology and the spirit of science, on a rational view of life, a secular approach to social relations, a feeling for justice in public affairs, and, above all else, on the acceptance in the political realm of the belief that the prime unit of the polity should be the nation state."[27] It is the diffusion of this world culture that weakens and destroys the structure of traditional societies—the old social, economic, and psychological commitments—but which is not easily able to reconstitute a more modernized society—new forms of commitment—at least not without some tension and chaos. The diffusion began about 400 years ago when European powers first traveled throughout the world to traditional societies, and through colonial rule introduced the seeds of change from a traditional and seemingly changeless order to a modern order that thrives on the absorption of change.[28]

The procedures by which operational measures of processes of social mobilization were constructed are in some ways similar to these used to measure democracy, but more complicated. Five indicators of social mobilization are used: urbanization, education, communication, industrialization, and economic development. For each of these, two kinds of indices are employed—level and rate of change. Each of these five major indices is a combination of several indicators; for example, urbanization includes percentage of the national population in cities of 50,000 or more and in cities of 100,000 or more. And finally, the time period for the level of social mobilization measured is 1960. The rate of change indices are average annual change (almost invariably increases, not decreases) for the period 1946-66. Table 1-7 summarizes the operational definition of the 10 level and rate-of-change indices, and their components. For each index, each of the components was *T*-scored, the *T*-scores summed, and the sum *T*-scored. Table 1-7 presents all of these indices of social mobilization.

These are five indices that measure levels of social mobilization in the year 1960 and five indices that measure rates of change of the processes of social mobilization over the 20 year span of 1946-66. Each of the 10 indices is made up of from two to as many as seven separate indicators or aspects of social mobilization. The 34 indicators that are used to comprise the 10 indices were chosen from a total of 50 separate indicators, 25 of levels and 25 of rates of change of social mobilization. In the cases of both the level and rate indices, the indicators that had the closest relationships (based on Pearsonian correlation coefficients) to the dependent variables (democracy) were chosen, so that some of the indices, (e.g., education) use different indicators in the level and change categories.

Eighty-five nations are included in the study. The selection of cases is based solely on the availability of data; for example, there were 85 countries for which

Table 1-7
Indices of Social Mobilization

Levels of Social Mobilization (1960)

1. Urbanization
   a. Population in cities of 50,000 or more, per capita
   b. Population in cities of 100,000 or more, per capita
2. Education
   a. University school enrollment per 1,000 inhabitants
   b. Total school enrollment per 1,000 inhabitants
   c. Percent literate, 1960
3. Communication
   a. Number of telephones per 1,000 inhabitants
   b. Number of televisions per 1,000 inhabitants
   c. Number of pieces of domestic mail per capita
   d. Newspaper circulation per capita
4. Industrialization
   a. Steel consumption in kilograms per capita
   b. Energy consumption in kilograms per capita
   c. Gross domestic product originating in industrial activity, in U.S. dollars per capita
   d. Industrial percentage of total employed labor force
   e. Ancillary service percentage of total employed labor force
   f. Percent of gross domestic product originating in industry
   g. Percent of gross domestic product originating in ancillary services
5. Economic Development
   a. Gross domestic product per capita, in U.S. dollars
   b. Gross national income in U.S. dollars, per capita
   c. Gross national product in U.S. dollars, per capita

Rates of Social Mobilization (Average Annual Change, 1946-66)

1. Urbanization
   a. Population in cities of 50,000 or more
   b. Population in cities of 100,000 or more
2. Education
   a. Primary school enrollment per 1,000 inhabitants
   b. Secondary school enrollment per 1,000 inhabitants
   c. University school enrollment per 1,000 inhabitants
   d. Total school enrollment per 1,000 inhabitants
   e. Percent literate
3. Communication
   a. Number of telephones per 1,000 inhabitants
   b. Pieces of domestic mail per capita
   c. Newsprint consumption per capita
4. Industrialization
   a. Energy consumption in kilograms per capita
   b. Steel consumption in kilograms per capita
5. Economic Development
   a. Gross national product in U.S. dollars per capita
   b. Gross national income in U.S. dollars per capita
   c. Gross domestic product in U.S. per capita

democracy and social mobilization data were available. The time point or period for which most of the data were gathered was 1960 or a 20 year period, 1950-70 (in the case of competitiveness) or 1946-66 (in the case of social-mobilization variables). Thus an effort was made to collect descriptive data that refer to each country either at a given point in time or a given period in recent history, after World War II.

Deutsch maintains that the indicators of processes of social mobilization tend to be coherent, to cluster; as urbanization processes proceed, they are accompanied by industrialization processes, which are clustered with education processes, and so forth throughout the range of indicators. Presumably, not only levels of social mobilization, but rates of change of social-mobilization indicators tend to be coherent. Deutsch says nothing about the possible relationships between levels and rates of change of social-mobilization indices. Presumably rate of change is, at least in part, a function of level, at least in some circumstances. For example, a nation that is 95 percent literate cannot experience a high, sustained rate of increase in literacy—similarly with urbanization. However, a nation could conceivably have three telephones per capita, or all college graduates, so with regard to certain variables, there is virtually no limit on the range and rate of increase. Table 1-8 presents the matrix of intercorrelations among 10 social-mobilization variables, five relating to levels and five to rates of change of mobilization processes.

Concentrating first on the extent of intercorrelation among levels of social mobilization (the upper left-hand quadrant of Table 1-8), most are fairly closely related. Urbanization and economic development are the weakest, with a correlation coefficient of 0.58. All are positive. Some are quite high, such as the relationship of communication with both industrialization ($r = 0.80$) and economic development ($r = 0.94$). But in general, the intercorrelations among social-mobilization levels, with coefficients ranging from 0.58 to 0.94, are approximately what Deutsch specified. There are, however, some discontinuities in some of the nations included in the study; some nations are highly mobilized on two or three processes and low on another two or three.

The strength of intercorrelation between levels and rates of social-mobilization processes is quite diverse. Urbanization level is only weakly related to urbanization rate ($r = 0.28$) in part because the more urbanized a nation is, the less urbanized it can become after a certain point. It is unrelated to education rate ($r = 0.02$) and only moderately related to communication, industrialization, or economic-development rates. Level of education is similarly related to the five rates indicators. Communication level is very slightly and inversely related to urbanization and education rates. However, communication level is strongly related to communication rate; the higher the level, the greater the rate of communication growth. A similar relationship prevails between communication level and rate of economic development. Communication level is only moderately related to industrialization rate ($r = 0.66$).

Table 1-8
Matrix of Intercorrelations Among 10 Social-Mobilization Indicators

	Levels (1960)					Rates (1946-1966)				
	1	2	3	4	5	6	7	8	9	10
1. Urbanization level	1.00	0.67	0.60	0.60	0.58	0.28	0.02	0.60	0.49	0.54
2. Education level	–	1.00	0.67	0.73	0.70	0.06	0.02	0.63	0.61	0.57
3. Communication level	–	–	1.00	0.80	0.94	–0.08	–0.16	0.90	0.66	0.82
4. Industrialization level	–	–	–	1.00	0.84	–0.06	–0.23	0.74	0.75	0.62
5. Economic-development level	–	–	–	–	1.00	–0.11	–0.11	0.88	0.65	0.83
6. Urbanization rate	–	–	–	–	–	1.00	0.06	–0.08	0.10	–0.10
7. Education rate	–	–	–	–	–	–	1.00	–0.18	–0.23	–0.06
8. Communication rate	–	–	–	–	–	–	–	1.00	0.66	0.84
9. Industrialization rate	–	–	–	–	–	–	–	–	1.00	0.49
10. Economic-development rate	–	–	–	–	–	–	–	–	–	1.00

Industrialization level is negatively and only very slightly related to urbanization (–0.06) and communication (–0.23) rates, fairly strongly related to communication (0.74) and industrialization (0.75) rates, and moderately related to economic-development rate (0.62). Economic-development level is negatively but only slightly related to urbanization or education rates of change, both at –0.11, strongly related to communication and economic-development rates, 0.88 and 0.83 respectively, and moderately related to the industrialization rate at 0.65.

The third comparison, between rates of change, is the most mixed of all. The rate of urbanization is virtually unrelated to the rates of change of other social-mobilization indicators, and negatively in two cases. Similarly, the rate of educational change is evidently unrelated to the other four processes, and in these cases, although the coefficients are quite small, they are uniformly negative. The rate of the spread and development of communications is correlated with neither urbanization nor education rate (–0.08 and –0.18 respectively), but it is moderately correlated with the industrialization rate (0.66) and strongly correlated with the economic-development rate (0.84). The rate of industrialization is virtually unrelated to urbanization and education rates, 0.10 and –0.23 respectively, moderately associated with communication rate (0.66), and only modestly correlated with economic-development rate. Finally, the rate of economic development is strongly associated with only one other indicator of social change—communication rate at 0.84.

In summary, first, the correlation coefficients among levels of social-mobilization processes tend to range from moderate to very high. Second, the degree of association between levels and rates of mobilization varies considerably. Neither urbanization nor education rates tend to be related to any of the other nine levels or rates of social mobilization. They vary independently. However, the other correlations range from modest to rather strong. In general, the higher the levels of social mobilization, the more rapid the rates of increase of communication, industrialization, and economic development over the period 1946-66. But again, distinct discontinuities are evident. Third, the only one of four possible relationships between rates of change that is strong is between communication and economic development; all the others are moderate or weak. Rates of change coefficients also demonstrate prominent discontinuities. It is possible to conclude, tentatively, that there is a tendency toward coherence among the levels and rates of social-mobilization processes, when they are examined cross-nationally. However, disequilibrium among the levels and rates of these processes is strong enough to suggest the thorough examination of the large minority of cases in which coherence is absent. Through the cross-national examination of these deviant cases, important qualifiers to the hypothesis can be devised and the explanatory utility of the theory sharpened.

Some Guiding Hypotheses

In summary, this research examines the political consequences of social mobilization; specifically it hypothesizes that liberal democracy is, at least in part, one consequence of social mobilization. However, social science things are never as simple as they may seem, and this certainly applies to the relationships between social mobilization and liberal democracy. There are numerous complicating factors in this relationship that are to be explored. First, liberal democracy, as herein defined, comprises at least three separate, related, but perhaps contradictory or conflicting dimensions—competitiveness, participation, and liberties. The effects of social mobilization on liberal democracy have to be interpreted in terms of its effects on each of the three dimensions, and the effects on the three dimensions may well differ from one to the next. As Table 2-6 suggests, in global terms, the three dimensions of democracy do tend to cluster, more or less, but the extent of correlation between each of the possible pairs varies considerably. Therefore, it seems quite probable that social mobilization is not related to each dimension in the same fashion, that is, in the same (positive or negative) direction and to the same extent or strength. Nevertheless, even though conceptualizing democracy in three dimensions complicates the analysis, it is necessary in order to capture as much as possible of the full essence of liberal democracy.

A second complicating factor involves the conceptualization of social mobilization. Both levels and rates of social mobilization are included as explanatory factors. Presumably both have consequences for liberal democracy, but the strength of association of each and liberal democracy and the degree to which each has independent effect on liberal democracy are not known. As stated earlier, Deutsch prefers to think of the rate of change of social mobilization as more important as a conditioner of political phenomena. In addition to the inclusion of both levels and rates is the measurement of each in terms of five separate indices (never mind that each index comprises several related variables!). Urbanization, education, communication, industrialization, and economic development—both levels and rates of change—are used to try to explain liberal democracy. Already, the mind boggles at the potential complexity of this system of social-political relationships.

A third set of complications is the introduction of regions into the analysis as a "controlling" nominal attribute. That is, the relationships between levels and rates of social mobilization, on the one hand, and liberal democracy, on the other, can be examined both globally and regionally. Both are cross-national analysis, but the differences are apparent. More is said of this later. Suffice it to say, for the moment, that the global and regional analysis are not expected to produce the same results. Making sense of the differences (and similarities) is complicated.

Although this study is in part exploratory and seeks, therefore, to generate some new hypotheses, it does rest initially on several hypotheses that are adopted to guide the research rather than to place it in a theoretical straightjacket. In support of the theory of social mobilization as posited by Deutsch and Eisenstadt, it is hypothesized here that the processes of social mobilization tend to produce increasingly greater tendencies toward liberal democratization. The higher the levels of urbanization, education, communication, industrialization, and economic development, the greater the tendency toward the development of political competitiveness, participation, and public liberties, that is, liberal democracy. This hypothesis is clear in three of the consequences of social mobilization postulated by Deutsch and Eisenstadt: (1) expansion of the politically relevant strata of the population, (2) increased political participation, and (3) increased tendencies toward democratic or at least populistic control. Second, increasing rates of social mobilization, as measured by the five indices of change, tend to produce increasing tendencies toward the institution of liberal democratic practices. However, it is expected that rates of increase which are too rapid, for example, cases in which the first step of social mobilization—uprooting or breaking away from traditional commitments—is completed but the second stage—induction of persons into new commitments—is delayed, may fail to produce increased tendencies toward liberal democracy. Rather, political instability, chaos, suppression, rebellion, and repression may characterize nations where social mobilization is too slow in creating new habits and loyalties. And in cases where there is pronounced disequilibrium between one or more levels of mobilization or rates of increase (such as between urbanization and industrialization), nondemocratic tendencies may manifest themselves for a considerable time.

The empirical testing of these two straightforward hypotheses seems simple enough. The difficulty as well as the importance of such an enterprise lies in untangling the relationships of three dimensions of democracy, five measures of levels of social mobilization, five measures of rates of change of social mobilization, in one global and four regional perspectives.[29]

2 The Global Model of Liberal Democracy

This chapter discusses the results of a multiple-regression analysis of the relationships between social mobilization and liberal democracy in the global perspective, for all eighty-five nations. Relationships between both the levels and rates of change of social mobilization, on the one hand, and liberal democracy and each of its three components, on the other, are examined. The first purpose is to determine to what extent liberal democracy and its three dimensions are related to levels and rates of social mobilization. The second purpose is to identify sources of disequilibrium and, perhaps, conflict in the complex of relationships brought on by such conditions as the fairly strong positive intercorrelation of two social-mobilization variables (either levels or rates of change), both of which are fairly strongly correlated with liberal democracy, one positively and one negatively; or conditions in which a single indicator of social mobilization is strongly correlated negatively with one dimension of democracy and positively with another. Third, considerable attention is given to an analysis of cases that are most optimal, those which are most over-democratized, and those which are most under-democratized. An *optimal case* is one whose degree of liberal democracy is exactly or very close to that degree predicted by its level (or rate of change) of social mobilization, in the context of the other nations included in the analysis, such as a global model; that is, they deviate very little or not at all from the regression line.[1] *Over-democratized cases* are nations whose level of liberal democracy is considerably greater than that predicted by the regression equation. *Under-democratized nations* are those whose level of liberal democracy is quite a bit lower than that predicted by the regression equation. A scattergram visually presents the distribution of nations about the regression line, and the analysis of residuals (differences between predicted and actual liberal democracy scores) seeks to explain optimality, over-democratization, and under-democratization in terms of social mobilization.

Levels of Social Mobilization

Table 2-1 presents the matrix of simple-correlation coefficients (r), the multiple-correlation coefficients (R), the coefficients of multiple determination (R^2), and the standardized-regression coefficients or beta weights (β) for measures of liberal democracy and measures of levels of social mobilization.

Among the simple correlation coefficients (r), the findings presented in Table

Table 2-1
Simple- and Multiple-Correlation Coefficients for Measures of Liberal Democracy and Levels of Social Mobilization for 85 Nations

	Urbanization		Education		Communication		Industrialization		Economic Development			
	r	*β*	*r*	*β*	*r*	*β*	*r*	*β*	*r*	*β*	*R*	R^2
Competitiveness	0.45	0.09	0.52	0.19	0.61	0.13	0.48	0.27	0.62	0.54	0.65	43%
Participation	0.23	0.16	0.41	0.28	0.40	0.17	0.40	0.11	0.41	0.05	0.46	21%
Liberties	0.35	0.06	0.38	0.06	0.48	0.17	0.40	0.09	0.49	0.32	0.50	25%
Liberal democracy	0.45	0.00	0.58	0.23	0.66	0.21	0.56	0.11	0.67	0.40	0.69	48%

2-1 generally tend to confirm the hypothesis that democratic development is in part a function of levels of social mobilization; there is a moderate positive, relationship between most of the social mobilization indices and of the indices of liberal democracy. For the political-competitiveness dimension of liberal democracy, none of the simple correlations falls below 0.45; the strongest relationship is with economic-development level at 0.62 (and with communication at 0.61). The participation dimension is certainly less stronger associated with social mobilization—hardly at all with urbanization and only moderately with education, communication, industrialization, and economic development at about 0.40. The democratic dimension of public liberties presents a fairly similar case; the correlations are either rather weak (for example, urbanization and education) or only moderate (communication, industrialization, and economic development). Although the general hypothesis is at least weakly confirmed, two additional and perhaps more important points ought to be stressed. First, communication and economic-development indices are far stronger as explanatory (or predictive) variables than the other three measures of social mobilization, at least in the simple-correlation analysis. Particularly with regard to the strength of the correlation between communications development and liberal democracy, the thesis advanced by Daniel Lerner and defended by Donald J. McCrone and Charles F. Cnudde[2] seems to be indirectly upheld; of the first three variables, communication appears to be closer to democratic development. Just slightly stronger is the correlation with economic development, a general indicator of the level of national income and national product. As suggested by social-mobilization theory, certain processes of social mobilization tend strongly to cluster together; in this case, communication and economic development have a simple correlation coefficient of 0.94. This helps to explain in part their strong relationships with measures of liberal democracy. A second point concerns the size of the correlation coefficients between competitiveness and each of the social mobilization indices; this dimension of democratic development is more closely related to social mobilization than the other two. A final point suggests the importance of conceiving of liberal democracy in terms of several dimensions. Variations in the strength of association between the three dimensions of liberal democracy and each of the five social-mobilization indices tends to confirm the supposition described in Chapter 1—that liberal democracy is an extremely complicated phenomenon and that all of its dimensions are not necessarily nor at all times mutually reinforcing or even in harmony. They may in fact be incompatible under certain conditions at certain stages of social mobilization. It is clearly possible, however, for the dimensions of democracy to be compatible under the appropriate conditions. The variations of strength of association presented in Table 2-1 reflect both of these possibilities cross-nationally.

Even though liberal democracy is a complex multidimensional political phenomenon, it is possible to conceive of it in holistic terms, especially with the notion of summarizing the degree to which most people most of the time in a given nation experience varying levels of liberal democracy—in all three of its dimensions. The composite index of liberal democracy is included in Table 2-1 for that purpose. The most pertinent finding with regard to the liberal democracy index is that in all five cases, its relationship with social mobilization is stronger or at least as strong as any of its individual dimensions. The smallest coefficient is that between liberal democracy and urbanization, a moderate 0.45. However, education and industrialization are both stronger at 0.58 and 0.56 respectively. Still stronger are the coefficients of correlation with communication (0.66) and economic development (0.67). It is clear that the three dimensions are additive. Although the three dimensions are not all strongly intercorrelated, when they are added together, the resulting index is more strongly related to social-mobilization indicators than any of the single measures of liberal democracy. Just as social-mobilization theory stipulates that its processes tend to be coherent in developmental terms, liberal-democratic practices also demonstrate a slight tendency to cluster, but there are important exceptions. If the correlation coefficient for each social-mobilization index and the three dimensions are averaged (for example, urbanization with competitiveness, participation, and liberties averages 0.34) and compared with the coefficient of the same social-mobilization index and the index of liberal democracy (for example, urbanization with liberal democracy is 0.45), the latter is in all cases substantially higher than the former. For urbanization it is 0.11 higher (0.45 minus 0.34); for education it is 0.14 higher (0.58 minus 0.44); for communication, 0.16 higher (0.66 minus 0.50); for industrialization, 0.13 higher (0.56 minus 0.43); and for economic development, 0.16 higher (0.67 minus 0.51). In combination, the dimensions of democracy seem to take on added strength and meaning.

However, the beta coefficients included in Table 2-1 permit several important modifications to be made to the general interpretation of the empirical findings. The relationships between levels of social mobilization and dimensions of liberal democracy are neither as simple nor as straightforward as they at first appear. Four particular points stand out when one examines the beta weights that indicate the increase or decrease (in standard deviation units, that is, as a proportion of the standard deviation) in the dependent variable for each one unit increase in a given independent variable. A beta coefficient also takes into account the relationship of each of the other independent variables to the dependent variable in the multiple-regression equation.

First, a one-unit increase in the level of urbanization produces little or no change in the level of any of the three dimensions or in the level of liberal democracy itself. The simple correlations with urbanization are weakest, and so are the beta coefficients. The direct influence of urbanization on democratic-political development, in cross-national perspective, seems to be vastly overrated.[3] In fact, when the influence of other independent variables is taken into account, a one-unit increase in the level of urbanization produces a 0.16 decrease in the level of participation. Urbanization is in reality slightly but negatively related to level of popular participation. Second, the beta coefficients of economic development and measures of liberal democracy are all fairly high—the highest, except for participation. A unit increase in economic development produces a 0.54 unit increase in competitiveness, a 0.32 unit increase in public liberties, and a 0.40 unit increase in liberal democracy. Economic development apparently has virtually no impact on participation with a beta coefficient of 0.05. Again, participation emerges as independent of and, therefore, least well explained by levels of social mobilization.

Third, increase in the level of industrialization produces decreases in competitiveness, liberties, and liberal democracy ($\beta = -0.27$, -0.09, and -0.11 respectively). Although only the competitiveness beta coefficient is moderately strong, when the influence of the other four social-mobilizations variables is held constant, industrialization has a slight negative relationship with all but participation. In addition, it should be noted that industrialization, like urbanization, is related positively to two dimensions of liberal democracy and negatively to one. Thus there is the distinct possibility that a one-unit increase in industrialization produces conflicting consequences, such as greater popular participation and less liberty or less competitiveness.

Closely related to the tension possibly produced by industrialization's positive and negative relationships with different dimensions of liberal democracy is the situation brought about by the relationships of industrialization and economic development with dimensions of liberal democracy and liberal democracy itself. Both of these independent variables have an appreciable independent influence on competitiveness but the beta coefficient for the former is negative, −0.27, and for the latter it is positive, 0.54. The intercorrelation between these two independent variables is 0.84. The implication of this set of relationships is evident. Industrialization and economic development tend, as social-mobilization theory suggests, to be strongly and positively related. As one increases, cross-nationally, the other tends to increase; as one decreases, the other tends to decrease. So the two cluster. Yet, as they cluster, they tend to have opposite effects on level of competitiveness, at least at some levels of social mobilization, viewed cross-nationally. Such a situation is virtually certain to yield tension and disequilibrium.

When all five social-mobilization processes are considered as independent variables, the multiple-correlation coefficients (R) are produced. The order of strength of association between social mobilization and dimensions of liberal democracy is first, competitiveness (0.65); second, political liberties (0.50); and third, participation (0.46); these coefficients indicate that the percent of variation in those dimensions of democracy that is explained by social mobilization processes (R^2) is 43 percent, 25 percent, and 21 percent respectively. Again, it seems that political competitiveness is the dimension of democracy that is most causally sensitive to social mobilization. Finally, Table 2-1 presents the multiple-correlation coefficients for the composite index of liberal democracy and the five independent variables: 0.69, which means that almost half (48%) of the cross-national variation in liberal democracy is accounted for in terms of social-mobilization processes. This leaves about half of the variation in degree of liberal democracy unexplained in terms of the global model. A closer examination of which cases conform most closely to the global-regression model and which deviate most widely (both over-.and under-democratized) and to some reasons why their behavior is either typical or deviant is undertaken in the latter section of this chapter and in later chapters.

Rates of Social Mobilization

Social mobilization theory actually posits that it is not the levels of social mobilization but the rates of change of its processes that are most significantly productive of political consequences, at least in the short-run terms of a period of 20 years. Naturally, increasing rates of change produce increasingly higher levels, and to some extent, the height of the level serves as at least a mild constraint upon the extent to which further increases (and certainly further accelerations of increases) can occur. Yet levels and rates of increases are to some extent independent and at least conceptually distinct. Table 2-2 presents the simple, multiple, and beta coefficients for a cross-national comparison of rates of social mobilization and degrees of liberal democratic development.[4] It should be remembered that the rates of change of social-mobilization processes are average annual change for the period 1946 through 1966.[5] The democratic development indices are either for the year 1960 or summarize the tendency for the period 1950-70.

Examining first the simple correlation coefficients in Table 2-2, it is clear that neither urbanization increases nor education increases are closely related to any of the three liberal-democracy dimensions. Rather, although the association is uniformly weak or nonexistent in these categories, it is a negative relationship; as the rate of urbanization increases there is a very slight tendency for the level of competitiveness to be lower ($r = -0.10$). Increases in the rates of social mobilization in this case tend to be unrelated to each of the three dimensions, with a slight tendency toward depressing the levels of these measures of democracy.

With regard to the competitiveness dimension, however, it is evident that the rates of change of the remaining three social-mobilization processes are more strongly associated. Both communication increases and increases in the rate of economic development are strongly related to competitiveness ($r = 0.65$ and 0.68 respectively), while the relationship of competitiveness and industrialization is weak at 0.26. Rates of increase in communication and economic

Table 2-2

Simple- and Multiple-Correlation Coefficients for Measures of Liberal Democracy and Measures of Rates of Change of Social Mobilization

	Rates of Change of Social Mobilization											
	Urbanization		Education		Communication		Industrialization		Economic Development			
	r	β	r	β	r	β	r	β	r	β	R	R^2
Competitiveness	−0.10	0.00	−0.05	0.00	0.65	0.49	0.26	−0.26	0.68	0.39	0.72	52%
Participation	−0.07	−0.14	0.02	0.17	0.37	0.08	0.51	0.54	0.29	−0.05	0.56	31%
Liberties	0.00	0.11	−0.09	−0.09	0.51	0.33	0.15	−0.33	0.57	0.47	0.63	40%
Liberal democracy	−0.07	−0.01	−0.05	0.04	0.67	0.40	0.41	−0.01	0.67	0.35	0.71	50%

development are only weakly correlated with popular participation (r = 0.37 and 0.29 respectively), whereas increases in the rate of industrialization tend to produce a higher level of electoral turnout (r = 0.51). The pattern of relationship between public liberties and communication, industrialization, and economic development resembles that of competitiveness, although all three measures of association are lower.

When the three measures of liberal democracy are combined into a single index, both urbanization and education rates are negatively but extremely weakly related, hardly an unexpected finding in view of the relationships of these two social-mobilization processes to the individual dimensions of democracy. But both communication increases and economic development increases are fairly closely related to the degree of liberal democracy; as the rates of these two social processes increase, so does the likelihood that degree of liberal democracy is higher. The relationship with industrialization is a modest 0.41.

When using the beta coefficients to assess the relative importance of each of the independent variables in the explanatory regression equation, it is evident, first, that both urbanization and education make only negligible or no contributions. An increase in urbanization rate of one unit produces a slight decrease in the level of participation (–0.14). A one-unit increase in the rate of educational change raises the participation level by 0.17. However, the rate of increase of communications is fairly important in three of the four dependent variables. Increasing the communications rate by one unit results in a 0.49 increase in competitiveness, a 0.33 increase in liberties, and a 0.40 increase in liberal democracy, all in the positive direction. Increasing the communications rate produces no change in the level of participation.

The rate of industrialization is fairly important for competitiveness (β = –0.26); increases tend to depress competitiveness. However, participation increases by 0.54 units when industrialization rates accelerate by one unit. The beta weight for liberties (–0.33) indicates a negative relationship with industrialization, and the beta for liberal democracy, the composite measure, is a –0.01.

Economic-development rate increases of one unit produce increases of 0.39 in competitiveness, 0.47 in liberties, and 0.35 in liberal democracy. Its effect on participation seems insignificant.

By way of summary, it is apparent that different aspects of social-mobilization rates of change have important and variable consequences for liberal democracy and for its three dimensions. Of the five rates of social mobilization, communication and economic development are relatively more important, with industrialization of secondary importance as its rate increases tend to have a depressing effect. In explaining participation levels, industrialization rate is clearly the only factor of importance. Economic-development rate is the most important factor in the regression equation when explaining public liberties; the other four rates have little influence. Finally, liberal democracy as a whole is most closely related to rates of communication and economic development, but not to urbanization, education, or industrialization.

Again the possibilities for disequilibrium and tension arising from contrary and conflicting tendencies produced by different social-mobilization rates are evident. Rates of change of communication and industrialization are fairly strongly intercorrelated ($r = 0.66$), and therefore there is some tendency for increases of one rate to be accompanied by increases in the other rate and similarly with decreases. Yet as they cluster, industrialization rate produces decreases in the level of liberties ($\beta = -0.33$) and communication rate produces increases in the level of liberties ($\beta = 0.47$). This set of relationships certainly makes the achievement of increasingly higher levels of stable public liberties difficult to achieve. Similarly, changes in the rates of industrialization produce strikingly incompatible tendencies with regard to participation ($\beta = 0.54$) and public liberties ($\beta =- -0.33$).

When all five social-mobilization variables are used to explain levels of liberal democracy, it is competitiveness, among the individual dimensions, whose cross-national variations are best accounted for; rates of social mobilization account for 52 percent of the variation in competitiveness. Only 31 percent of the variation in participation and 40 percent of the variation in public liberties are similarly statistically explained. The three-dimensional indicator of liberal democracy is quite strongly influenced by rates of change; the multiple-correlation coefficient is 0.71, exactly half of its variation being explained as a function of changes in social-mobilization processes.

A comparison of the findings in Tables 2-1 (levels) and 2-2 (rates) suggests three tentative conclusions. First, rates of change of social-mobilization processes are more important in explaining liberal democratic development than are levels of social mobilization, at least in the short run. The multiple-correlation coefficients for the change variables are uniformly higher than those of the levels of mobilization. Second, communication and economic-development variables, both levels and rates of these processes, are the two variables most strongly correlated with two of the single dimensions of liberal democracy (competitive and liberties) and with the composite indicator of liberal democracy. Third, of the three dimensions of liberal democracy, competitiveness is clearly the most strongly affected by both levels and rates of social mobilization. In fact, when rates of change are used as the explanatory variables, the explained variation of competitiveness is just slightly greater than that of the composite indicator of liberal democracy. Public liberties follows competitiveness in extent of explained variation, and last is the degree of popular participation. And finally, whether using level or rate-of-change variables, approximately half of the variation in democratic development is accounted for. In the case of both levels and rates of change, popular participation seems to be impervious to the influence of social mobilization; 79 percent of the participation is unaccounted for by levels of social mobilization, and 69 percent is unaccounted for by rates of change. And, given these low degrees of explained variation in participation, the most important variable in each regression equation is different from all the other most important variables. Whereas communications and economic-development levels and rates are most important in explaining competition, liberties, and even liberal democracy, it is education level and industrialization rate that are most important in explaining participation, although only weakly. Some of the sources of this apparent incompatibility have already been suggested. Later in this chapter they are dealt with more fully and attention is given to some of their probable causes.

Relative Influence of Levels and Rates of Social Mobilization

A final question that must be answered with regard to the nature of the relationship of both levels and rates of change to liberal-democratic characteristics concerns the relationship between levels and rates of social mobilization. That is, what is the effect of level of social mobilization on dimensions of democracy when the rate of social mobilization is held constant? Or what is the relationship between the rate of change of a particular process of social mobilization and liberal democracy when the level of social mobilization is held constant?

The best way to determine more exactly the nature of the relationships between social mobilization and liberal democracy is to compute multiple-partial-correlation coefficients.[6] These coefficients reveal the degree of association between a dependent variable and several independent variables while holding constant the effects of several other independent variables. That is, it is possible to determine the degree of correlation between levels of social mobilization and liberal democracy while partialling out or controlling for the influence of rates of change of social mobilization, and similarly, the influence of rates of change of social mobilization on democracy can be computed while holding constant the effects of levels of social mobilization. Table 2-3 contains these computations.

For direct comparability, the first two columns in Table 2-3 contain the multiple-correlation coefficients originally presented in the earlier Tables 2-1 and 2-2—levels and rates of social mobilization correlated with each of the three dimensions of liberal democracy and the composite indicator of liberal democracy. Column three in Table 2-3 presents new multiple-correlation coefficients between each of the measures of democracy and all 10 of the social-mobilization indicators, both levels and rates. By comparing the third column with the first and second columns, it is easy to see that all 10 social-mobilization variables explain very little more of the variation in the dependent variable than does the set of five mobilization-rate variables alone. All 10 variables do, however, account for substantially more of the democratic variation than does the set of five mobilization-level variables. This suggests additional support for what was originally hypothesized: that rates of mobilization are more important than levels of mobilization with regard to political consequences.

Table 2-3
Multiple- and Multiple-Partial-Correlation Coefficient for Levels and Rates of Social Mobilization and Liberal Democracy

	Multiple-Correlation Coefficients			Multiple-Partial-Correlation Coefficients	
	1	2	3	4	5
	Levels	Rates	Levels and Rates	Levels w/Rates Constant	Rates w/Levels Constant
Competitiveness	0.65	0.72	0.75	0.13	0.42
Participation	0.46	0.56	0.58	0.10	0.36
Public liberties	0.50	0.63	0.67	0.03	0.45
Liberal democracy	0.69	0.71	0.73	0.19	0.28

Table 2-4
Simple- and Partial-Correlation Coefficients for Measures of Democracy and Both Levels and Rates of Social Mobilization[a]

	Political Competitiveness		Popular Participation		Public Liberties		Liberal Democracy	
	sim.	par.	sim.	par.	sim.	par.	sim.	par.
Level of:								
Urbanization	0.45	0.28	0.23	−0.04	0.35	0.05	0.45	0.06
Education	0.52	0.29	0.41	0.10	0.38	0.19	0.58	0.27
Communication	0.61	0.03	0.40	0.10	0.48	0.03	0.66	0.08
Industrialization	0.48	0.17	0.40	0.00	0.40	0.23	0.56	0.19
Economic development	0.62	0.10	0.41	0.10	0.49	0.07	0.67	0.13
Rate of:								
Urbanization	−0.10	−0.13	−0.07	−0.02	0.00	0.02	−0.07	−0.06
Education	−0.05	−0.06	0.02	0.10	−0.09	−0.07	−0.05	−0.01
Communication	0.65	0.25	0.37	0.02	0.51	0.17	0.67	0.21
Industrialization	0.26	−0.28	0.51	0.33	0.15	−0.32	0.41	−0.12
Economic development	0.68	0.33	0.29	-0.09	0.57	0.34	0.67	0.28

[a]A partial correlation coefficient for either set of independent variables is based on holding constant the effects of the other set of five independent variables.

The greater effect of rates of change on political life is even more strongly supported through a comparison of columns four and five with columns one and two in Table 2-3. In column four there are four multiple-partial-correlation coefficients, each using five levels of social mobilization as independent variables while controlling for the influence of five rates of mobilization variables. It is rather obvious in all four cases that the size of the coefficients in column one (levels of mobilization correlated with liberal democratic variables) is reduced considerably in column four (levels of social mobilization correlated with liberal democratic variables while controlling for rates of mobilization). When the rate of change is held constant, the level of social mobilization actually has only the slightest impact on competitiveness, participation, or liberties, with multiple-partial coefficients of 0.13, 0.10, and 0.03 respectively. Only in the case of the composite index of liberal democracy could it be argued that levels of social mobilization have any appreciable influence regardless of rates of change. However, even in this case, with a multiple-partial coefficient of only 0.19, the argument is less than compelling.

A comparison of column five with column two in Table 2-3 also demonstrates the extent to which the size of the coefficients of multiple correlation between rates of mobilization and democracy variables is reduced when the influence of levels of mobilization is controlled for. However, the size of the reduction is not as great; in fact, there are some fairly respectable coefficients remaining even when levels of mobilization are held constant. The multiple-partial coefficient between rates and competitiveness, with levels constant, is 0.42; this compares fairly well with the multiple coefficient of 0.72 when the effects of levels were not partialled. Similarly, even when the effects of levels are controlled, the multiple-partial coefficient between participation and rates of mobilization stands at 0.36. The highest multiple-partial is between rates of mobilization and public liberties, 0.45; the lowest is between rates and the composite index of liberal democracy, 0.28.

On the basis of these relationships, it is possible to conclude that not only is rate of change more important than the level of social mobilization with regard to liberal democracy, but that rate of mobilization retains much of its explanatory utility even when the effect of level of mobilization is controlled for. Therefore it seems that motion, not position, on the social-mobilization scale is what is important. The probability that a nation will institute increasingly liberal-democratic practices is enhanced as its rate of social mobilization increases. But, the fact that it has reached a higher level of social mobilization at a slow rate may have very little relationship to its probability of instituting liberal democracy.

These conclusions are well supported by the data in Table 2-3, at least in terms of broad, general processes of social mobilization, rates and levels, in the global model. It is possible to analyze still further the relative influence of levels and rates of social mobilization in terms of specific processes that comprise them, for example, education, communication, etc. The question to be answered here, stated in general terms, is, "What is the strength of influence of the level of a single social-mobilization process (such as, urbanization) when the influence of all five of the mobilization-rates processes is controlled for?" Table 2-4 shows the partial-correlation coefficients that answer questions such as these. For each partial-correlation coefficient between a "level" variable and democracy, all "rate" variables (that is, the rate of social mobilization) are held constant. For each partial correlation coefficient between a "rate" variable and liberal democracy, the effects of all "level" variables (that is, the level of social mobilization) have been controlled for. In addition, for the convenience of comparison of simple and partial correlation coefficients, the simple correlation coefficients from Tables 2-1 and 2-2 are also included in Table 2-4.

Selection of an arbitrary cutoff point of 0.25 for partial correlations makes possible the identification of most of the important relationships and simplifies discussion. The first point that emerges from Table 2-4 is, again, the extreme complexity of relationships between and among the social-mobilization and democracy variables. When five measures of both levels and rates of social mobilization are employed, and three separate measures of liberal democracy are used, conceptualizing the relationships is most difficult. However, it is evident from this table that almost all of the simple-correlation coefficients are reduced in size (some drastically) when the effects of the other set of variables are controlled. That is, for example, when a partial between a level variable and democracy is computed, while holding constant the effects of all five rate variables, the partial is considerably smaller than the simple correlation. When a rate variable is correlated with a democratic variable holding constant all level variables, the partial coefficient is smaller than the simple coefficient.

Nonetheless, some of the partial-correlation coefficients remain large enough to suggest several important conclusions. First, regardless of the rate of social mobilization, both urbanization level (0.28) and education level (0.29) appear to have some independent positive effect on the degree of political competitiveness. That is, when rates of social mobilization are held constant, urbanization and education still retain some independent effect on competitiveness, even though considerably less than that suggested by the respective simple-correlation coefficients. Similarly, education level retains some independent effect on liberal democracy when the rate of social mobilization is controlled for (0.27). Otherwise, for all the other moderate-to-strong simple correlations between levels of social mobilization and dimensions of democracy, when rates of social mobilization are held constant, they either disappear or are severely reduced in strength. This applies even to economic-development level, which has the highest simple correlations with democracy.

Although the strength of correlation between rates of social mobilization and democracy also tends to be appreciably reduced when levels of social mobilization are held constant, the reduction in the size of the correlations is neither as complete nor as great. Seven of the partials remain at or above the arbitrary 0.25. Regardless of the level of social mobilization, both communication and economic-development rates have an independent, positive effect, and industrialization rate has an independent negative effect, on political competitiveness, with partial coefficients of 0.25, 0.33, and –0.28 respectively. No matter what the level of social mobilization, fast rates of industrialization tend to produce a slight decrease in political competitiveness. Likewise, no matter what the level of social mobilization, high rates of communication and economic development tend to produce a slight increase in competitiveness.

Popular participation seems to be a function of only one rate of social-mobilization variable, when level of social mobilization is held constant. Regardless of the level of social mobilization, industrialization rate has independent positive relationship with participation (0.33).

With regard to public liberties, if levels of social mobilization are held constant, industrialization rate retains an independent negative effect (–0.32), and economic development retains an independent positive effect (0.34). Finally, only economic-development rate seems to have an independent effect on liberal democracy when the effects of social-mobilization level are controlled; the partial there is 0.28.

The hypothesis is confirmed: rates of social mobilization have more important political consequences than levels of mobilization. However, several significant qualifications to and extensions of this basic proposition, as revealed in Tables 2-3 and 2-4, need to be added in order to strengthen the explanatory theory. First, although rates of mobilization are more important than levels, the levels of urbanization and education remain fairly important for political competitiveness, even when the influence of rates of mobilization is partialled out; the partial coefficients are 0.28 and 0.29 respectively. Second, with regard to liberal democracy, education level retains importance (a partial of 0.27), even when the influence of rates of mobilization are controlled for. The independent influence of education and industrialization level on public liberties might be mentioned (partials of 0.19 and 0.23), but otherwise, the influence of levels of social mobilization virtually disappears when the rate of change of mobilization is controlled for. Third, given that rates of social mobilization are more important than levels, it is mainly the influence of communication, industrialization, and economic-development rates that is most important, when level of mobilization is held constant. Political competitiveness is independently effected by all three of these rates of change. Mass participation is independently affected by industrialization. Industrialization and economic development have strong independent effects on public liberties; the former is negatively related to liberties, the latter positively. Fourth, when the level of mobilization is held constant, liberal democracy is independently influenced mainly by economic-development rate and to a lesser extent by communication rate. Finally, in spite of all the internal conflicts among the relationships of individual mobilization levels and rates with individual dimensions of liberal democracy (for example, two positively correlated levels or rates, one of which is positively and one of which is negatively correlated with a given dimension of democracy), the following conclusion seems justified, at least as a clarification of the basic theoretical proposition: liberal democracy tends mainly to be a function of high levels of education (and to a lesser extent industrialization) and high rates of communication and economic development.

Optimal, Under-Democratized, and Over-Democratized Nations

Figures 2-1, 2-2, and 2-3 present visual displays of the relationship between both levels and rates of social mobilization and liberal democracy, between levels of social mobilization and liberal democracy, then rates of social mobilization and liberal democracy, respectively. In these figures, each of the 85 nations is plotted in terms of its liberal-democracy score and its social-mobilization scores; the

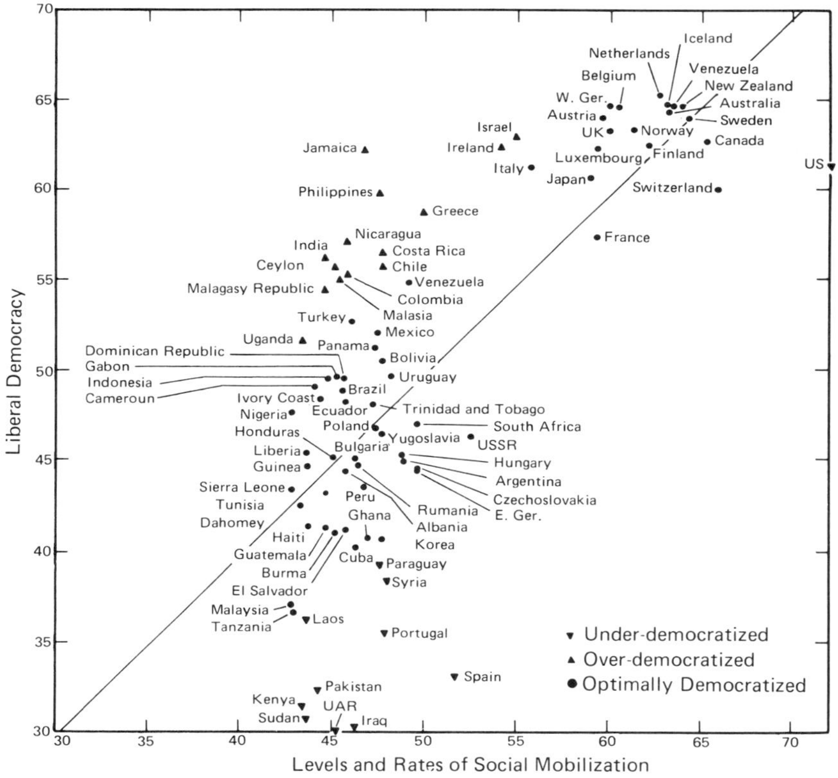

Figure 2-1. Scattergram of Social Mobilization and Liberal Democracy ($R = 0.73$)

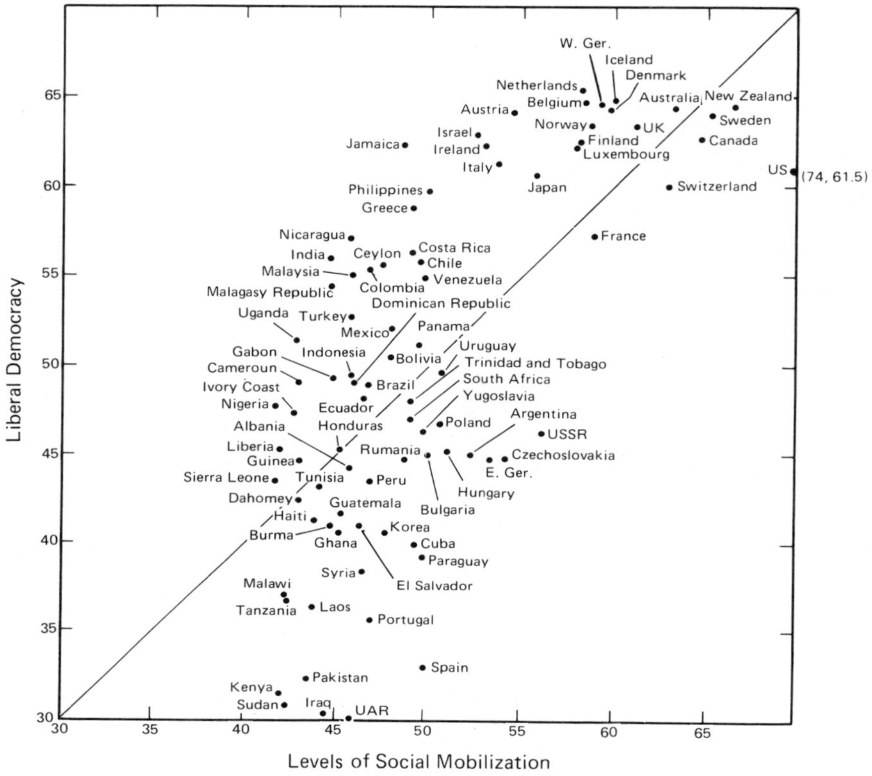

Figure 2-2. Scattergram of Levels of Social Mobilization and Liberal Democracy ($R = 0.69$)

scattergrams visually present the multiple regression of liberal democracy on the levels or rates of social mobilization or both. The diagonal line in the scattergram is the line of regression. The multiple-regression computation minimizes the deviation of the points (nations) about this regression line. Examination of the multivariate distribution graphically displayed in these figures permits not only the determination of the extent of positive and negative deviation about the regression line, but also the specific identification of the optimal and deviant nations. Cases below the line, especially more than one standard error of the estimate (7.03) below the line are considered under-democratized nations. Nations which are 7.03 or more points above the regression line are considered over-democratized. Nations within the plus or minus 7.03 are considered optimal cases in that their degree of liberal democracy is approximately what is

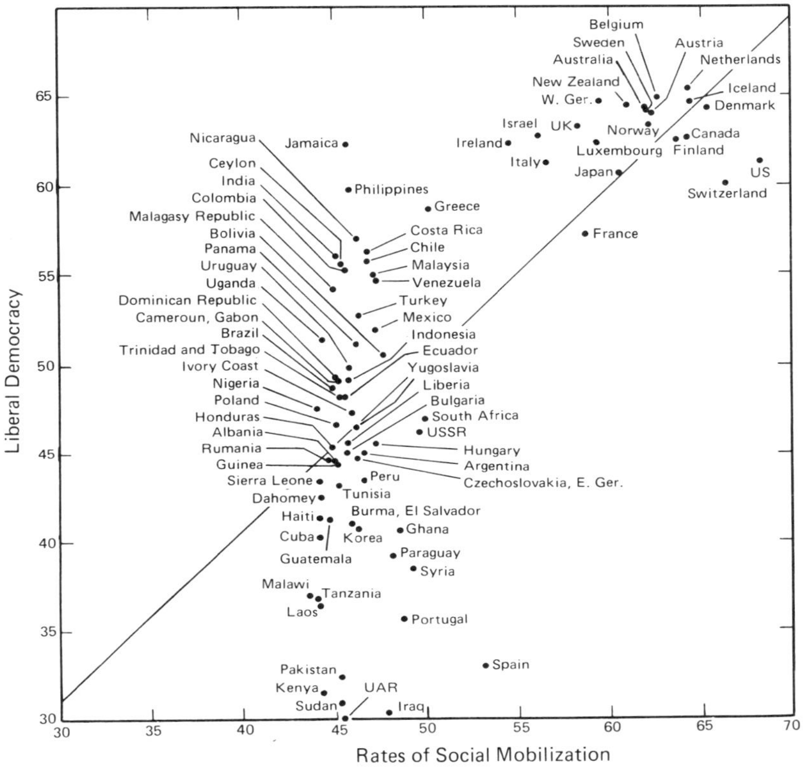

Figure 2-3. Scattergram of Rates of Social Mobilization and Liberal Democracy ($R = 0.71$)

theoretically expected, given their levels and rates of social mobilization. The degree of liberal democracy of these optimal cases that fall within one standard error of the regression line are, therefore, considered adequately explained in terms of social-mobilization theory.[7] The degree of liberal democracy of nations which are over-democratized or under-democratized deviates from theoretical expectations and therefore must be explained in some other terms. It should be remembered that these designations are made in the global perspective of all 85 nations.

Table 2-5 lists the most under-democratized nations and the extent of their under-democratization, that is, the number of points below the regression line.

The most immediately apparent feature of Table 2-5 is its similarity to Table 1-4, which lists the traditional hegemonies, those nations characterized by the

Table 2-5
Under-Democratized Nations

1.	Spain	−19
2.	UAR	−16
3.	Iraq	−15
4.	Sudan	−13
5.	Kenya	−12
6.	Portugal	−12
7.	Pakistan	−11
8.	U.S.	−11
9.	Syria	−10
10.	Paraguay	− 8
11.	Laos	− 7

opposite of liberal democracy in terms of all three dimensions. Nine of the 11 nations (all except the United States and Syria) that appear in Table 2-5 also appear in Table 1-4. In other words, the condition of under-democratization, in terms of the relationship between social mobilization and liberal democracy, seems to be mainly a characteristic of traditional-hegemonic regimes. Only one non-hegemonic regime (the United States) is under-democratized. In addition, it is extremely socially mobilized, whereas all the other under-democratized nations have, during the period of study, undergone only a low degree of social mobilization. The only other under-democratized nation that is not a traditional hegemony, Syria, misses being so classified by a very narrow margin. Syria's polity is monopolistic, exclusive, and just barely moderately libertarian; with regard to the latter criterion, a three-point difference would have placed Syria in the coercive category and thus qualified her as a traditional hegemony. Nonetheless, nine of the 11 under-democratized nations are traditional hegemonies, and nine of the traditional hegemonies (all except Ghana and South Korea, which are narrow misses with deviations from the regression line of 6.29 and 5.97 respectively) are under-democratized.

An explanation for the under-democratization of the 11 nations in Table 2-5 is easy to provide. With one exception (the United States), these countries have had a rather uniform experience with regard to both levels and rates of social mobilization—low in both categories. The breaking of old norms, habits, customs, traditions, mores, etc. and the induction of persons into new ways of thinking, evaluating, and behaving have reached only low levels and were (in the period 1950-70) proceeding only quite slowly. In these nations, expectations are low; much of the population is accustomed to the political status quo and does not really hope for different arrangements. In the case of Spain, with the highest level and rate of social mobilization, a combination of the attribution of legitimacy to the polity by the people and the imposition of the polity on the people by political leaders explains its under-democratization in spite of some social mobilization. In regard to social-mobilization theory, these appreciably under-democratized nations should experience considerable strain, tension, and disequilibrium, for quite obviously, their political systems are in substantial discordance with their social systems, or with their levels and rates of social mobilization. Perhaps the best explanation of this condition of under-democratization is that these polities are traditional hegemonies because they must be. Only a combination of deliberate authoritarian leadership and traditional normative orientation on the part of the population can keep a nation so under-democratized and politically resistant to social mobilization.

In contrast, Table 2-6 presents the most over-democratized nations—those above the regression line by 7.03 or more.

The only similarity between the over-democratized and under-democratized nations is their relatively low degree of social mobilization. The 14 over-democratized nations do not tend toward homogeneity with regard to any of the characteristics that might be intuitively anticipated: kind of regime, region of the world, colonial experience, ethnicity, etc. In global perspective, they simply stand as deviant cases, and the only way to explain them in global perspective is to identify numerous idiosyncratic characteristics that tend to make each of the countries unique. Thus the explanations of each country's deviance would tend to be unique to that particular country. An attempt to explain their deviance is postponed until later chapters that deal with regional patterns of social mobilization and liberal democracy.

It is evident from the groups of over- and under-democratized nations that those having considerably less experience with social mobilization can range from very over-democratized to very under-democratized. In contrast, past the midpoint of social mobilization there is a strong tendency for nations to be only slightly over-democratized. It seems that considerably less mobilized nations can produce polities of great variety, in terms of the degree of liberal democracy, but that considerably more mobilized nations tend to produce only polities in

Table 2-6
Over-Democratized Nations

1. Jamaica	+15	8. Ceylon	+9
2. Nicaragua	+12	9. Malaysia	+9
3. Philippines	+12	10. Chile	+8
4. India	+11	11. Costa Rica	+8
5. Malagasy Rep.	+10	12. Ireland	+8
6. Colombia	+ 9	13. Israel	+8
7. Greece	+ 9	14. Uganda	+8

harmony with their social mobilization. It should be noted that nations of less mobilization can also produce polities in harmony with their mobilization levels and rates (for instance, Poland and Honduras).

Still another point that emerges from Figure 2-1 concerns the position of the eastern European nations in the global multiple regression. Generally the argument runs that these nations are deviant (under-democratized) cases because they are rather more socially mobilized and rather less democratic. Usually there are two related reasons offered in explanation of this assumption: first, Communist political ideology dictates the appropriateness of a more authoritarian regime, and, second, the so-called nation-states of eastern Europe are actually colonies of the Soviet Union and are managed politically the way colonies are managed, that is, in an authoritarian fashion. However, in terms of the global model, these presumptions do not appear to be valid. In actuality, the nations of eastern Europe are about as democratic as their social-mobilization levels and rates predict. Although all nine of the eastern European nations are under-democratized, as might be expected, their average number of points below the regression line is only −2.89, clearly within one standard error, and rather close to the regression line. Neither Communist political ideology nor Soviet domination seems to be distorting the expected relationship between social mobilization and liberal democracy. Figures 2-2 and 2-3, which show visually the relationship of liberal democracy to levels and rates of mobilization separately, indicate two important pieces of evidence that bear on this generalization. First, if only level of social mobilization is considered, eastern European nations do tend to be more under-democratized. If only rate of mobilization is considered, these nine nations cling closely to the regression line and turn out to be optimal cases. So care must be exercised when generalizing about the relationship between social mobilization and liberal democracy in eastern Europe; the degree of liberal democracy there tends to be closely related to rates but not as closely related to levels of social mobilization.

Finally, the extremely deviant case of the United States should be mentioned. It is grossly under-democratized, given its exceedingly high level and rate of social mobilization. Even though the United States ranks fairly high on the scale of liberal democracy (tied for 18th), both the level and rate of social mobilization are so incredibly high relative to the rest of the nations of the world that it appears greatly under-democratized. Even if the mass-participation rate were quite high (which it is not), social mobilization in the United States is so high that changes in kind of democracy, rather than degree, might be necessary in order to bring the United States close to the regression line.

To get an overall sense of the extent to which degree of deviation, positive or negative, of nations on one dimension is related to degree of deviation on each of the other two dimensions, a table of intercorrelations of residuals (errors of prediction) is presented. The higher the correlation coefficient, the greater is the degree of correspondence between the countries on two given residuals or deviations, and nations which have more competitiveness than expected also have more liberties, and so forth. Positive coefficients indicate a positive relationship, and negative coefficients indicate an inverse relationship. Table 2-7 presents these coefficients.

The expectation is that there is a moderate to high correlation between any two measures of degree of deviation from the regression line. If a nation is over-democratic on one dimension, it is expected to be similarly over-democratic on the other two, and so forth for optimality over-, and under-democraticness. Yet that is quite obviously not the case with regard to numerous measures of congruence in Table 2-7.

Essentially, any correlation coefficient in Table 2-7 that relates participation deviance (based on level or rate) with any other measure of deviance from the regression line is extremely low and in two cases (with competitiveness and liberties deviance based on level of social mobilization) they are negative. Otherwise, with only one exception, all the coefficients range from 0.50 to 0.90; the single exception is the relationship between public-liberties deviance (based on level of social mobilization) and competitiveness deviance (based on rate of change) at 0.42. But it is clear that the varying extents to which a nation is over-democratized, under-democratized, or optimally-democratized, (with regard to levels or rates of social mobilization) on measures of competitiveness, liberties, or liberal democracy are fairly strongly and positively interrelated. However, it is just as clear that variation on the participation-deviation scale is not related to variation on the other scales of democratic deviance.

Summary and Conclusions

Before turning to a more specific examination of social mobilization and liberal democracy in the four regions themselves and to the development of four

Table 2-7
Matrix of Intercorrelations of Deviation (Residuals of Prediction) for Competitiveness, Participation, and Liberties by Levels and Rates of Social Mobilization

	1	2	3	4	5	6	7	8
1. Competitiveness	1.00	−0.09	0.59	0.71	0.85	0.01	0.44	0.58
2. Participation		1.00	−0.03	0.48	0.00	0.90	0.10	0.51
3. Liberties			1.00	0.78	0.42	0.13	0.88	0.67
4. Liberal democracy				1.00	0.61	0.56	0.72	0.89
5. Competitiveness					1.00	0.07	0.50	0.70
6. Participation						1.00	0.17	0.63
7. Liberties							1.00	0.78
8. Liberal democracy								1.00

regional models, it is useful to summarize the propositions that the global model suggests as empirically defensible. It should be remembered that these propositions flow from the global model and therefore tend to apply generally to all of the nations in the study. Only the more important propositions are included here; many more could be added.

1. Liberal democracy has a fairly strong relationship to level of social mobilization.
2. Economic-development level is most strongly related to liberal democracy, while the strength of relationship of education and communication with liberal democracy is considerably less, and urbanization is virtually not related to liberal democracy.
3. Industrialization level is negatively related to liberal democracy.
4. Of the three separate dimensions of liberal democracy, competitiveness is most closely associated with level of social mobilization, liberties next, and participation last.
5. Of the five variables of social mobilization, economic-development level has the strongest impact on competitiveness while urbanization, education, and communication have substantially less.
6. Increases in industrialization level produce decreases in the level of competitiveness.
7. Education level is the social-mobilization variable most closely associated with participation, although not too strongly so. Communication, education, and economic levels are not closely related to participation.
8. Urbanization level is negatively related to participation, but only weakly so.
9. Economic-development level is the social-mobilization variable most strongly related to liberties; urbanization, communication, and education levels much less so.
10. Industrialization level is negatively related to liberties, but only weakly so.
11. Of the five measures of social-mobilization level, economic-development level is the most useful in explaining liberal democracy and its three dimensions.
12. With the exception of participation, industrialization level is negatively related to the measures of liberal democracy.
13. Liberal democracy is strongly associated with rate of social mobilization.
14. Communication and economic-development rates are the most important social-mobilization rates in the explanation of liberal democracy; the other three rates are of no consequence.
15. Competitiveness is strongly associated with rate of social mobilization; communication and economic-development rates are most important; urbanization and education rates of no consequence; and industrialization rate negatively related.
16. Participation is fairly strongly related to social-mobilization rate; of predominant importance is industrialization rate.

17. Liberties are fairly strongly related to social-mobilization rate; communication and economic-development rates are most important, while urbanization, education, and industrialization rates are not.
18. Rate of social mobilization has a greater consequence for liberal democracy than does level of social mobilization.
19. When level of social mobilization is held constant, rate of mobilization retains most of its explanatory power with regard to liberal democracy; however, when rate of mobilization is held constant, level of mobilization loses most of its explanatory power.
20. When rate of social mobilization is held constant, education level retains the greatest explanatory power with regard to liberal democracy; when level of mobilization is held constant, communication and economic-development rate retain the greatest explanatory power.
21. The most under-democratized nations are, by and large, traditional hegemonies.

Having cataloged the major propositions that flow from the global model, we now turn to a more specific examination of social mobilization and liberal democracy in each of four geocultural regions. In this way it is possible to develop four regional models with which to analyze the regions and with which the global model can be compared. Although each regional model is based upon the same variables, it differs from the global model in that it rests on the nature of the relationships between variables in the countries of that region and only those countries. Thus each regional model seeks to incorporate indigenous regional political experiences and political values to the extent that they shape the relationship between social mobilization and liberal democracy in the countries of that region. In addition, each of the following four chapters which deals with a regional model seeks to go beyond the systematic examination of social mobilization theory there and to deal with some of the more idiosyncratic and unsystematized variables that have serious implications for liberal democracy.

3 Geocultural Regions and Political Traditions

In each of the following four chapters, the relationship between social mobilization and liberal democracy is examined in the context of a group of countries in a geocultural region of the world. In this way, four additional models can be designed, each based on geocultural region—Anglo-Europa,[1] Iberia and Latin American,[2] Africa,[3] and the Near East and Far East.[4] While it hardly needs to be emphasized that reasonable people might disagree over questions about the placement of some countries in one geocultural category or another,[5] decisions have to be made about which countries belong in which categories. The problem is probably more difficult because the categories of analysis are both geographical and cultural, that is, they are characterized by physical proximity and/or cultural similarity. In some cases they are proximate but culturally dissimilar (Italy and Switzerland); in others they are distant but culturally similar (Canada and New Zealand). Ultimately, no matter how the categorizations are managed, there is substantial room to quibble at the margins of categories. Such is the risk of attempting to categorize whole polities. Nonetheless, it seems important to examine the impact of social mobilization on liberal-democratic politics among the nations of each of the geocultural regions for at least three reasons.

Elements of Geocultural Regionalism

First, the regions themselves are inherently interesting and important. Although disputes over the validity and importance of area studies within political science rage now and then in the professional journals, many serious scholars spend a lot of time trying to master the politics of just one region.[6] Second, and probably more important with regard to political theory, is the substantial probability (perhaps the certainty) that the nature of the fundamental human social context differs from one geocultural region to another. That is, there are social, political, and historical contexts in which both social mobilization and politics emerge and are (or are not) related, which determine or at least condition the existence and nature of that relationship, and which, therefore, give meaning to the relationship. These contexts, these political traditions, differ among geocultural regions. What comprises these human political traditions? How do the various geocultural contexts differ? The third reason for the construction of geocultural models of social mobilization and liberal democracy attempts to answer these questions.[7] The presumption is that .by performing an analysis among polities within a region, one or more of the following results is achieved: (a) the variation of certain variables is held constant, that is, certain more-or-less uniquely regional variables; (2) the magnitude of variation of certain variables is reduced; or (3) certain variables are eliminated from the analysis altogether. In all three cases, the regional variables are not measured and used in the analysis, in part because they may not be known. And, as discussed in Chapter 2, some of these regional variables may be natural discrete, nominal polychotomies; they are qualitative attributes that do not extend across the entire array of world nation-states, but are operative only within their indigenous social context. Stated differently, the phenomena in the social context that are relevant may be different from one context to another.

It seems likely, however, that intraregional analyses would involve the exercise of some control of some of the following kinds of variables, the cumulative effects of which can be summarized in the term "political tradition":[8] (1) values, including political, social, religious, ethical, and other cultural values; (2) geography and geographical proximity, including both the geographical and physical properties and resources of the countries of the region as well as their existence over time in physical proximity; (3) race; (4) language; and the dominant modes of organizing, combining, and synthesizing these phenomena. Also included in the cumulative historical impact of shared historical experiences are participation in war, imperialism, colonialism, and empire, either as perpetrator or victim. All of these factors that tend to differentiate geocultural regions exert continuing and profound impact on the political tradition of the peoples of a region.[9] It affects such basic human attributes as organizational capacity at the societal or even geocultural regional level, such as, the ability and "need to create more effective, more adaptive, more complex, and more rationalized organizations."[10]

Political Implications of Geocultural Regionalism

The characteristics that nations of a geocultural region tend to hold in common are presumed to be at least partly responsible for conditioning whether or not social mobilization and liberal democracy are related, and if they are, in what ways—which variables in particular and how strongly. What is more or less unique to a region must be, or is at least suspected of being, the important cluster of variables that makes the regional correlation coefficients different from each other and different from the global model.[11] Thus, it is possible to learn, in terms of the analysis of the global-model relationships, exactly where social mobilization produces levels of liberal democracy (and which dimensions in particular) and presumably why it does—and where it does not and why not. If, for example, compared with the global model, the relationship between social-mobilization variables and liberal-democratic variables is substantially weaker for the countries of a given geocultural region, then cumulative effect of common historical experiences of the countries, their political tradition, ought to be the source of or at least provide clues about an explanation of the weak or nonexistent relationships. This is especially the case when one regional model differs substantially from another.

An instructive result of the arguments between country specialists and global macrotheorists is the sensitizing of research to both the particular and the general, the unique and the common, the local and the global. Different political, social, and economic patterns, institutions, or other phenomena and events have different meanings, we are told, not only in different geocultural regions of the world, but also in different societies within regions,[12] and even in different sections or areas of a single, small country.[13] It is quite well known that political structures and political functions do not always or necessarily coincide neatly.[14] Armies sometimes legislate; interest groups adjudicate; parties articulate interests; and the church may have considerably stronger regulative and extractive capabilities than the state. A military coup d'état is not the same phenomenon in all incidences; it can have different meanings in Canada, Chile, and Ghana.[15]

In short, in cross-national comparative-political analysis, the validity of that crucial assumption of comparability is simply more probable within a geocultural region than in a global or random selection of polities.[16] The task in the following four chapters is to characterize geocultural regions and to examine the nature of the relationship of social mobilization and liberal democracy with reference to the geocultural context in which the relationship evolved and exists. The presumption is that the characteristics of geocultural regions condition whether the relationship between social-mobilization variables and liberal-democracy variables is strong, moderate, or weak, and relevant or irrelevant. Lucian W. Pye is undoubtedly correct in stating that a world culture is spreading,[17] but it seems equally correct to expect that the application of any aspect of the world culture in a specific regional context will not only alter the nature and meaning of the context (as Pye asserts) but also may alter the nature and meaning of that aspect of the world culture itself. The level or rate of change of education, for example, may have rather different impacts and interpretations in Japan and Portugal, or Turkey and Haiti. It is, in one important sense, the complete social context that gives birth, meaning, and consequences to the social-mobilization processes. Following the example of education levels and rates, it is obvious and important that there is a content to the education process; young people can be educated, or socialized, in a variety of ways and with a variety of contents. Education content can be religious or secular, conservative or revolutionary, pragmatic or ideological, etc. A first-grade textbook in reading can be about Dick and Jane, or about the oppressiveness of the big landowners, or about the misery of life in the barrios. The point is that what education is and what it does depends largely upon where it takes place, who is involved, what is the purpose, etc. Although it may be in some ways a universal phenomenon (as may be the case with the other indices of social mobilization), its nature is dependent on its social and cultural context, and its relationship to political practices is seriously mediated (inhibited or encouraged) by this same set of social and cultural values that permeate a given society.[18]

In the four chapters to follow, each of the four geocultural regions provides a separate context in which the political consequences of social mobilization are analyzed. These analyses also provide the opportunity to identify the deviant cases that are over-democratized or under-democratized with reference to the mobilization-democracy relationship in their geocultural context.

Liberal Democracy and Social Mobilization in the Geocultural Regions

By way of a comparative introduction to the characteristics of each of the four regions, Table 3-1 presents the mean average, standard deviation, and coefficient of variability[19] for each of the 14 variables for each of the four geocultural regions. These descriptive statistics permit some comparisons of the degree to which the central tendencies of the regions differ for the numerous variables and the extent to which their degrees of dispersion or variability differ. These comparisons reveal which regions tend to be higher or lower than other regions in terms of both levels and rates of change of social mobilization variables as well as in terms of the liberal democracy variables.

The average value of the Anglo-European nations on the dependent and independent variables is high, but there are two exceptions. All the means are in the mid fifties to lower sixties except rate of education (48.8). With these two exceptions, the Anglo-European averages are all higher than those of any of the other three regions. Levels of communication, industrialization, and economic development are the highest, and yet rate of communication is about equally high. Although the level of communication is quite high, the rate of increase of communication is also quite high. The coefficients of variability indicate that variation within the variables is rather uniform; 14 of them are between 15 and 20. Only popular participation (*CRV* = 6) has really low variability.

African nations tend to be low in all liberal democratic and social-mobilization variables; they range from the mid thirties to the upper forties. With only a few exceptions, the variability within these variables is considerably lower than that of other regions. African nations are all at approximately the same level of social mobilization and are mobilizing the same speed. However, although they tend to be low on both levels and rates of mobilization and to exhibit very little relative dispersion within those variables, they are also low on the liberal-democ-

Table 3-1

Means, Standard Deviations, and Coefficients of Variability of Liberal-Democratic and Social-Mobilization Variables by Region[a]

	Anglo-Europa (*N* = 29)			Africa (*N* = 16)			Iberia and Latin America (*N* = 24)			Near East and Far East (*N* = 16)		
	Mean	SD	CV	Mean	SD	CV	Mean	SD	CV	Mean	SD	CV
1. Political competitiveness	55.0	11.0	20	43.5	6.8	16	49.5	8.1	16	48.2	9.0	19
2. Popular participation	58.3	3.7	6	45.8	11.1	24	45.8	8.3	18	45.3	10.0	22
3. Public liberties	53.5	10.5	20	46.3	10.4	22	49.3	8.2	17	48.4	10.0	21
4. Liberal democracy	57.3	8.4	15	43.7	6.8	15	49.0	6.0	12	46.5	11.4	24
5. Level of urbanization	56.1	9.1	16	40.0	5.5	14	51.4	7.2	14	46.7	10.0	21
6. Level of education	58.8	5.9	10	37.0	4.9	13	49.8	6.2	12	47.3	8.7	18
7. Level of communication	60.2	10.3	17	42.6	1.2	3	46.1	3.8	8	44.7	4.7	10
8. Level of industrialization	60.1	8.1	13	42.7	6.3	15	46.5	5.6	12	44.0	6.1	14
9. Level of economic development	60.4	10.6	17	42.9	1.9	4	45.9	2.8	6	44.5	3.4	8
10. Rate of urbanization	49.0	9.5	19	47.5	8.6	18	52.3	11.1	21	50.7	10.5	21
11. Rate of education	48.8	10.7	22	47.8	2.5	5	49.2	6.2	13	55.3	9.6	17

Table 3-1 (cont.)

	Anglo-Europa (N = 29)			Africa (N = 16)			Iberia and Latin America (N = 24)			Near East and Far East (N = 16)		
	Mean	SD	CV	Mean	SD	CV	Mean	SD	CV	Mean	SD	CV
12. Rate of communication	60.0	10.1	17	43.5	2.3	5	44.3	2.7	6	46.6	7.0	15
13. Rate of industrialization	59.9	9.0	15	43.6	3.5	8	44.6	3.5	8	46.6	9.4	20
14. Rate of economic development	58.3	12.4	21	43.9	2.0	4	46.4	3.4	7	46.4	6.4	14

[a]For all 85 nations in the global model, the mean is 50, the standard deviation is 10, and the coefficient of variability is 20 for all variables.

racy variables but have considerably higher coefficients of variability. They are not all at about the same level on the three dimensions of liberal democracy.

The Iberian and Latin American nations tend to be a little higher in general on all the variables, their means ranging from the mid forties to the low fifties. It appears that both the level and rate of urbanization are high, in fact higher than in Africa or the Near East and Far East. And although the level of urbanization is not as high in the Iberic and Latin American region as it is among Anglo-European nations, the Iberic-Latin rate of urbanization is higher than in Anglo-Europa. The dispersion or variation around the central tendency within each variable tends to be comparatively small among these Iberic and Latin American nations.

The Near Eastern and Far Eastern nations range from the mid forties to the mid fifties. The rates of urbanization and education are both relatively high, even when compared with the nations of Anglo-Europa. Yet while the Near Eastern and Far Eastern countries tend to rank approximately next to Anglo-Europa and higher than Africa or the Latin American and Iberic nations, the East exhibits greater variability. Finally, the Near East and Far East resembles Africa with regard to degree of liberal democracy, but the former's coefficients of variation are even greater, indicating a wider diversity of political variation among these nations.

The next step in the regional analysis is to move beyond these descriptive statistical data to the precise identification of correlations between the social-mobilization variables and the liberal-democracy variables. In this way, four separate regression models will specify exactly the similarities and differences of relationships and suggest the manner in which the political tradition permeates and affects the relationships.

4 The Anglo-European Model of Liberal Democracy

Included in the Anglo-European geocultural region are the following 29 nation-states: Albania, Australia, Austria, Belgium, Bulgaria, Canada, Czechoslovakia, Denmark, Eastern Germany, Finland, France, Greece, Hungary, Iceland, Ireland, Italy, Luxemburg, Netherlands, New Zealand, Norway, Poland, Rumania, Sweden, Switzerland, United Kingdom, United States, Union of Soviet Socialist Republics, Western Germany, and Yugoslavia. For these countries the correlations between the various pairs of measures of liberal democracy range from moderately strong to extremely strong, as exhibited in Table 4-1.

The correlation coefficients in Table 4-1 are all extremely high except for two, both with participation, and even these two are moderately strong. However, the two intercorrelations between participation, on the one hand, and both competitiveness and public liberties, on the other, are negative at −0.69 and −0.70 respectively. In Anglo-Europa, wherever political competitiveness or public liberties are high, the level of popular participation tends to be low, and vice versa. The split between east and west is largely responsible for this inverse relationship, for among eastern European nations popular participation is extremely high while competitiveness and liberties tend to be considerably lower. The list of 29 Anglo-European nations includes 17 liberal-democratic polities (see Table 1-2) and nine modern-hegemonic polities (see Table 1-3) from eastern Europe.

An equally interesting and unanticipated finding revealed by Table 4-1 concerns the comparison of the global and Anglo-European models with regard to intercorrelations among democratic variables. For Anglo-European nations, these intercorrelations are all substantially stronger, except that between participation and liberal democracy, which is about the same in both. Additionally, whereas the correlations between participation and the other two dimensions of liberal democracy are quite small and positive in the global model, they are fairly strong and negative in Anglo-Europa. A glance back at Table 1-6 enables a direct comparison of the two sets of intercorrelations. The quantitative association of qualities of democracy seems to assume different configurations in the global and Anglo-European models.

Similar kinds of comparisons can be made between the 85 nation grouping and the geocultural region for variables of social-mobilization levels and rates of change. Table 4-2 presents these intercorrelations between 10 social mobilization indicators.

Focusing first on the upper-left quadrant of Table 4-2, the correlations

Table 4-1
Matrix of Intercorrelations Among Measures of Liberal Democracy for Anglo-European Countries

	Competi-tiveness	Participa-tion	Liberties	Liberal Democracy
Competitiveness	1.00	–0.69	0.97	0.98
Participation		1.00	–0.70	0.60
Liberties			1.00	0.98
Liberal democracy				1.00

between levels of social mobilization, it is evident that in general the coefficients are considerably lower than for all 85 nations in the global model (see Table 1-8). Deutsch's exposition of social-mobilization theory makes it clear that these indicators should be quite strongly related,[1] but with the exception of the relationship between communication level and economic-development level ($r = 0.93$), such is not appreciably the case. In fact, six of the correlations are below 0.50 and only four are above. A moderately strong relationship is evident between communication and industrialization levels ($r = 0.67$) and between industrialization and economic-development levels ($r = 0.72$). Perhaps the clear absence of a strong relationship between either urbanization or education levels and any of the other variables suggests that the Anglo-European nations are more mature or modern than nations of the world in general, in the sense claimed implicitly by Daniel Lerner.[2] That is, urbanization, for example, is the initial mobilization process in a developing nation at the initial phase of development. In the more developed nations of Anglo-Europa, urbanization is no longer an important process in terms of its relation to social mobilization. It has essentially already happened and its consequences already manifested themselves; long before 1960, it had run its course. However, the data do not permit a direct or conclusive test of such a speculative hypothesis.

For Anglo-Europa, the 25 correlations between levels and rates of social mobilization (upper right hand quadrant of Table 4-2) are, like that for the global model, quite diverse. Neither urbanization nor education level is strongly related to any of the rates of mobilization. Communication level is strongly related only to communication and economic-development rates; it is negatively related to both urbanization and education rates, as are industrialization and economic-development levels. The industrialization level is not closely associated with any rate variable, and economic-development level is strongly related only to communication and economic-development rates. Table 1-8, which contains the same data for all 85 nations, provides some interesting contrasts with the data for Anglo-Europa. In general, the coefficients for the global model are higher.

Table 4-2

Matrix of Intercorrelations Among Measures of Social-Mobilization Indicators for Anglo-European Nations

	Levels (1960)					Rates (1946-66)				
	1	2	3	4	5	6	7	8	9	10
1. Urbanization level	1.00	0.45	0.38	0.45	0.42	0.08	0.08	0.50	0.08	0.35
2. Education level		1.00	0.47	0.44	0.57	0.02	0.25	0.40	0.20	0.31
3. Communication level			1.00	0.67	0.93	−0.31	−0.17	0.84	0.17	0.70
4. Industrialization level				1.00	0.72	−0.32	−0.27	0.52	0.48	0.28
5. Economic development level					1.00	−0.31	−0.05	0.81	0.19	0.73
6. Urbanization rate						1.00	0.09	−0.35	0.15	0.30
7. Education rate							1.00	−0.23	−0.30	0.05
8. Communication rate								1.00	0.05	0.73
9. Industrialization rate									1.00	−0.11
10. Economic development rate										1.00

Finally, in the lower right quadrant of Table 4-2 are coefficients of association between rates of change of social-mobilization variables. They are all quite low, with the single exception of that between communication and economic-development rate at 0.73. And in general, the correlations in this quadrant are lower than those for the global model in Table 1-8.

Thus it seems that in Anglo-Europa, where rates of social mobilization are generally high even though levels of mobilization are also generally high, many of the characteristics of social-mobilization processes discussed in Chapter 1 seem not to apply. In particular, the characteristics of coherence, reinforcement, positive relationships, and interchangeability are not found in the data for the 29 Anglo-European polities. Levels and rates of social mobilization are not related in the same way among these nations as they are among a global selection of nations; social mobilization may well be and mean different things to different geocultural regions. This proposition is explored further as we examine its relationship to liberal democracy.

Levels of Social Mobilization

Table 4-3 contains simple-correlation coefficients, beta weights, multiple-correlation coefficients, and coefficients of multiple determination for the five independent social-mobilization variables and the four dependent liberal-democracy variables.

It is quite evident that a large proportion of the variation of the four liberal-democratic variables is accounted for by the social-mobilization variables. An examination of the multiple coefficients of correlation and determination reveals that about half (49%) of the variation in participation is accounted for, almost two-thirds (62%) of public liberties variation is statistically explained, and fully 72 percent of the cross-national variation in competitiveness is accounted for. These coefficients are substantially larger than those for the global model of 85 nations. In fact, these coefficients are almost twice as large as those of the global model.[3]

Although the simple-correlation coefficients can be informative about relationships between pairs of the variables, it is probably more useful to focus attention on the beta weights. They indicate the extent to which a change in a given independent variable produces change in the dependent variable, in standardized units. Clearly, with regard to political competitiveness, the influence of economic development is preeminent.[4] A one-unit increase in the level of economic development produces a 0.66 unit increase in the level of competitiveness. Also of interest is the fact that a one-unit increase in education and industrialization produces a decrease of –0.31 and –0.36 respectively in the degree of competitiveness. With the exception of these two negative beta weights, Anglo-European political competitiveness tends to resemble that of the

Table 4-3

Simple- and Multiple-Correlation Coefficients for Measures of Liberal Democracy and Levels of Social Mobilization for Anglo-Europa

	Urban-ization		Educa-tion		Communi-cation		Industri-alization		Economic Development			
	r	β	r	β	r	β	r	β	r	β	R	R^2
Competitiveness	0.47	0.33	0.18	−0.31	0.73	0.35	0.31	−0.36	0.71	0.66	0.85	72%
Participation	−0.15	0.03	−0.18	0.10	−0.56	−0.31	−0.08	0.57	−0.55	−0.72	0.70	49%
Liberties	0.52	0.40	0.19	−0.30	0.63	0.14	0.26	−0.39	0.64	0.76	0.79	62%
Liberal democracy	0.53	0.41	0.18	−0.33	0.66	0.22	0.31	−0.33	0.66	0.68	0.81	68%

global model, except the beta weights and multiple coefficients are clearly higher in the former.

Although only about half the participation is explained by the five levels of mobilization, it is clearly economic development and, to a lesser extent, industrialization, that are responsible for variations in participation.[5] A one-unit increase in the level of economic development is reflected in a −0.72 unit decrease in participation; an increase of one-unit in the level of industrialization produces a positive increase of 0.57 in participation. Apparently, as industrialization increases, with its concomitant or consequential increase in the organization and political organization of the urban laboring classes, there is an increase in the turnout at national election. However, as nations continue into affluence—beyond industrial society into postindustrial society[6]—there appears to be a decided tendency toward a decrease in popular participation in national elections. And again, the grouping of eastern Europe with western Europe and the Anglo nations, that is, lower level of economic development with extremely high turnout and higher level of economic development and considerably lower turnout, the partial result is that industrialization is positively and economic development negatively related to participation.[7]

In a contrary manner, economic-development level is strongly and positively related to public liberties[8] ($\beta = 0.76$) and industrialization level is negatively related to public liberties ($\beta = -0.39$). And urbanization level has a somewhat higher beta weight ($\beta = 0.40$) with regard to public liberties than it does with competitiveness or participation. The pattern of relationships between social-mobilization levels and the composite indicator of liberal democracy resembles that of public liberties. Again, economic-development level with a beta weight of 0.68 is the variable most strongly related to liberal democracy,[9] and industrialization level is negatively related ($\beta = -0.33$). And, again similar to public liberties, a unit increase in urbanization level produces a 0.41 increase in liberal democracy. This contrasts drastically with the pattern of relationships between urbanization level and the four measures of liberal democracy for the global model (the highest beta weight of which is 0.16).

A final comment on the data in Table 4-3 concerns the general evenness of the size of the beta coefficients. None is extremely high; many are in the middle range; and only four are below 0.30. Although economic-development level seems to have a preponderant influence on liberal democracy, and four of the beta weights are below 0.30, there seems to be a kind of overall evenness or generality of influence of level of social-mobilization variables on liberal-democracy variables. A look at similar beta weights for the global model in Table 2-1 shows that all but three of them were under 0.30.

Rates of Social Mobilization

As Table 3-1 showed previously, not only are levels of social mobilization highest in Anglo-Europa of all the four geocultural regions, but the rates of change in that region are also the greatest. And similarly, rates of change are quite closely associated with liberal-democratic variables, as the social-mobilization theory hypothesizes. Table 4-4 presents these correlation coefficients.

Competitiveness is affected most by economic development and communication rates,[10] with beta weights of 0.52 and 0.49 respectively. Rate of industrialization has a negative impact; a unit increase in this rate produces a decrease of –0.27 units. As is rather well known, high industrialization rates are found in the one-party states (extremely low on competitiveness) of eastern Europe, and more competitiveness is found among the states that, though continuing to experience high rates of economic development, experience slower rates of industrialization. Some of them may, in fact, have negative rates as they make the transformation from industrial to post-industrial societies; the percent of the labor force employed in industrial occupations actually decreases, and the percent of the labor force employed in ancillary services rapidly increases.[11] With economic development and communication rates the most prominent, the five rates of social mobilization statistically account for fully 90.1 percent of the total variation in degree of competitiveness, a remarkably large coefficient of determination. Urbanization, education, and industrialization rates contribute very little to this high level of statistical explanation.

With regard to popular participation, it is rate of economic development, again, which is clearly most influential,[12] with a beta weight of 0.53. Industrialization rate has a considerably smaller degree of effect on participation ($\beta = 0.32$) and communication rate has a negative influence ($\beta = -0.27$), although it is also quite small. But among the five social-mobilization rates, almost 58 percent of the variation in participation can be accounted for. This degree of explanation is almost twice as great as that for the global model ($R^2 = 31\%$). Although some rates of social mobilization are positively and some negatively related to popular participation, they are fairly strongly related in the Anglo-European nations. A similar situation holds for variation in public liberties. However, in this case, an extremely high 86.5 percent of the variation is accounted for. Similar to previous analyses of Anglo-European nations, economic-development and communication rates are the strong influences ($\beta = 0.51$ and 0.45 respectively). Industrialization rate has a small negative beta weight (–0.27).[13]

Finally, the composite indicator of liberal democracy is quite strongly correlated with rates of mobilization; almost 93 percent of the variation is accounted for—impressive to say the least. Not surprisingly, economic-development and communication rates are largely responsible for the high level of statistical explanation.[14] And also not surprisingly, industrialization and education rates have small but negative beta weights. Urbanization has a small positive beta weight. The pattern of association of liberal democracy and rates of social mobilization is very similar to that for competitiveness and mobilization. And a comparison of the four coefficients of multiple determination for the global model with those of the Anglo-European model shows that the latter are almost

Table 4-4
Simple- and Multiple-Correlation Coefficients for Measures of Liberal Democracy and Rates of Social Mobilization for Anglo-Europa

	Urbanization		Education		Communication		Industrialization		Economic Development			
	r	β	r	β	r	β	r	β	r	β	R	R^2
Competitiveness	−0.28	0.11	−0.08	−0.05	0.84	0.49	−0.27	−0.22	0.88	0.52	0.95	90.1
Participation	−0.09	−0.23	0.17	0.26	−0.54	−0.27	0.34	0.32	−0.61	0.53	0.76	57.9
Liberties	−0.23	0.17	−0.09	−0.13	0.79	0.45	−0.35	−0.27	0.84	0.51	0.93	86.5
Liberal democracy	−0.27	0.11	−0.06	−0.05	0.82	0.47	−0.29	−0.23	0.85	0.50	0.93	92.9

double the former in three cases (competitiveness, participation, and the composite indicator of liberal democracy) and more than double for another (liberties). There is an obvious strength and cohesiveness of the relationship between levels and rates of social mobilization and liberal democracy in Anglo-Europa that is not at all evident in the global model. Among the 29 nations of Anglo-Europa, liberal democracy is largely a function of certain aspects of social mobilization. That seems certain, given the overwhelming confirmation of the mobilization theory hypotheses contained in Tables 4-3 and 4-4. What remains is to determine whether level or rate of mobilization is more important in terms of their impact on this prime characteristic of national politics, degree of liberal democracy.

Relative Influence of Levels and Rates of Social Mobilization

The same test used to examine relative contribution of level of social mobilization while holding constant rate (and vice versa) for the global model is used for the Anglo-European countries. In this way, it can be determined whether achieving a certain high level of social mobilization or continuing to mobilize at a high rate is more important, or if they are of roughly equal importance. Table 4-5 presents the evidence that suggests that rate of mobilization is the prime determinant.

First, the multiple-correlation coefficients based on the influence of all 10 independent variables are only a very little or not at all greater than those which use five measures of rate of mobilization to explain liberal democracy. But actually, three of the mobilization-rate coefficients are already so high ($R = 0.76$ or better as in column 2 of Table 4-5) that much improvement in these

Table 4-5
Multiple- and Multiple-Partial-Correlation Coefficients for Levels and Rates of Social Mobilization and Liberal Democracy for Anglo-Europa

	Multiple Correlation Coefficients			Multiple-Partial-Correlation Coefficients	
	1	2	3	4	5
	Levels	Rates	Levels and Rates	Levels w/Rates Constant	Rates w/Levels Constant
Competitiveness	0.85	0.95	0.95	0.21	0.83
Participation	0.70	0.76	0.79	0.32	0.50
Liberties	0.79	0.93	0.94	0.16	0.82
Liberal democracy	0.81	0.93	0.93	0.22	0.78

coefficients could hardly be expected. For the case of the lower coefficient of multiple correlation, that of participation, there is a slight increase in the strength of association over either set of mobilization variables alone when both sets are used. The coefficient of correlation of both level and rate is increased three percentage points over that of rates alone. However, the more revealing part of Table 4-5 is contained in columns 4 and 5. When rate of mobilization is held constant, there is very little association between level of mobilization and democracy in the Anglo-European nations. The coefficient for competitiveness is reduced from $R = 0.85$ to $R = 0.21$; participation is reduced from 0.70 to 0.32; liberties is decreased from 0.79 to 0.16; and liberal democracy falls from 0.81 to 0.22. When the influence of rate of change is controlled for, the level of mobilization is found to be of limited importance. Ironically, it is popular participation whose correlation coefficient is least reduced when rate of change is held constant. It has been participation all along whose variation is least well accounted for by mobilization variables.

In column 5 of Table 4-5, the other half of the answer is provided. When rate of social mobilization is used to explain liberal democracy and the influence of level of mobilization is partialled out, rate maintains a substantially high level of association with liberal-democracy variables. The coefficient for competitiveness is reduced from $R = 0.95$ to $R = 0.83$; that for participation goes from 0.76 to 0.50; the liberties from 0.93 to 0.82; and that of liberal democracy is lowered from 0.93 to 0.78. This represents a remarkably consistent maintenance of a high degree of explanatory power on the part of rates of social mobilization, even when the effects of levels of mobilization are controlled for. And this in spite of the fact that levels of mobilization are extraordinarily high in Anglo-European nations in terms of global standards. The pattern of relationships of the multiple- and multiple-partial-correlation coefficients for Anglo-Europa is very similar to that for the global model, except for two differences. First, in the global model, the size of the coefficients between level and democracy variables, holding constant rate of change, is reduced even more drastically. And second, in the global model, although the coefficients between rate of change and democratic variables, holding constant the influence of level of mobilization, remain fairly high, they are not nearly as large as in the case of the Anglo-European model. A glance back at Table 2-3 provides these comparisons.

Unexplained Variation and the Deviant Cases

Since such a large proportion of the total variation of the variables of liberal democracy is accounted for by level and especially rate of social mobilization, the problem is to describe the political tradition of the geocultural region which permits or is conducive to the development of such a strong association between independent and dependent variables, not to explain why there is so little or no association. Nevertheless, not all the democratic variation is statistically explained by the 10 independent social-mobilization variables; there is unexplained variation, and there are, therefore, some deviant cases. The scattergram in Figure 4-1 displays the relationship between social mobilization (both levels and rates) and liberal democracy for the 29 Anglo-European nations.

At least four features of this regression become clear at first glance; and only a separate geocultural regional analysis of this kind reveals such features. In the first instance, the nations are, on the whole, very close to the regression line, as the multiple-correlation coefficient of $R = 0.93$ indicates in summary form. There is, quite apparently, some geocultural coherence at work here that

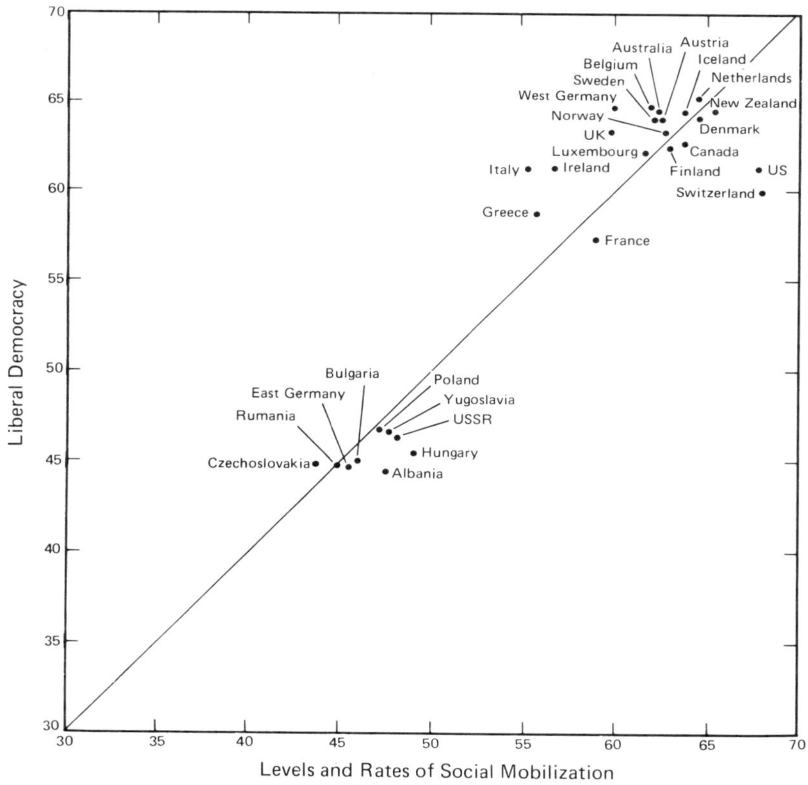

Figure 4-1. Scattergram of Liberal Democracy and Social Mobilization for Anglo-European Nations ($R = 0.93$)

produces such a close regression of liberal democracy on social mobilization. Second, there are two distinct clusters of nations, eastern Europe and western Europe plus the other English-speaking nations. Low social mobilization is associated with low liberal democracy, as demonstrated by the eastern European cluster of countries in the lower left corner of the scattergram. High social mobilization is associated with high liberal democracy, as demonstrated by the cluster of polities in the upper right corner of the scattergram. A third feature of the scattergram concerns the relative closeness to the regression line of the two major clusters—east and west. The eastern European cluster of modern hegemonic regimes, those with inclusive participation but monopolistic competition and coercive nonliberties, are actually clustered closer to the regression line than is the western European group of nations. Social mobilization has a greater impact, of the sort predicted, on the liberal democratic aspect of polities in eastern Europe than in western Europe where liberal democracy was born. Or, stated in a slightly different way, although the nations of eastern Europe rank rather low on liberal democracy, they actually have quite precisely the degree of liberal democracy that they *ought* to have in terms of their social mobilization. In terms of social-mobilization theory and their geocultural context, these nations are not under-democratized at all; rather, they are about optimally democratized.[15]

A fourth point, which follows from the second and third points about the existence of two clusters of nations one of which (eastern Europe) is closer to the line, is that the deviant cases are, by and large, from the western European cluster. Table 4-6 reveals the over- and under-democratized nations.[16]

These are the only nations in the Anglo-European group that are more than one standard error above or below the regression line. The standard error in this regression is 3.1. All of the over-democratized cases are from the western bloc and two or half of the under-democratized cases are from that bloc. However, since the correlation coefficient for this regression is $R = 0.93$ with a standard error of the estimate of only 3.1, these eight cases, though deviant in terms of the criterion being of one standard error or more above or below the regression line, are not really very deviant.[17] The main purpose is, therefore, to suggest reasons for the statistical explanation of 83.5 percent of the variation of liberal

Table 4-6
Under-Democratized and Over-Democratized Nations in Anglo-Europa

Over-Democratized		Under-Democratized	
Ireland	5.6	Switzerland	−8.0
Italy	4.8	United States	−6.6
Western Germany	4.0	Albania	−3.3
United Kingdom	3.5	Hungary	−3.8

democracy, not to belabor an attempt to account for the unexplained variation of 16.5 percent. And that purpose is best served by looking into the political tradition more or less shared by nation states of the Anglo-European region.

The Political Tradition of Anglo-Europa: Liberal Secularism

The political tradition in which social mobilization and liberal democracy are so closely associated is essentially one characterized by a secular political culture which supports a differentiated polity; it is a modern political tradition. This characterization of the Anglo-European context has received considerable attention in political science literature, and therefore, it will not be elaborated in detail here.[18] However, the central features of this context will be generally described mainly in terms of their connection with the relationship between social mobilization and liberal democracy.

The Anglo-European political tradition is, in terms of a continuum from traditional to secular, considerably more secular than that of most of the nations or regions of the world. It is a rational-calculating, bargaining, multivalued, experimental, relatively homogeneous, pragmatic, "game-like" political tradition. Rational-calculating means the conscious establishment of a connection between means and ends so that the practice of politics will be productive in terms of more or less well defined tasks or goals. The style of political action is primarily that of bargaining in the political marketplace. Decisions taken or bargains struck are viewed as experimental and tentative in long-run terms and are therefore subject to revision and change. With regard to the homogeneity of political culture in Anglo-Europa, there is a sharing of means and ends in politics; and shared values that knit the political system together include preeminently those of freedom, mass welfare, and security. Another important aspect of the secular political tradition is the high degree of individuation and autonomy among various political roles. Because of this individualistic conception of political action and roles, there is to a considerable extent a bargaining relationship among political roles, politics is saturated with the atmosphere of the economic market, and office holders are conceived of as agents and instrumentalities or brokers who are located at various points in the bargaining process. The whole political system is viewed as a laboratory in which policies are considered, to a large extent, to be hypotheses, and the consequences of legislation, the nature of which is quickly and effectively communicated throughout the political system, are looked upon as constituting an approximate empirical test of the hypotheses. These characteristics are part of the pragmatic, empirical approach to politics prominent in Anglo-Europa. The "game" of politics is played pragmatically and it is, at least in part, viewed as fun. Political terminology such as "the outcome is in doubt," "winners and losers," reflects this "game" conception of politics.

Growing out of this political tradition is a type of political system distinguished chiefly by its relatively high degree of structural differentiation. Political structures and political roles are differentiated, that is, they tend to pursue specialized functions. They tend to be autonomous, although they are interdependent. And not only are political structures highly differentiated, but most political interests tend to be manifest, organized, and bureaucratized. Naturally, the poor, the ignorant, and the dispossessed have interests that are at best only vaguely and ineffectively organized, but compared to world standards, Anglo-European political interests are highly organized and bureaucratized. There is a concomitantly high level of stability in the functions of roles. Ordinarily, functions are not substitutable; bureaucracies function as bureaucracies, generals as generals, legislative bodies as legislative bodies, media of mass communication as media of mass communication, etc. The political division of labor is more complex, more explicit, and more stable in Anglo-Europa than tends to be the case in the rest of the world. Finally, there is a wider diffusion of political (and other kinds of) power and influence within the Anglo-European systems than there is elsewhere. It is in this geocultural region that the participant political culture is best developed and most widely distributed.[19]

Naturally, when attempting to generalize about the political tradition and character of 29 nation-states, much that actually varies is considered to be constant. There are conflicting traditions and subcultures, particularly in polities like France, Italy, Belgium, and Canada, which, although small in some cases, do persist and are important. But at the macropolitical level, the central tendency of each and all of these polities clearly distinguishes it from other geocultural regions that might be conceived. And even where such contrasting traditions or subcultures do exist, the polities have been built on the spirit and institutionalization of accommodative practices.[20] Flemings and Walloons have grave policy differences but Belgium accommodates both groups, survives, prospers, and maintains relative harmony, stability, and democracy.[21] Reinhold Neibuhr argues, for example, that a prominent part of the explanation of Anglo-European character and culture is based on three prerequisites: community solidarity and literacy, individual freedom, and justice and an equilibrium of power.[22] All three of these features, but particularly the first, are closely connected with the development of cultural and technical forms of competence.

The ethnic and linguistic unification of most Anglo-European nations preceded the rise of free government; national communities triumphed over ethnic, linguistic, and cultural diversities. In some cases, such as that of the United States, nations realized the hazards of religio-cultural diversity and therefore deliberately set about to establish freedom for the sake of national unity. In all the Anglo-European nations, the invention of printing and literacy made all this possible; they were in part a result of and in part produced cultural and technical forms of competence. In the first place, literacy and printing support communal unity by helping one language to triumph over various dialects and by enabling communities of interest and vocation to acquire some degree of social cohesion based on ties not related to the political problems that divide the nation at a given point in time. Second, they permit individual freedom by giving individuals the ability and the inclination to transcend or defy traditional organic loyalties and commitments as well as the capacity to trust in their own ability to defend their own interests and to organize for the protection and attainment of their goals. In addition, the religio-cultural foundations for individual selfhood were laid by the Judeo-Christian faith and later elaborated in the structures of free societies. The result was bourgeois social and political emphasis on the individual's emancipation from the organic, traditional cohesiveness of the older cultures. Bourgeois voluntarism and individualism overcame the organic and collective factors of community of human existence. Bourgeois democracy either destroyed feudalism or gradually transmuted it. Liberal democracy slowly evolved from these kinds of contingent circumstances.

Summary and Conclusions

It seems evident from the data presented in this chapter that the secular political values and the institutions resting on these values in Anglo-European nations promote or at least permit a strong association between social mobilization processes and liberal democracy. In terms of this relationship, Anglo-Europa demonstrates a reasonably high degree of geocultural regional cohesiveness. When the nations of this secular, differentiated Anglo-European cultural region are the basis of the analysis, the relationship between social mobilization and liberal democracy increases in strength. It is a presumption, not a certainty, that when geocultural region (for example, Anglo-Europa) is held constant, the identity and amount of the variables or attributes that are being held constant are actually known. But the relevant literature of political science indicates rather clearly the kinds of political traditions generally shared by these 29 polities.

When considered separately, both level and rate of social mobilization are strongly associated with liberal-democratic variables. Levels of industrialization and economic development are the two most prominently correlated with liberal democracy. Rates of communication and economic development are the two most strongly related to democracy. When the influence of level of mobilization is partialled out, rate of mobilization retains much of its explanatory power, although the coefficient is reduced in size. When rate of mobilization is held constant, however, the coefficient measuring association between level of mobilization and liberal democracy is virtually reduced to nothing. And in Anglo-Europa, not only are levels of mobilization the highest in the world, but rates of change are also greatest among regions of the world. Nonetheless, it is true that level and rate of social mobilization, when taken together, account for an extremely large portion of the variation in liberal-democracy variables.

Another point concerns the problematic nature of popular participation. This dimension of liberal democracy is fairly strongly *negatively* associated with both of the other two dimensions, competitiveness and liberties. No causation is meant to be implied here, but it seems that participation remains one of the significant problems of liberal democracy. How is it possible to increase the degree of popular participation in politics without decreasing the degree of competitiveness and liberties? Or, alternatively, how is it possible to increase the degree of competitiveness and/or liberties while at the same time increasing the degree of popular participation in politics, not to mention the expansion of the scope and kinds of participation in politics through interest groups, workplace, school, municipality, etc.? Similarly, when competitiveness and liberties are positively associated with a given level or rate of mobilization, participation is almost invariably negatively associated with that variable.

Finally, although a list of eight deviant cases was presented in Table 4-6, there are in reality only two deviant cases: Switzerland and the United States are both under-democratized. The other six cases may be slightly more than one standard error above or below the regression line, but in this particular regression, the standard error is rather small. The explanations for the two truely deviant cases are simple. Switzerland allowed women the franchise in national elections only in 1971; the turnout rate in presidential elections in the United States is notoriously low. But probably more importantly, in both Switzerland and the United States levels of industrialization and economic development are extremely high and rates of communication and economic development are extremely high. And it is these two levels and two rates of social mobilization that have the greatest explanatory power vis-à-vis liberal-democratic variables. Yet they are so very high in Switzerland and the United States that a concomitantly high level of liberal democracy is simply not attained.[23] But the central point is that there are only two deviant cases; the other 27 cases are quite close to the regression line as predicted. Anglo-Europa is a geocultural region in which social mobilization and liberal democracy are quite closely associated. The Anglo-European political tradition is a secular, differentiated political tradition.

5 The Iberic-Latin Model of Liberal Democracy

Included in the Iberic-Latin American geocultural region are the following 22 nations: Argentina, Bolivia, Brazil, Chile, Colombia, Costa Rica, Cuba, Dominican Republic, Ecuador, El Salvador, Guatemala, Haiti, Honduras, Jamaica, Mexico, Nicaragua, Paraguay, Peru, Portugal, Spain, Trinidad and Tobago, Uruguay, and Venezuela.[1] As will be demonstrated in this chapter, the pattern of relationships between social mobilization and liberal democracy among these countries is radically different from that of the global model. But first, an examination of the intercorrelations among liberal-democracy dimensions is informative. It, too, contrasts to the global model.

The data contained in Table 5-1 strongly suggest that there is simply very little or no relationship between any of the pairs of variables measuring dimensions of liberal democracy in the Iberic-Latin American region. There is only a slight association between competitiveness and either participation ($r = 0.24$) or liberties ($r = 0.32$). There is no relationship whatsoever between participation and liberties ($r = 0.00$!). Whether the countries of this region have a high or low degree of one dimension of liberal democracy is simply not related to whether they have a high or low degree of another dimension of democracy. But it should be added that these nations nonetheless do demonstrate all positive coefficients. That is, there is not a negative relationship between participation and either of the two other democracy variables; there is simply not much relationship at all. And, in addition, the relationship of each dimension with the composite indicator of liberal democracy is considerably smaller than that of the group of 85 nations in the global model. In brief, and this point will be discussed more elaborately later, the data in Table 5-1 suggest that liberal democracy is not a very useful concept in the Iberic-Latin region.

Turning next to a similar kind of assessment of the interrelationships between pairs of social-mobilization variables, both levels and rates, it is evident in Table 5-2 that the results can be characterized only as mixed.

Looking at the upper left quadrant that contains the coefficients relating levels of social mobilization, it is evident that Karl Deutsch's statement of high levels of association does not hold true in all cases. The relationship of education to industrialization and economic-development levels is fairly strong ($r = 0.85$). The remainder of the coefficients are small. It should be noted that none of the coefficients is negative.

When levels and rates of mobilization are intercorrelated, the results are similar. Only one is above the arbitrary minimum of $r = 0.60$, and that is the

Table 5-1
Matrix of Intercorrelations Among Measures of Liberal Democracy for Iberic-Latin Countries

	Competi-tiveness	Partici-pation	Liberties	Liberal Democracy
Competitiveness	1.00	0.24	0.32	0.77
Participation		1.00	0.00	0.62
Liberties			1.00	0.64
Liberal democracy				1.00

relationship between level of economic development and industrialization rate at $r = 0.70$. There simply seems to be very little association between the level of mobilization and the rate of continuing mobilization among the 22 Iberic-Latin nations.

The coefficients of correlation between rates of mobilization are perhaps most disappointing of all. There the highest is only $r = 0.41$, urbanization rate with communication rate. Equally unanticipated is the negative, though small, association between communication rate and economic-development rate. This is in drastic contrast to the global model, where this coefficient is large and positive.[2] With regard to the relationships between levels, between rates, and between levels and rates, social mobilization in Iberic-Latin nations is extremely uneven or unbalanced, fragmented, and inconsistent.[3]

Now that the data have shown that in Iberic-Latin nations there is little or no relationship between measures of liberal democracy and little or no relationship between measures of levels and rates of social mobilization, it would appear unlikely that strong relationships between mobilization and democracy variables would appear. It is to an examination of this hypothesis that we now turn.

Levels of Social Mobilization

Table 5-3 presents the simple- and multiple-correlation coefficients and beta weights for measures of levels of social mobilization and the four measures of liberal democracy.

Before discussing the discrete findings embodied in Table 5-3 in detail, the obvious probably deserves emphatic statement: in the Iberic-Latin nations, the level of social mobilization has little or nothing to do with the degree of liberal democracy, however measured. The one possible exception is that of public liberties, with a multiple-determination coefficient of 46.2 percent. This exception will be discussed later.

In terms of details, political competitiveness is hardly influenced by any or all

Table 5-2
Matrix of Intercorrelations Among Social-Mobilization Indicators for Iberic-Latin Nations

	Levels (1960)					Rates (1946-66)				
	1	2	3	4	5	6	7	8	9	10
1. Urbanization level	1.00	0.30	0.52	0.41	0.38	0.50	0.42	0.27	0.43	0.24
2. Education level		1.00	0.17	0.77	0.66	−0.03	0.01	0.22	0.44	0.34
3. Communication level			1.00	0.32	0.21	0.05	0.18	−0.19	0.20	0.52
4. Industrialization level				1.00	0.85	0.19	0.01	0.23	0.49	0.49
5. Economic-development level					1.00	0.16	0.04	0.22	0.70	0.27
6. Urbanization rate						1.00	0.38	0.41	0.13	−0.05
7. Education rate							1.00	0.20	0.27	0.04
8. Communication rate								1.00	0.16	−0.24
9. Industrialization rate									1.00	0.24
10. Economic-development rate										1.00

Table 5-3
Simple- and Multiple-Correlation Coefficients for Measures of Liberal Democracy and Levels of Social Mobilization for Iberic-Latin Nations

	Urbani-zation		Educa-tion		Communi-cation		Industri-alization		Economic Development			
	r	β	r	β	r	β	r	β	r	β	R	R^2
Competitiveness	0.03	0.13	0.09	−0.06	−0.16	−0.30	0.12	0.31	0.10	−0.10	0.28	7.8%
Participation	0.20	0.23	0.03	0.30	0.02	0.25	−0.11	−1.07	0.12	−0.68	0.53	28.1%
Liberties	0.22	0.11	0.30	−0.30	0.16	−0.15	0.20	1.38	0.29	−0.72	0.68	46.2%
Liberal democracy	0.23	0.24	0.20	−0.04	0.01	−0.20	0.05	0.27	0.26	0.00	0.34	11.6%

of the five levels of social mobilization. The beta coefficients of three of the mobilization variables (education, communication, and economic-development levels) are negative, although quite small. And only 7.8 percent of the total variation in degree of political competitiveness is accounted for by levels of social mobilization. This proportion of explained variation is considerably smaller than that of the global model.[4]

For participation, only 28.1 percent of the variation is explained: this proportion is slightly greater than that of the global model.[5] It is clear that of that 28.1 percent, most of the statistical explanation is contributed by two variables: industrialization and economic-development levels. But the beta coefficients are *negative*! If the level of industrialization is incremented by one unit, the degree of participation is decreased by −1.07 units; an increment of one unit in the level of economic development produces a decrease of −0.68 unit in participation. A glance back at Table 5-1 reveals that these two independent variables are positively related ($r = 0.49$).

Slightly less than half (46.2%) of the variation in public liberties is accounted for by all five mobilization-level variables in combination; this is a higher percentage of the variation explained than is the case in the global model.[6] Three of the beta weights are negative: education ($\beta = -0.30$), communication ($\beta = -0.15$), and economic development ($\beta = -0.72$). However, the largest change produced in liberties by a one-unit increase in any independent variable is that produced by industrialization; here the beta weight is 1.38. It is evident that the largest contributions are made positively by industrialization and negatively by economic development ($\beta = -0.72$); as mentioned above, these two independent variables are positively related to each other ($r = 0.49$). As one increases (or decreases) the other tends also to increase (or decrease); and, as industrialization increases, liberties tends to increase, and as economic development increases, liberties tends to decrease. More will be said of these and similar kinds of inconsistencies and possible resultant tensions later.

Finally, with regard to the composite index of liberal democracy, the proportion of explained variation is quite small, $R^2 = 11.6\%$.[7] Naturally, with a coefficient of determination that small, no single independent variable makes a very large contribution to explained variation. Yet it might be mentioned, again, that two of the beta weights are negative, and three are positive. Also, even though the beta coefficients of economic development with two of the three dimensions of democracy are fairly large, an increase of one unit of economic development produces no change whatsoever in the degree of liberal democracy. It should be remembered, as is shown in Table 5-1, that the relationships between dimensions of democracy are small or nonexistent.

A final note on these relationships as measured in Table 5-3 pertains to evidence of imbalance and potential tension in Iberic-Latin nations. A chief example of such evidence is the relationship of industrialization to each of the three dimensions of democracy. Whereas an increase of one unit in industrialization level produces a decrease of −1.07 in participation, it produces an increase of 1.38 units in public liberties. And industrialization level is the single most important variable for both participation and liberties. And, to add to the confusion, the simple-correlation coefficient between participation and liberties is $r = 0.00$! Increased participation tends to bring on an increasingly larger number of demands made on the political system, demands that most Iberic-Latin governments cannot, in the absence of more wealth and resources, adequately meet. Therefore, the governments must either reduce the participation or safeguard constitutional stability by seriously constraining public liberties.[8] In these Iberic-Latin nations, wherever industrialization is high, participation is low and liberties is high; where industrialization is low, participation is high and liberties is low. However, it must be repeated that since the coefficients of multiple correlation are not large, these statements characterizing the relationships among industrialization, participation, and liberties are tentative.

Rates of Social Mobilization

As will be seen in Table 5-4 below, the relationship between rates of mobilization and dimensions of liberal democracy is about the same as levels of mobilization and democracy—weak and inconsistent.[9]

The findings contained in Table 5-4 are rather easy to summarize; the relationships documented in that table are simply weak, at best. Only participation, with 32.8 percent of its variation explained by rates of social mobilization, is at all associated with the independent variables. Industrialization and economic-development levels make the largest contributions to the explained variation of participation with beta weights of $\beta = 0.41$ and $\beta = -0.40$ respectively, presenting the same sort of situation as was documented with levels of mobilization and democracy (two independent variables that are positively related, $r = 0.24$, one of which is negatively and one of which is positively related to a dependent variable, namely participation). However, the present case is less problematic because of the lower level of correlation between the two independent variables.

Rate of social mobilization apparently has little impact on political competitiveness (R^2 = 6.0%). Variations in public liberties and liberal democracy in general seem almost equally impervious to the expected forces of social-mobilization change, with multiple-determination coefficients of 15.6 percent and 13.4 percent respectively. When the multiple coefficients are that small, it makes little statistical or political sense to examine the contributions of individual variables in detail. Suffice it to say that for liberties, three of the beta weights are negative, and for the composite indicator of liberal democracy, three of the beta weights are negative. But they are not the same three beta weights in both cases.

Table 5-4

Simple- and Multiple-Correlation Coefficients for Measures of Liberal Democracy and Rates of Social Mobilization for Iberic-Latin Nations

	Urbanization		Education		Communication		Industrialization		Economic Development			
	r	β	r	β	r	β	r	β	r	β	R	R^2
Competitiveness	0.03	0.00	0.17	0.18	−0.13	−0.05	−0.12	−0.08	−0.16	−0.10	0.26	6.0%
Participation	−0.12	−0.10	0.14	0.12	−0.38	0.24	−0.03	0.41	−0.36	−0.40	0.57	32.8%
Liberties	0.20	0.35	−0.11	−0.20	−0.09	−0.13	−0.17	−0.22	0.04	0.18	0.39	15.6%
Liberal democracy	0.05	0.10	0.10	0.05	−0.30	−0.30	−0.16	0.06	−0.24	−0.15	0.36	13.4%

Relative Influence of Levels and Rates of Social Mobilization

It is still possible, however, that when the combined influence of levels and rates of social mobilization is taken into account, a substantial proportion of the variation in some or all of the dimensions of democracy could be statistically explained. This is an especially appealing proposition, since it is already known that there are not large coefficients of simple correlation between most of the pairs of levels and rates of social mobilization. It might even be expected that the combined influence of levels and rates might be almost as great as the sum of separate influences of levels and rates related to a given dimension of democracy. However, such is clearly not the case. Table 5-5 demonstrates that the two sets of independent variables combined explain more of the variation than either set alone, but still not as much as might be anticipated.

In Table 5-5, the multiple-correlation coefficients produced when competition and liberties are regressed on level of social mobilization (column 1) are slightly higher than when they are regressed on rate (column 2). In contrast, the coefficients produced when participation and the composite indicator of liberal democracy are regressed on rate are larger than when they are regressed on level of social mobilization. When regressed on both level and rate of social mobilization (column 3), the coefficients of all four measures of democracy are increased in size, although only liberal democracy is increased appreciably. The point is, even when the influence of both level and rate of social mobilization is taken into account, the proportion of the variation in Latin-Iberic democracy that is statistically explained is not large. Almost half of liberties variation is accounted for, (R^2 = 49%) but for the other three dependent variables the proportion of explained variation is small. Only 15.2 percent of the variation in competitiveness is accounted for, only 43.6 percent of the variation in participation, and only 28.1 percent of the variation in liberal democracy.[10]

Table 5-5
Multiple- and Multiple-Partial-Correlation Coefficients for Social Mobilization and Liberal Democracy in Iberic-Latin Nations

	Multiple Correlation Coefficients			Multiple-Partial Correlation Coefficients	
	1	2	3	4	5
	Levels	Rates	Levels and Rates	Level w/ Rate Constant	Rate w/ Level Constant
Competition	0.28	0.26	0.39	0.30	0.28
Participation	0.53	0.57	0.66	0.39	0.46
Liberties	0.68	0.39	0.70	0.64	0.25
Liberal democracy	0.34	0.36	0.53	0.42	0.44

Columns 4 and 5 of Table 5-5 provide the multiple-partial-correlation coefficients. When the rate of mobilization is held constant, and the relationship between level of mobilization and a dimension of democracy is examined, the coefficients are substantially higher than might be expected. Although the multiple-correlation coefficients for level of mobilization and competitiveness (in column 1 of Table 5-5) are low to start with, the multiple-partial coefficient between level of mobilization and competitiveness with the influence of rate held constant is actually increased slightly from 0.28 to 0.30. Again, comparing column 1 and 4 in Table 5-5, the coefficient for participation decreases from 0.53 to 0.39. Similarly, the coefficient for public liberties decreases only slightly from 0.68 to 0.64. Finally, the coefficient for liberal democracy increases from 0.34 to 0.42.

When level of mobilization is held constant and the relationship between rate and measures of democracy is examined, a similar pattern is found. A comparison of columns 2 and 5 indicates that the coefficient for competitiveness changes from 0.26 to 0.28; that for participation from 0.57 to 0.46; that for liberties from 0.30 to 0.25; and that for liberal democracy from 0.36 to 0.44. The point here is that the multiple-partial coefficients, when rate of mobilization is held constant, are reduced in size in two cases and increased in size in two cases. Holding constant the influence of level of mobilization does not substantially eradicate the influence of rate of mobilization. Similarly, partialling out the effect of rate of mobilization does not appreciably alter the relationship between level of mobilization and measures of liberal democracy. This Iberic-Latin pattern of relationships, although the coefficients are generally low compared with those in the global model, stand in obvious contrast to the pattern of relationships in the global model. In the global model, when level of mobilization was held constant, rate of mobilization retained much of its explanatory power; when rate was held constant, level lost much of its explanatory power. However, in the nations of the Iberic-Latin geocultural region, although neither level nor rate accounts for a large proportion of the variation in any of the four dependent variables of liberal democracy, when one is held constant, the other continues to account for about the same proportion of variation of a given dependent variable. Rate of mobilization is clearly not the dominant explanatory variable in the Iberic-Latin nations, as it was in the global model. Level of mobilization in the Iberic-Latin nations is clearly more important vis-à-vis rate of mobilization than it is in the global model. However, it should be reemphasized: neither level nor rate nor both is all that strongly related to measures of democracy among Iberic-Latin nations.

Unexplained Variation and the Deviant Cases

The foregoing analysis casts considerable doubt on a major hypothesis of social-mobilization theory: that social mobilization produces liberal democracy, in the geocultural context of the Iberic-Latin nations. There is a relationship, but it is rather weak, especially when compared with the global model. Figure 5-1 presents the extent of relationship between social mobilization and liberal democracy visually, and it permits the identification of individual Iberic-Latin nations in terms of their closeness to the regression line, above or below.

In general, the scatter is shaped like a gourd upside down with Spain and Portugal at the small end. These two nations are lowest of all 24 Iberic-Latin countries on both liberal democracy and social mobilization. The heteroscedasticity of the scatter is due to the rather closer relationship between social mobilization and liberal democracy in the lower reaches of the domain of those two scales and the considerably weaker relationship in the upper reaches. In other words, the strength of the association weakens with movement from low toward high on the two scales, producing the large end of the gourd with Jamaica the outstanding case. A sizeable number of cases, particularly above the regression line, moves away from the regression line with an increase in both scales.

Of the nine nations with liberal democracy scores of 50 or greater, only two (Venezuela and Panama) are below the regression line and therefore tend to be somewhat under-democratized. Of the 13 cases with liberal-democracy scores below fifty, only two are above the regression line and therefore more or less over-democratized. These patterns suggest that in the Iberic-Latin geocultural region, democratic nations tend to be over-democratized relative to their social mobilization and nondemocratic or authoritarian nations tend to be under-democratized relative to their social mobilization. It should also be noted that of the 15 nations below the regression line, those more or less under-democratized, none is more than one standard error of the estimate below the line. In contrast, of the nine nations above the line and thus more or less over-democratized, fully five are more than one standard error of the estimate above the line.

The deviant cases, those which lie more than one standard error of the estimate away from the regression line, are listed in Table 5-6. Since none actually falls more than one standard error below the line, the criterion for classifying a nation as under-democratized has been relaxed just a bit to include the four nations that come very close.

A look back at Table 2-8 reveals that the five Iberic-Latin nations that are most over-democratized in Iberic-Latin terms are also most over-democratized in global terms. And similarly, the four nations that are most under-democratized in terms of their own geocultural region are also under-democratized relative to the global model.

The results of the analyses of the scattergram (Figure 5-1) and the over-democratized and under-democratized nations simply continue to support the conclusion already drawn from the regression and correlation analyses: that social mobilization has considerably less to do with liberal democracy in Iberic-Latin nations than was originally hypothesized and even less than was

Table 5-6
Over-Democratized and Under-Democratized Nations of the Iberic-Latin Region

Over-Democratized		Under-Democratized	
Jamaica	16.2	Paraguay	−6.4
Nicaragua	9.5	El Salvador	−6.2
Costa Rica	9.4	Spain	−6.1
Bolivia	7.9	Peru	−6.1
Chile	7.0		

found to be the case in the global model. The problem becomes one of trying to account for the relative failure of social-mobilization theory to explain liberal democracy, rather than to describe the ways in which it does explain liberal democracy. Only 15.2 percent of the variation in political competitiveness is accounted for, only 43.6 percent of popular participation, 49 percent of public liberties, and only 28.1 percent of the variation in liberal democracy. The next section is devoted to the description of the Iberic-Latin political tradition, political culture and institutions, with regard to the ways in which they tend to affect the relationship between social mobilization and liberal democracy. It is a political tradition that is hostile to liberal democracy and to the optimization of the relationship between social mobilization and liberal democracy. The Iberic-Latin political tradition is one in which, for a variety of reasons discussed below, the practices of liberal democracy are largely irrelevant. Just how this came to be and why it continues are dealt with in the next section.

The Iberic-Latin Political Tradition: Corporatism

The concepts of cultural secularization and structural differentiation are, as they were in the case of Anglo-Europa, useful again in the analysis of patterns of Iberic-Latin politics. It is clear that in most respects, Iberic-Latin political institutions tend not to be well differentiated, and they are embedded in a political culture and society that are not highly secularized in orientation. But because it is just as clear that there can be numerous variants of the traditional, undifferentiated polity, simply specifying that these two latter features characterize the Iberic-Latin geocultural region is obviously insufficient. The question becomes, what particular combination of values and structures best characterizes the Iberic-Latin political tradition and makes it distinctive, that is, different from the central values and structures of African or Near and Far Eastern political systems. It is hypothesized that these cultural and structural properties

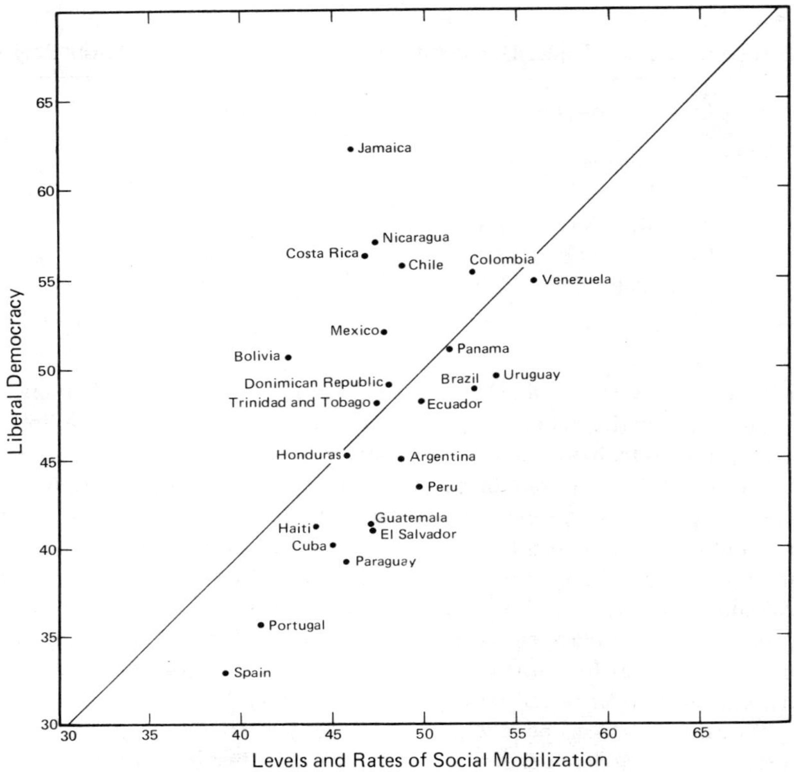

Figure 5-1. Scattergram of Social Mobilization and Liberal Democracy for Iberic-Latin Nations ($R = 0.53$)

are largely responsible for the virtual absence of a relationship between social mobilization and liberal democracy. The position argued here is that, although elements of culture, society, and state tend to be mixed and fused in bewildering complexity, the Iberic-Latin political culture is best described as "organicist-corporatist," and the polity itself is best characterized as "patrimonialist-corporatist."[11] In short, Iberic-Latin societies and states are corporatist and manifest little cultural secularization or structural differentiation in political terms.

Howard J. Wiarda has captured the essential properties of Iberic-Latin political culture in the following definition:

[a long] cultural-historical tradition stretching back to the origins of the Iberic-Latin systems and embodying a dominant form of socio-political organiza-

tion that is . . . hierarchical, elitist authoritarian, bureaucratic, Catholic, patrimonialist, and corporatist to its core.[12]

Iberic-Latin political culture (and the society that rests on its values) is based on a strong philosophic tradition or cultural predisposition toward organic harmony of all values, interests, and institutions. This basis is moral idealism or a unified moral purpose, and its origin is traceable to the Roman heritage of the Iberic-Latin region[13] and to Christianity, most emphatically and predominantly to the religious and philosophical certainty of Catholicism. These fundamental values of religio-philosophical thought add up to a unified, organic-corporate conception of society and state, and they are authoritarian, traditional, conservative, elitist, patrimonial, Catholic, horizontally stratified, vertically segmented, hierarchical, and both class- and caste-based.[14] They include as well as support the bases for the impressive historical continuity of Iberic-Latin political institutions and political values. Again, these values and conceptions can easily be traced to the pervasive influence of Roman law and early Christian theological sources. These are the values that have historically conditioned the thought and action of leaders and masses in the Iberic-Latin mode.

Yet between 1850 and 1900, currents of change, including industrialization, urbanization, and ideology, began to affect the political culture of this region, particularly Spain and Portugal initially. Their philosophers began to face up to the questions of change and modernization raised, even forced, by such powerful social forces, and based their work largely on newer and reformist currents coming out of the Catholic church and on their own very strong philosophical tradition. They produced, well within the organicist-corporatist framework, a modified philosophical system for thought and action that blended the traditional concern for order and hierarchy with the developing necessity for change and modernization.[15] These political cultural values, as well as the political institutions, which developed out of this gradual and evolutionary transformation, yielded a political tradition that has a remarkable capacity for permeability, absorption, adjustment, accommodation, co-optation, flexibility, and adaptation. In short, these values and institutions are extremely resilient. They respond to social change and the forces of modernization by grafting them onto their institutions but without appreciably transforming those institutions. They undergo the shocks and strains of change without themselves being changed.[16] This genuinely resilient and flexible value system and set of political institutions that it supports bend but do not break, and they have a remarkably strong tendency to return subtly to their original shapes. Environmental changes and challenges are absorbed and transformed into supportive forces by the Iberic-Latin organicist-corporatist political culture.

The way in which this process occurs and the nature of the political structures that it produces are closely related and can both be discussed in the same context—that of the patrimonialist-corporatist polity. Again relying on Wiarda's definition, the patrimonialist-corporatist polity is a

> system of authority and interest representation, derived chiefly (though not exclusively) from Catholic thought, stressing factional representation, the integration of labor and capital into a vast web of hierarchically ordered 'harmonies', monopolistic, and functionally determined units (or 'corporations'), and guided and directed by the State.[17]

In addition, it should be pointed out that there can be such systems of authority and interest representation which are progressive, leftist regimes and systems which are regressive and rightist regimes. A patrimonialist-corporatist regime may or may not undertake a variety of "modernizing" plans and programs.[18]

This kind of political structure is, as earlier stated, based on a vertically and horizontally segmented hierarchy of class and caste stratifications, social rank orders, functional corporations, estates, juridical groupings, and interests, all of which are closely linked to and in fact derive their authority and legitimacy from the central state or its leader.

All of the adjectives that were used to describe the political culture also apply with mostly similar precision to the political institutions themselves.[19] The political process and institutions are dominated by a heterogeneous elite that is itself composed of functionally differentiated, bureaucratically organized "orders." These noncompetitive orders have been heavily penetrated by the state. Therefore, it is rather easy for the state, through its leader, to control crucial political processes such as interest representation and leadership selection. Although the orders are, according to corporatist-political culture, supposed to be equal, they are not; the military order frequently predominates for obvious reasons.[20] The processes of electoral selection and legislative decision-making are, for example, frequently dominated by a single or hegemonic-political party.

In addition to the political-cultural values that pervade and give meaning to Iberic-Latin political life, the explanation for this executive-statist dominance is related to the virtually complete bureaucratization of politics. In fact, politics has been substantially both depoliticized and de-ideologized. Political problems, old and new, are as quickly as possible converted into legal-administrative issues and given bureaucratic solutions. This form of super-administrative state operates on the basis of vertical, compartmentalized interactions, which it encourages. However, horizontal communications and interactions, for example on the basis of socioeconomic class or geographical region, are not only discouraged but prohibited. When the executive is not able to manage challenges to existing policy and processes routinely, through their conversion to legal-administrative issues and then their bureaucratic administration, he usually initiates a plan of co-optation and selective privilege rather than substantial modification of policies or processes. If co-optation and selective privilege fail, large-scale repression of the challenging groups is the alternative usually followed.

The state and its leader have this kind of variable- and flexible-response capability in part because they neither monopolize access to important political roles nor enforce rigid adherence to an ideological system. These two features also explain in part the high degree to which the state and leader are accorded widespread legitimacy by the orders and masses. The leader quite consciously cultivates numerous bases of legitimacy, for example, a deliberate blending of traditional, charismatic, and rational-legal bases of legitimacy. And all that is demanded of subjects by the state in terms of their orientations toward the state's legitimacy, is simple compliance, not active support or positive enthusiasm.

Executive political power in Iberic-Latin polities has, over the decades, achieved considerable autonomy from socioeconomic class, economic sectoral, or regional interests as well as from the political party or parties. In this position, the executive and the state can usually remain remarkably resistant to change and modernization. In cases or during periods in which the demands for change are too strong to subdue and/or subsume, the state is usually able effectively to control and otherwise favorably manipulate the political consequences of change or to move forcefully and preemptively.

The patrimonialist and organicist corporatism of the Iberic-Latin region is the outcome of centuries of slow political evolution. Development in these nation-states involved, as in other regions of the world, the results of two more or less conflicting processes of structural change, the diffusion of power and the concentration of resources in societies. However, in the Iberic-Latin region, three distinctive contingent properties of these social systems, perhaps necessary and sufficient conditions, produced corporatism rather than some other political tradition: (1) these nations experienced and continue to experience unusual longevity and historical continuity on the part of their major institutions; (2) the state assumed and retained full responsibility for the concentration of emergent resources; and (3) the state managed to subordinate, control, and manipulate various kinds of representative associations that would otherwise probably have become more or less autonomous associational interest groups. All these conditions and contingencies were by and large fulfilled in each of the Iberic-Latin nations and the political outcomes are, though hardly identical in all, roughly the same—a corporatist culture, society, and state.

Iberic-Latin levels of social mobilization were, in the period under study, higher than those of any other geocultural region except Anglo-Europa. Iberic-Latin rates of change, increases in all cases, were also higher than Africa and the Near and Far East, except in the two cases of education rate and industrialization rate (in both cases, lower than the Near and Far East but higher than Africa). Yet in spite of these relatively high levels and rates of indicators of social mobilization, the expected effects of such social processes are not evident in the Iberic-Latin region. There seems to be only a weak, tenuous, and indirect relationship, if any, between social mobilization and liberal democracy. First, although urbanization, education, communication, industrialization, and economic-development levels and rates in the Iberic-Latin nations are comparatively high, social mobilization is not necessarily occurring there. Neither has the erosion of old habits, customs, mores, outlooks, patterns of behavior, attitudes, etc., nor the emergence of new such habits, customs, etc., accompanied the processes of urbanization, education, communication, industrialization, and economic development. Standing between these processes and the expected or usual practices of liberal democracy are the organicist-corporatist political culture and the patrimonialist-corporatist state. This kind of culture and state absorb the shocks of the five social-mobilization processes without being themselves transformed, obliterated, or simply allowed to wither while new cultural norms and new political institutions emerge. At the risk of arguing in circles, it seems that the organicist-corporatist Iberic-Latin political culture, now several centuries old, can be viewed as partly responsible for producing the patrimonial-corporatist Iberic-Latin state, and that the state, over the centuries, has been extremely effective in cultivating the political culture as the basis of its own survival and prosperity. The state was able to establish and maintain its superordination vis-à-vis any and all other classes, groups, and sectors, nascent or organized, because of the nature and strength of the political tradition, and to manipulate and dominate them. The culture remained virtually unchanged largely because the authoritarian state made change highly difficult. And so forth for several centuries.

Wiarda, probably the most perceptive student of corporatist culture and institutions, has come to a similar kind of conclusion through the examination of Iberic-Latin political and social history and theory. For example, he states that,[21]

> . . . if one uses corporatism in the broadest historical and political-cultural sense, and sees the 1930s experiments with "corporatism" as close to and essentially a modern-day adaptation and relabeling of that older tradition, then the model of society and polity we have been presenting is useful in studying an even wider range of phenomena: class relations, patrimonialism, the nature of the state, the economic system, social structure and behavior, *patron*-client patterns, the nature of the change process, etc. In this more general sense, corporatism seems closely attuned to the prevailing value system, a part of the natural Iberic-Latin systems function, *an historic response that often renders inapplicable the pluralist-democratic model on the one hand or the fascist-totalitarian one on the other.* [italics added]

6 The African Model of Liberal Democracy

The African model is based on data from the following 16 sub-Saharan countries: Cameroun, Dahomey, Gabon, Ghana, Guinea, Ivory Coast, Kenya, Liberia, Malagasy Republic, Malawi, Nigeria, Sierra Leone, South Africa, Sudan, Tanzania, and Uganda.[1] As Table 6-1 demonstrates, there seems to be little coherence among dimensions of liberal democracy in these 16 African countries.

In the case of Africa, the intercorrelations between pairs of liberal-democracy dimensions are either low or negative. For example, the relationship between competitiveness and participation is negative and almost large enough to call strong (–0.37). In Africa, where political competitiveness tends to be high, mass participation tends to be low, and similarly, the nations in which there are greater levels of participation tend to have little or no political competitiveness.[2] Although the coefficient is positive, the relationship between political competitiveness and public liberties is small, $r = 0.16$; the distribution of these two democratic practices among African nations tends to be random, that is, there can be considerable public liberty in the absence of competitiveness and politically competitive situations that permit little or no liberty. Finally, with a coefficient of simple correlation of –0.01 between mass participation and public liberties, it is possible to conclude only that no relationship exists; these two variables are completely independent of each other in the African political experience. In short, the elements of liberal democracy in Africa are so incoherent as to be irrelevant to African politics. This means that not only do levels of liberal democracy tend to be low and, therefore, do not vary much from country to country, but also that even when there is some variation in liberal democratic practices from country to country, there is very little covariance between any two democracy variables.

In general, with regard to social mobilization in African nations, levels tend to be fairly strongly intercorrelated, levels and rates mixed but with some noticeably strong correlations, and rates of social mobilization are, with one exception, only very weakly intercorrelated. Table 6-2 shows the complete matrix of intercorrelation between all pairs of social-mobilization variables.

All of the coefficients of correlation for levels of social mobilization are high except industrialization and the other four level variables. Levels of urbanization, education, communication, and economic development are strongly covariant, while the relationships between each of these and industrialization tends to be considerably weaker. In the upper right quadrant of Table 6-2 are coefficients measuring the relationship between levels and rates of social mobilization. Of the

Table 6-1
Matrix of Intercorrelations Between Dimensions of Democracy for African Countries

	1	2	3	4
1. Competitiveness	1.00	−0.37	0.16	0.27
2. Participation		1.00	−0.01	0.54
3. Liberties			1.00	0.73
4. Liberal democracy				1.00

25 coefficients, only eight are strong. Four of the strong relationships are between rates of communication and levels or urbanization ($r = 0.81$), education ($r = 0.75$), communication ($r = 0.90$), and economic development ($r = 0.85$). The other four large coefficients are between rates of economic development and levels of education ($r = 0.60$), communication ($r = 0.76$), industrialization ($r = 0.73$), and economic development ($r = 0.89$). Among all 25 coefficients there are mainly strong or weak relationships, and almost none in the moderate range. This complex set of relationships between levels and rates of mobilization assumes added importance when one examines the interrelationships between different rates of mobilization. The only two rates with a high coefficient are communication and economic development, the same two that produced the only high coefficients in the intercorrelations between levels and rates of mobilization. The coefficient of correlation between communication and industrialization rates is 0.73, indicating that the rates of change, increase in most cases, of these two variables are strongly covariant, and also that these two rates of change are strongly associated with levels of social mobilization (with two exceptions). It should be noted that all of these high coefficients are positive. Now we proceed to examine the extent to which social-mobilization indicators can explain the variability of liberal democracy.

Levels of Social Mobilization

Table 6-3 presents the various measures of association between levels of social mobilization and the four measures of liberal democracy.

The relationships documented in Table 6-3 are complex, conflicting, contrasting, and in many ways unexpected. It is evident that they do not support the theory and hypotheses relating social-mobilization and liberal-democratic practices; in fact, these findings generally tend to disconfirm the major hypotheses. First, regarding the relationship between political competitiveness and social mobilization, the two most important explanatory variables are levels of communication and economic development with beta weights of 1.44 and −1.06

Table 6-2

Matrix of Intercorrelations Among Social-Mobilization Indicators for African Nations

	Levels (1960)					Rates (1946-66)				
	1	2	3	4	5	6	7	8	9	10
1. Urbanization level	1.00	0.74	0.90	0.40	0.85	0.19	0.35	0.81	0.41	0.60
2. Education level		1.00	0.82	0.44	0.84	0.12	0.15	0.75	0.28	0.76
3. Communication level			1.00	0.44	0.94	0.11	0.14	0.90	0.52	0.73
4. Industrialization level				1.00	0.44	−0.05	−0.31	0.24	0.41	0.42
5. Economic-development level					1.00	0.04	0.23	0.85	0.48	0.89
6. Urbanization rate						1.00	0.21	0.02	−0.15	−0.07
7. Education rate							1.00	0.30	−0.08	0.24
8. Communication rate								1.00	0.43	0.73
9. Industrialization rate									1.00	0.38
10. Economic-development rate										1.00

Table 6-3
Simple- and Multiple-Correlation Coefficients for Levels of Social Mobilization and Liberal Democracy for African Nations

	Levels of Social Mobilization											
	Urbanization		Education		Communication		Industrialization		Economic Development			
	r	β	r	β	r	β	r	β	r	β	R	R^2
Competitiveness	0.67	−0.27	0.72	0.57	0.73	1.44	0.37	0.04	0.62	−1.06	0.84	70.6%
Participation	−0.26	0.59	−0.17	−0.04	−0.33	−2.81	−0.33	−0.26	−0.08	2.16	0.82	67.2%
Liberties	0.00	−0.31	0.08	0.23	0.04	0.53	0.08	0.05	0.00	−0.45	0.20	4.0%
Liberal democracy	0.11	−0.11	0.25	0.37	0.11	−0.97	−0.02	−0.14	0.21	0.78	0.41	16.8%

respectively. Among African nations, level of communication is positively and level of economic development negatively related to degree of political competitiveness. It was previously shown in Table 6-2 that these two independent variables have an intercorrelation coefficient that is both strong and positive, $r = 0.94$. The disequilibrating tendencies are obvious in such cases.

The situation is similar in the case of mass political participation as well. An increase of one unit in economic development produces an increase of 2.16 in the level of participation, while an increase of one unit in the level of communication produces a decrease of –2.81 in the degree of participation. The conflicting forces are even more extreme in the case of participation. It is also worth noting, in a comparison of competitiveness and participation, that the directions of the relationships for communication and economic-development levels are reversed. That is, the beta for communication level is positive for competitiveness and negative for participation; the beta for economic development is negative for competitiveness and positive for participation. Thus the imbalance and strain are very complex; high communication levels are associated with high competitiveness and low participation; high economic-development levels are associated with low competitiveness and high participation; high communication levels are strongly associated with high economic-development levels; although competitiveness and participation are only moderately related, the relationship is negative, $r = -0.37$. This condition represents potential for societal disequilibrium in the extreme.

Although the same situation tends to persist with regard to public liberties, it is considerably less pronounced. Communication level is positively related ($\beta = 0.53$) and economic-development level negatively related ($\beta = -0.45$) to public liberties. However, as will be shown, the proportion of liberties variation that is explained by level of social mobilization is small.

The composite indicator of liberal democracy shows the same kind of disequilibrium demonstrated by participation. Liberal democracy is positively related to communication level ($\beta = 0.97$) and negatively related to economic-development level ($\beta = -0.78$). The other three social-mobilization levels are only weakly related to liberal democracy.

When the influence of all five mobilization levels is considered, a large proportion of the variation in both political competitiveness and participation is statistically explained; $R^2 = 0.70.6\%$ and 67.2% respectively. However, knowing the nature of the internal relationships between levels of communication and economic development and the two dimensions of democracy, competitiveness and participation, it is difficult to state precisely the meaning of these high coefficients of multiple determination. As mentioned earlier, African experience has tended to produce national-political regimes that are either monopolistic-participatory or competitive-exclusive, in terms of competitiveness and participation. It seems that the ways in which levels of communication and economic development are interpreted and managed by African political systems and their leaders are radically different.

Public liberties in African states seems not to be associated with levels of social mobilization; the coefficient of multiple determination is only 4.0 percent. The same generalization applies, but with less force, to the relationship between social mobilization and the composite indicator of liberal democracy. Here the coefficient of multiple determination is only 16.8 percent.[3] This latter finding is hardly surprising in view of the conflicts and disequilibria within and between both independent and dependent variables. As will be seen next, the complex of relationships is similar when rate of social mobilization is considered.

Rates of Social Mobilization

Table 6-4 presents the results of regression analysis of rates of social-mobilization and liberal-democracy measures.

Variations in the level of political competitiveness seem to be most closely associated with only one social-mobilization rate, that of communication; an increase of one unit in communication rate produces an increase of 0.85 units in political competitiveness. None of the other mobilization rates is closely associated with competitiveness. Mass participation variations are closely linked to both communication rate and economic-development rate, but again one relationship is negative and the other is positive. A one-unit increase in communication rate produces a decrease of –0.95 in participation, while a one unit increase in economic-development rate produces an increase in participation of 0.79. It should be recalled at this point that these are the only two rates of social mobilization that are highly intercorrelated ($r = 0.73$). The rates of both communication and economic development are accelerating together but simultaneously producing conflicting results with regard to the practice of liberal democracy.

No mobilization-rate variable is closely related to variations in public liberties or in the composite indicator of liberal democracy. One-unit increases in communication and economic development produce conflicting but small increments in liberal democracy.

When the influence of all five independent variables is taken into account, the coefficient of multiple correlation for competitiveness is $R = 0.76$; thus 57.7 percent of the variation is statistically accounted for. Similarly, almost half, $R^2 = 49.0$ percent, of the variation in participation is explained by the five social-mobilization rates. Neither of these is as large as the same two coefficients using levels of mobilization. The multiple-correlation coefficient for public liberties is, again, quite small, $R = 0.29$ and the coefficient for liberal democracy is not much bigger, $R = 0.39$.[4]

As was the case with levels of social mobilization, competitiveness and participation variables seem to be closely connected only with variations in communication and economic-development rates and not with the other three

Table 6-4
Simple- and Multiple-Correlation Coefficients for Rates of Social Mobilization and Liberal Democracy for African Nations

	Rates of Social Mobilization											
	Urbanization		Education		Communication		Industrialization		Economic Development			
	r	β	r	β	r	β	r	β	r	β	R	R^2
Competitiveness	−0.10	−0.14	−0.07	−0.29	0.65	0.85	0.49	0.16	0.41	−0.15	0.76	57.7%
Participation	−0.09	−0.02	0.25	0.36	−0.26	−0.95	0.21	−0.09	0.18	0.79	0.70	49.0%
Liberties	0.15	0.19	−0.15	−0.08	−0.06	-0.17	0.13	0.22	−0.04	0.03	0.29	8.4%
Liberal democracy	0.00	0.05	0.04	0.04	0.05	−0.42	0.15	0.14	0.29	0.51	0.39	15.2%

rates of social mobilization. But it also should be remembered that, with regard to these two democracy variables, level of mobilization seemed to have considerably more explanatory power. It remains to be seen to what extent, if any, either level or rate of social mobilization retains its explanatory power when the influence of the other is partialled out.

Relative Influence of Levels and Rates of Social Mobilization

Table 6-5 repeats multiple-correlation coefficients from the previous two tables and also includes similar coefficients when both level and rate of mobilization are used to account for variations in liberal democracy. It also indicates the strength of association between democratic variables and each of the sets of independent variables while holding constant the influence of the other set (columns 4 and 5).

Column 3 of Table 6-5 can be compared with columns 1 and 2. When both level and rate of social mobilization are used to explain variations in competitiveness ($R = 0.85$), the enlargement in the size of the correlation coefficient is negligible. This is little improvement over the coefficient using only level of mobilization. No improvement over the use of only level of mobilization is found when both level and rate are used to explain participation; the coefficient for the latter correlation is $R = 0.82$, the same as that for level alone. Similarly, there is not much difference for liberal democracy. Level and rate of social mobilization seem to predict equally well. However, an examination of columns 4 and 5 in Table 6-5 strongly indicate that it is primarily the level of social mobilization, and not so much the rate, that is associated with variations in liberal-democratic practices in Africa.

Table 6-5
Multiple- and Multiple-Partial-Correlation Coefficients for Levels and Rates of Social Mobilization and Liberal Democracy for African Nations

	Multiple Correlation Coefficients			Multiple-Partial-Correlation Coefficients	
	1	2	3	4	5
	Level	Rate	Level and Rate	Level w/Rate Constant	Rate w/Level Constant
Competitiveness	0.84	0.76	0.85	0.58	0.18
Participation	0.82	0.70	0.82	0.60	−0.03
Liberties	0.20	0.29	0.30	0.19	0.23
Liberal democracy	0.41	0.39	0.44	0.23	0.20

When the influence of rate of mobilization is held constant, the size of the coefficients of correlation between competitiveness and level of mobilization is not severely reduced; the coefficient in column 4 is 0.58. Similarly, level of mobilization retains much of its explanatory power when the influence of rate of mobilization is partialled out; in this case $R = 0.60$. Since the original multiple-correlation coefficients for public liberties and liberal democracy were small (columns 1 and 2), they remain small in both the multiple-partial coefficients.

In contrast, partialling out the influence of level of mobilization virtually eradicates the explanatory utility of rate of mobilization. This finding is apparent when columns 2 and 5 in Table 6-5 are compared. Considering only the two dependent variables which seem at all influenced by variations in social mobilization (competitiveness and participation), the coefficients are reduced in size from 0.76 to 0.18 and from 0.70 to –0.03, for rate of mobilization when level is held constant. With regard to the attainment and maintenance of political competitiveness and mass participation, in Africa it is the level of achievement and not the rate of achievement of social mobilization that seems to be important. Since the African average level of social mobilization on all five indicators is the lowest of any geocultural region, it is reasonable to speculate that the African rate of increase has no liberal democratic consequences at the African level of social mobilization. In other words, even high rates of mobilization have no immediate political consequences when level of mobilization is extremely low.[5] Once rate of increase is sufficient to build up, over time, the level of mobilization past the inhibiting threshold, rate may (or may not) then have the theoretically anticipated liberal-democratic consequences.

What is more certain, however, is that the pattern of the multiple-partial relationships of level and rate of social mobilization with liberal democratic variables in Africa is quite the reverse of what it is in the global model. When all 85 nations are included in the regressions, rate of change retains its explanatory utility, but level does not. In Africa, level of social mobilization retains its usefulness while rate of change does not.

Unexplained Variation and the Deviant Cases

When considering the regression of the composite indicator of liberal democracy on social mobilization, it should be remembered that the degree of explained variation is comparatively quite small; in this case $R = 0.44$. The scatter of cases in Figure 6-1 clearly reveals the weakness of the relationship. Social mobilization simply offers no explanation of liberal democracy in African nations. The cases that fall more than one standard error (7.6) from the regression line are Nigeria, Uganda, Malagasy Republic, all of which are over-democratized, and Kenya and

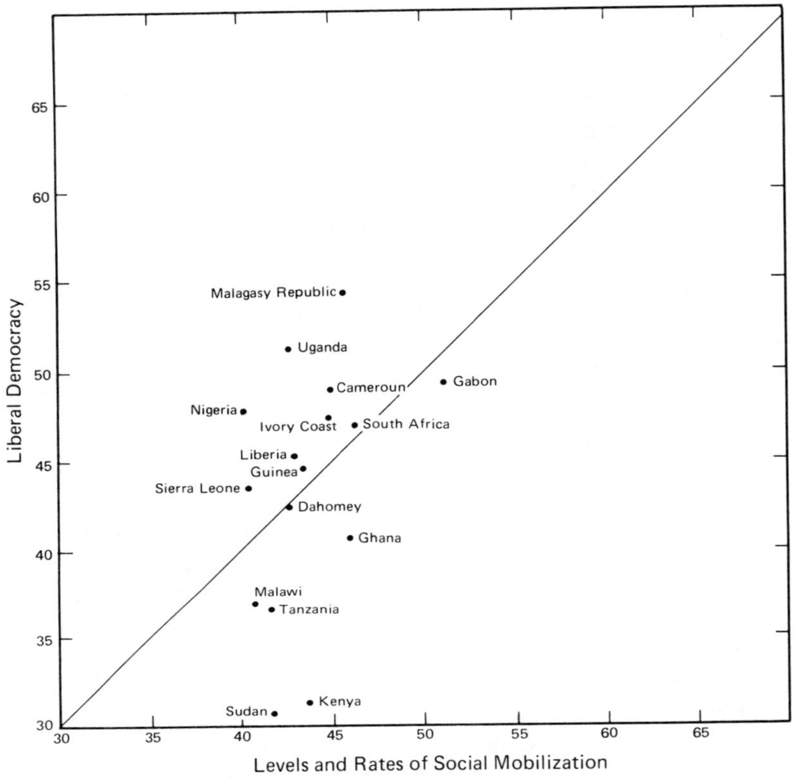

Figure 6-1. Scattergram of Social Mobilization and Liberal Democracy for African Nations ($R = 0.44$)

the Sudan, which are both under-democratized. Nigeria exceeds democratic expectations by 7.6 units, Uganda[6] by 8.8 units, and Malagasy Republic by 8.7 units. On the other hand, Kenya's liberal democracy score is 12.1 points lower than that predicted by her social mobilization, and the Sudan's liberal democracy score falls below expectations by 11 points.

Finally, Figure 6-1 reveals that Africa is not a place where liberal democracy flourishes; only Uganda and the Malagasy Republic actually score over 50.0 (the mean for all 85 countries) on the liberal democracy index. Similarly, African nations average lowest on all 10 measures of social mobilization.

It is apparent that, although political competitiveness and mass participation do seem to vary largely in response to variations in social mobilization in the African states, liberal democracy as such has not penetrated African polities.

Regimes that experience or permit high mass participation tend to have limited competitiveness. Nations which demonstrate considerable political competitiveness have little mass participation. Public liberties per se varies independently of social mobilization in Africa. Thus liberal democracy as a form of government is more random than patterned with respect to social mobilization. The problem in the next section is, therefore, to describe the traditions prominent in the African political experience that are responsible for the continuing failure of social mobilization to produce coherent liberal democracy.

The African Political Tradition: Communalism

In part the small degree of association between social mobilization and liberal democracy in Africa is explicable in terms of the extremely low levels and rates of mobilization. In comparison to the global model or any of the other three geocultural regional models, the means of African mobilization levels and rates are lowest.[7] Social-mobilization theory posits that before its various processes can have political consequences, they must reach a certain level. In African nations, not only are the levels low, but the rate at which these levels are increasing is the lowest. Thus it could be argued that social mobilization will, eventually, provide the basis for the development of increasingly coherent liberal-democratic political regimes, but not until the proper thresholds have been surpassed. But it should be remembered that the mean liberal-democratic score for African nations is also the lowest among the four regions and the world model. In spite of this, there is little shared variance between liberal democracy and any set of mobilization variables.

An additional and in many ways more satisfying answer for both the absence of a strong association between mobilization and democracy and for the weakness of liberal democracy in Africa can be found in the African political tradition. Two related concepts describe accurately the relevant central features of the political culture in Africa—traditionalism and communalism.

The political culture in African nations has undergone little secularization; rather it remains comparatively diffuse, parochial, and primitive.[8] The roles of the polity are not or at least not clearly differentiated from other societal roles, such as religious and economic. Political cultures characterized by diffuseness generally correspond to what are called "parochial" cultures. Parochial individuals in a political system are those who manifest highly diffuse social orientations and have little or no consciousness of the political system as a specific, distinct, specialized entity. A parochial has only the dimmest awareness of the existence of distinctly political structures at the national level. However, if such persons develop an awareness of a variety of governmental roles on the output side, such as tax collector, military officers, or police, but fail to conceive of themselves as legitimately able to make demands on government or to become aware of input structures like political parties or interest groups, they manifest a subject political orientation. The parochial or parochial-subject comprises a traditional political culture. The point is that the political culture has not become secularized.

Embedded in such a political culture, the polity tends strongly to be characterized by a minimum of structural differentiation and virtually no subsystem autonomy; the traditional and primitive political structures of such a polity are termed "intermittent." Gabriel A. Almond and G. Bingham Powell, Jr. cite as three different examples of the primitive, traditional system with undifferentiated, intermittent political structures these three African systems: the primitive bands of the Bergdama, the segmentary systems of the Nuer, and the pyramidal systems of the Ashanti.[9]

Although many of the polities of Africa tend toward the primitive, traditional, intermittent end of the spectrum, some do not. For example, Almond and Powell call Nigeria and Ghana "premobilized modern" systems, by which they mean that "the trappings of political modernity–parties, interest groups, and mass media–have been imposed upon highly traditional societies."[10] These apparently modern structures are, however, run by traditional elites in a traditional way. Only a small elite has been exposed to modernity, in terms of social mobilization, and although political awareness among the masses has been aroused by independence movements and the idea of economic betterment, political attitudes are primarily enmeshed in tradition. The ability and desire to engage in autonomous political participation is largely lacking in the populace, and even when the elites are able to arouse mass aspirations they are unable to satisfy them.

The basic reason for such a situation in these and many other African nations is that their more or less slightly differentiated political infrastructures exist primarily by accident; they were provided originally by colonialism or through the diffusion of ideas and institutions from the West long before African nations had the need, desire, or reason to develop such structures and cultures independently.[11]

In both the primitive and the premobilized modern political systems of Africa, three traditionalistic features stand out.[12] First, the low degree of structural differentiation means that many interests are latent and when they do assume political meaning, they frequently take the form of mob action or spontaneous violence. Political parties tend to be unstable; they appear, consolidate, reappear, fragment, etc. Political communication structures are intermittent, and unless the colonial legacy included an effective civil service, the bureaucratic structure is often weak and unreliable. Secondly, since political role orientations are so diffuse and unstable, there tends to be a high degree of substitutability among political roles. Bureaucracies often legislate, armies assume executive and judicial functions, political parties make national policy, etc. The division of labor, if indeed there is one at all, is quite unstable. Third, traditionalism encourages or at least permits the confusion of political roles. There may, for example, be a national legislative body that is formally based on a constitution, laws, and rules, but within the body there is a powerful family, an ethnic, racial, or linguistic group, a religious sect, or a group of chieftains who follow their traditional norms of behavior within the apparently modern legislature.

As is the case with an explanation of why social mobilization has not produced liberal democracy in the Iberic-Latin nations, the fact that African nations have traditional political systems, that is, diffuse cultures and undifferentiated structures, may be true but it is not by itself an adequate explanation. Both the description of political traditionalism in Africa and the reason why African politics has such a tradition can be understood only in relation to the phenomenon of "comunalism" and the "primordial sentiments"[13] of kinship, language, ethnicity, custom, tribe, race, and religion that comprise it. The strong primordial attachments in Africa inhibit the development and sustenance of liberal democracy because they inhibit national political integration, unity, and state-building.[14] If cultural heterogeneity is so strong that it prevents the construction of a nation-state, it also prevents the development of a liberal-democratic state.[15]

The term *communalism* in Africa refers to the political assertiveness of groups that have the following four characteristics:[16] (1) the membership of the group is comprised of people who share a common culture and identity and a "complementarity of communications";[17] (2) they include the entire array of demographic divisions within the wider society (for example, age and sex), and provide "for a network of groups and institutions extending throughout the individual's entire life cycle";[18] (3) resembling the greater society of which they are a part, they tend to be differentiated by wealth, power, and status; and (4) they share a common locality or territory.[19] In the case of many African communal groups, the "we" or "in-group" feeling is so strong that the groups are "candidates for nationhood."[20] Unlike economic, class, or intellectual groups that become dissatisfied and whose conflict can indeed become severe, primordial groups' discontent can "threaten to undermine the nation itself, because they . . . involve alternative definitions of what the nation is, of what its scope of reference is. . . ."[21] Primordial-political disaffection and assertiveness, based on language, culture, ethnicity, tribe, or kinship, "threatens partition, irredentism, or merger, a redrawing of the very limits of the state, a new dimension of its domain."[22] It is this kind of threat that makes nation- and state-building, and therefore liberal democracy, so very difficult in Africa. It is such primordial sentiments, natural and almost spiritual in nature, that serve seriously to distort the anticipated relationship between social mobilization and liberal democracy.

The term state-building refers "to the problem of integration and control," and the term nation-building refers to "the problem of group identity and loyalty."[23] State-building involves political penetration and integration, that which makes a society and political system cohere or hold together. State-building is accomplished through four basic processes: (1) territorial integration, or "establishing national central authority over subordinate units or regions which may or may not coincide with distinct cultural or social groups"; (2) elite-mass integration, or linking government with the governed; (3) value integration, or the integration of the citizen in a common political process; and (4) integrative behavior, referring to the integration of individuals into organizations for purposive activities.[24] In a similar vein, nation-building involves the development of loyalty and commitment to the state or political system, a process obviously related to the success or failure of state-building. A society characterized by cultural pluralism, in which each group has its own language and other self-conscious cultural identity, provides an extreme challenge to leaders who seek to create a sense of territorial nationality and to integrate diverse and discrete cultural loyalties into a single, unified national identity that overrides other more parochial affiliations. It is easy to see why African communalism has made difficult or prevented altogether any positive progress toward the building of viable nation-states.[25] Yet even more is involved. Under conditions of African communalism, not only does social mobilization fail to produce movement toward the establishment of stable, viable (liberal-democratic) nation-states, but it acts in a very negative way to produce instability, conflict, tension, extreme malintegration and occasionally insurrections, revolutions, and coups d'etat. The reasons for this situation also proved the explanation for the absence of the expected relationship between social-mobilization and liberal-democratic practices.

The first reason, which helps to explain why African nations make little or no forward progress toward stable, viable political systems, pertains to the kinds of traditionalism predominant in Africa. Following David E. Apter, African political traditionalism can be characterized either as instrumental-hierarchical or consummatory-pyramidal.[26] An instrumental system is one

> which can innovate easily by spreading the blanket of tradition upon change itself. In such systems, those who are called upon to arbitrate in matters of custom and to interpret in some official capacity are easily persuaded to find traditional counterparts in contemporary events. Such systems can innovate without appearing to alter their social institutions fundamentally. Rather, innovation is made to serve immemoriality. The characteristic structural expression of instrumental traditionalism is a military type of system, with hierarchical authority stemming from a single king or command figure. Appointive ranks in the system tend to underwrite the king as the central source of authority. Here, a heavy reliance on performance is a characteristic of office, and the chief who fails to serve his king loyally is subject to removal or death. Religion is decidedly secondary in such a system, which has a primary value service to the king or state.[27]

Apter's study of African states indicates that the instrumental-hierarchical type of traditionalism can accept change and innovate until the principle of the kingship and its authority are challenged. When this occurs, the entire system mobilizes to resist change. Apter's conclusion is that such a traditional system is resistant only to political change and innovation, not to other forms of modernization, "and in particular cannot easily supplant the hierarchical principle of authority with a representative one."[28] That is, instrumental-hierarchical tradition is specially resistant to changes that suggest liberal democratic practices.

The traditionalism of consummatory-pyramidal systems is considerably more complex, essentially because tradition is so closely tied to a strong primitive religious belief.

> Thus society, the state, authority, and the like are all part of an elaborately sustained, high-solidarity system in which religion as a cognitive guide is pervasive. Such systems have been hostile to innovation. Change has produced fundamental social upheavals such as migration to towns. Broken are warmth and intimacy of custom.[29]

The consummatory-pyramidal system is highly resistant to change of all kinds. When such systems are, for whatever reason, unable to resist change, the result is generally "external political groupings that form as new solidary associations cutting across the older ones."[30] In short, the instrumental-hierarchical tradition permits social mobilization and modernization but resists its implicit political consequences, whereas the consummatory-pyramidal tradition resists even the elemental modernizing processes of social mobilization.

In addition, the intrusion of modernizing forces accompanying social mobilization on African consummatory and instrumental tradition produces destabilizing or even retrogressive political consequences; naturally such consequences weaken or preclude state- and nation-building processes. First, in a culturally plural society, social mobilization generates competition and scarcity; the competition is defined largely in communal terms, and the scarcity undergirds communal hostilities.[31] In settings where social mobilization actually results in the erosion of old values, beliefs, and habits, and the reorientation of large numbers of people to a new system of rewards and paths to rewards, people begin to want, expect, and demand more goods and services, material and nonmaterial, in all sectors of life. Increasingly, more and more people come to want more and more, frequently more and more of the same thing. Competition, conflict, and antagonism result because people compete for the same things and because the society is unable to generate sufficient supply to meet the demand; there is increasing scarcity. Urbanization of the members of communal groups not only fails to secularize or "detribalize" and prevent or mute communal strife, but actually exacerbates communal conflict by throwing large numbers of people closely together in direct competition for scarce jobs, education, memberships in organizations, control of economic markets, and induction into the army.[32] In such a new, hostile, insecure environment tribalism provides considerable security. In addition, it provides opportunities for advancement, gain, and success, since urban people tend to view life largely in communal terms.

The rate of social mobilization is uneven among communal groups in a society or city, and differential rates of mobilization intensify communal conflict by increasing the number of concurrent and reinforcing social cleavages.[33] Characteristics of communal groups that cause differential rates of mobilization are the timing, intensity, and character of Western contact, environmental opportunities and resources, and cultural predispositions.[34] Some communal groups mobilize and modernize more quickly than others, and some modernize hardly at all. Soon, communal cleavages are reinforced by social, political, economic, religious, and power differentials, to the advantage of the more modernized and to the dismay of the less modernized. Cleavages become increasingly exaggerated, conflicts increasingly hostile, and struggles around issues of political subordination and superordination destructively militant and violent.

Under conditions of social mobilization there is a tendency, at the regional and national levels, for prominent social and political institutions to become identified with the interests of particular communal groups. When a communal group subordinates a political institution to its own interests, it not only weakens the level of institutionalization, but also weakens or destroys the legitimacy[35] accorded the institution by other communal groups.[36] *Institutionalization* means adaptability, complexity, coherence, and especially autonomy, rather than rigidity, simplicity, disunity, and subordination.[37] The seizure and control of a political institution by a communal group represents political decay, the opposite of development, in Samuel P. Huntington's terms, partially because it causes institutional ineffectiveness and produces challenges to the legitimacy of the institution by other, especially minority, communal groups.

In addition, the evidence also indicates that widespread mass participation, such as in elections, tends further to politicize and aggravate communal tensions, for at least two reasons.[38] First, cultural pluralism encourages aspiring politicians to rely upon communal loyalties to support them and to seek to protect and promote communal interests above all others. Communal loyalties tend to follow and reward communal appeals and protection. Politicians activate communal interests, which in turn leads to communal demands that their politicians represent only communal interests. In such a vicious cycle, militant-parochial politics drives out the moderate-universal politics, and liberal-democratic potential is undermined. Second, mass participation tends to encourage the making of inflated demands for government to undertake new and more and more expensive kinds of programs and functions with which it has had little or no independent experience. Even presuming some success in state- and nation-building, undertaking these new programs and tasks requires the continuous development of new patterns of elite-mass, value, and group-behavior integration. This further weakens the capabilities of the polity and militates against political integration.[39]

Interposed between social-mobilization processes and their liberal-democratic political consequences are low levels and rates of mobilization and traditionalism of two kinds, the newness of African independence with its attendant difficulty and incompleteness of nation- and state-building, and also, underlying and giving meaning to it all, communalism. African societies struggling to give birth to nation-states characterized by modernity and democracy still struggle with a problem long ago resolved in most of the older and more modern nation states—the primordial sentiments relating to fundamental identity and solidarity, such as tribe, language, ethnicity, race, and kinship. Whether continuing movement above the social-mobilization threshold will soon or eventually or ever produce political decisions that overcome communalism and lead to nation-statehood for many African societies remains an unanswered question.[40] Whether, once having attained nation statehood, African polities move toward some variant of liberal democracy is likewise unanswered and probably doubtful. Increases in urbanization, education, communication, industrialization, and economic development have been absorbed by the structure and dynamics of primordial communalism and have produced not liberal-democratic politics but political tensions, chaos, stagnation, instability, and coups. "The problem then of free government in Africa consists in avoiding both the extremes of repression and anarchy. To have free government, one must first have government. To have political liberty, one must first have a political community."[41]

7 The Near and Far Eastern Model of Liberal Democracy

Just as there were numerous unanticipated findings in the three previous geocultural regional analyses, the Near and Far Eastern model also provides some surprises. The 16 nation-states included in the analysis are Burma, Ceylon, India, Indonesia, Iraq, Israel, Japan, Laos, Malaysia, Pakistan, Philippines, South Korea, Syria, Tunisia, Turkey, and the United Arab Republic.[1] Among these nations liberal-democratic practices seem to be coherent, and their relationships to social mobilization tend to be as predicted by social-mobilization theory. First, an examination of the extent to which the three dimensions of democracy are interrelated is presented in Table 7-1.

What is most obvious in Table 7-1 is that the intercorrelations between pairs of liberal-democracy measures are all strong and positive. Compared with the global model findings, the three dimensions of liberal democracy are closely covariant. Particularly interesting is the fact that participation is positively related to both competitiveness and public liberties, in contrast to earlier findings in the global and other analyses. In terms of their distribution and covariance in the Near and Far East, the three kinds of practices of liberal democracy appear strongly coherent and mutually supportive, whether high, intermediate, or low, as demonstrated by separate intercorrelations and by the relationship of each separate dimension with the composite index of liberal democracy.

Given these strong relationships between pairs of liberal democracy variables, the nature of the intercorrelations between pairs of social-mobilization variables is certainly not unexpected. Table 7-2 presents these findings:

Social-mobilization theory stipulates that levels of development in different sectors of society should be approximately the same, that is, in a condition of balance. In fact, that appears to some extent to be the case in the nation-states of the Near and Far East. The smallest coefficient of intercorrelation between any pair of levels of mobilization is 0.46 (urbanization and education levels), and all the rest are above 0.50; five of the 10 are above 0.60. The strongest relationship is between communication and industrialization levels ($r = 0.91$).

Perhaps most remarkable of all is the generally high level of correlation between levels and rates of urbanization in the upper-right quadrant of Table 7-2. With some exceptions that will be discussed later, in the Near and Far Eastern nations, each level of social mobilization is a good predictor of its equivalent rate of mobilization. In general, nations with higher levels of mobilization are experiencing faster rates of change and nations with lower levels

Table 7-1
Matrix of Intercorrelations Among Measures of Liberal Democracy for Near and Far Eastern Nations

	Competi-tiveness	Partici-pation	Liberties	Liberal Democracy
Competitiveness	1.00	0.54	0.85	0.88
Participation		1.00	0.72	0.85
Liberties			1.00	0.96
Liberal democracy				1.00

are undergoing slower rates of change. The major set of exceptions involves the relationship of rate of education increase and the other mobilization-level variables. Rate of education is negatively correlated with all five mobilization-level variables; nations with low levels have high rates of increase and nations with higher levels are undergoing slow or not rate of increase in education. With the exception of education rate, there seems to be balanced levels and change rates among the indicators of social mobilization in the Near and Far East.

Turning to the lower right quadrant of Table 7-2, measures of association between rates of change in mobilization variables, the coefficients are all remarkably high. Only the relationship between education rate and economic-development rate is really lower than expected ($r = -0.50$); the other coefficients meet or exceed the arbitrary minimum of $r = 0.60$. What is not anticipated is the consistently negative relationship of education rate with each of the other four rates of social mobilization. As education rate increases, the rates of urbanization, communication, industrialization, and economic development tend to decrease, and vice versa. Clearly, there is an imbalance in rates of social mobilization represented by this series of negative relationships. Nonetheless, rates of mobilization in the nations of the Near and Far East do demonstrate more coherence than they do in the global model.

In summary, there are numerous interesting contrasts between the findings in Tables 7-1 and 7-2 and the equivalent results of the global model in Chapter 1. The social-mobilization patterns in the Near and Far East conform with considerably more strength to the hypotheses enunciated by Deutsch and others than do the global patterns of mobilization. The Near and Far East intercorrelations between democracy measures are not unlike those of the global model, in that they are all positive. However, they are considerably stronger than the global findings. Next we turn to an examination of the extent to which variations in social mobilization can explain liberal-democratic practices in the nations of the Near and Far East.

Table 7-2
Matrix of Intercorrelations Among Social-Mobilization Indicators for the Near and Far East

	Levels (1960)					Rates (1946-66)				
	1	2	3	4	5	6	7	8	9	10
1. Urbanization level	1.00	0.46	0.62	0.59	0.51	0.64	−0.36	0.64	0.61	0.52
2. Education level		1.00	0.61	0.64	0.56	0.16	−0.19	0.59	0.61	0.52
3. Communication level			1.00	0.78	0.91	0.53	−0.60	0.98	0.99	0.91
4. Industrialization level				1.00	0.85	0.39	−0.19	0.79	0.76	0.67
5. Economic-development level					1.00	0.38	−0.48	0.88	0.91	0.89
6. Urbanization rate						1.00	−0.71	0.72	0.70	0.58
7. Education rate							1.00	−0.60	−0.58	−0.50
8. Communication rate								1.00	0.98	0.86
9. Industrialization rate									1.00	0.91
10. Economic-development rate										1.00

Levels of Social Mobilization

Table 7-3 presents measures of the strength of association between levels of social mobilization and liberal democracy. The table contains the same four kinds of coefficients of association that have been presented in previous similar tables.

Again focusing on the size and sign of the beta coefficients,[2] it is evident in Table 7-3 that the pattern of relationships between levels of social mobilization and political competitiveness are quite different in the Near and Far East than they are in the global model. For example, whereas in the global model, industrialization and economic-development levels had the largest beta weights with regard to competitiveness, in the Near and Far Eastern model these two independent variables assume little explanatory importance. Urbanization and education levels are of little consequence in global terms, but the beta weights for these two variables are the largest ones for competitiveness in the Near and Far Eastern analysis. With a one-unit increase in urbanization, competitiveness decreases by –0.64; a similar one-unit increase in education produces an increase of 0.66 in competitiveness. Among the 16 nations of the Near and Far East, high political competitiveness seems to be a function mainly of high levels of urbanization.[3] When these and the other three levels of social mobilization are taken into account, fully 79.2 percent of the variation in competitiveness is statistically explained, almost double that of competitiveness in the global model.

The distribution of explanatory utility in the case of mass participation tends to be slightly more even, yet urbanization clearly makes the largest contribution to explanation of the variation in that dependent variable; the beta coefficient is negative, indicating a decrease in participation with an increase in urbanization. Communication level and participation are moderately related with $\beta = 0.46$. Less than half the variation in mass participation can be accounted for by levels of mobilization, $R^2 = 47.6$. However, this degree of explanation is over twice as large as the equivalent coefficient in the global analysis.

Variations in public liberties seem to be a function largely of urbanization; an increase of one unit in that indicator of social mobilization results in a decrease of –0.66 units of public liberties. Both education and communication levels and to a lesser degree industrialization level are positively related to liberties, with beta weights of 0.41, 0.39, and 0.35 respectively. The total explanatory power of levels of mobilization on liberties is fairly high: $R^2 = 62.4\%$. Like the other two dimensions of democracy, the degree of public liberties enjoyed in nations of the Near and Far East is closely related to the level of social mobilization. And although the simple-correlation coefficient between economic-development level and liberties is 0.52, when examined in the context of the regression equation that takes into account the influence of all five independent variables, economic development's explanatory power with regard to liberties is nil.

Table 7-3

Simple- and Multiple-Correlation Coefficients for Measures of Liberal Democracy and Levels of Social Mobilization for the Near and Far East

	Urbanization		Education		Communication		Industrialization		Economic Development			
	r	β	r	β	r	β	r	β	r	β	R	R^2
Competitiveness	0.02	−0.64	0.73	0.66	0.50	0.22	0.52	0.33	0.53	0.00	0.89	79.2%
Participation	−0.14	−0.59	0.33	0.20	0.42	0.46	0.25	−0.18	0.45	0.36	0.69	47.6%
Liberties	−0.04	−0.66	0.57	0.41	0.49	0.39	0.49	0.35	0.52	−0.02	0.79	62.4%
Liberal democracy	−0.02	−0.70	0.60	0.46	0.52	0.41	0.46	0.18	0.56	0.14	0.84	70.6%

Finally, the pattern of relationships between the composite index of liberal democracy and levels of mobilization is similar to that of the individual dimensions of democracy. With the composite index, the beta weight for urbanization is high and negative ($\beta = -0.70$). Education and communication levels assume secondary importance; increases of one unit of these variables produce increases of 0.46 and 0.41 respectively. And all together levels of mobilization explain over 70 percent of the variation in liberal democracy.

Urbanization level is most strongly and negatively related to all four of the measures of democracy presented in Table 7-3, as an inspection of the beta coefficient (β) column under urbanization suggests. Both the strength and negative value of these coefficients are quite in contrast with the global findings. In the Near and Far East, level of social mobilization appears to be a controlling factor in determining the degree and character of liberal democracy. However, it is also apparent that liberal democracy has a better chance to flourish in the less urbanized nations.[4]

Rates of Social Mobilization

Table 7-4 presents measures of association between rates of mobilization and liberal-democratic measures. As is evident, the results are mixed and inconsistent.

Again, examining the relationships between political competitiveness and each of the five rates of mobilization, it is evident that increases of one unit in communication and industrialization rates result in rather large increments in competitiveness, 1.79 and 3.42 respectively. It is clear that competitiveness in the Near and Far Eastern countries is relatively more sensitive to increases in the rates of these two mobilization variables. Similarly, an increase of one unit of economic development produces a -0.99 decrease in competitiveness. Yet as was described in Table 7-2, rates of communication and industrialization are quite strongly and positively correlated with rate of economic development. It might also be mentioned that the beta coefficient between rate of urbanization and competitiveness is -0.64. Two of these strongly and positively intercorrelated independent variables are positively related and two negatively related to competitiveness. This condition is interpreted as productive of social and economic imbalance and possible political tension and instability. Surprisingly, given the beta weights, only 54.2 percent of the total variation in political competitiveness is accounted for by rates of mobilization.

Mass participation variations appear to be a response mainly to rates of industrialization and economic development. However, as encountered in previous analyses, increases in industrialization rate and decreases in economic-development rate produce increases in the Near and Far Eastern mass participation. And only about a quarter (24.6%) of the variation in participation can be

Table 7-4

Simple- and Multiple-Correlation Coefficients for Measures of Liberal Democracy and Rates of Social Mobilization for the Near and Far East

	Urbanization		Education		Communication		Industrialization		Economic Development			
	r	β	r	β	r	β	r	β	r	β	R	R^2
Competitiveness	0.05	−0.64	−0.14	0.07	0.44	1.79	0.49	3.43	0.35	−0.99	0.74	54.2%
Participation	0.03	−0.24	−0.12	0.10	0.37	−0.82	0.40	1.78	0.33	−0.42	0.50	25.0%
Liberties	0.00	−0.31	0.02	0.16	0.41	−1.82	0.48	3.16	0.41	−0.60	0.73	52.9%
Liberal democracy	0.00	−0.37	−0.08	0.20	0.45	3.07	0.50	3.07	0.41	−0.73	0.71	50.6%

accounted for as a function of rates of mobilization. Neither urbanization nor education rate seems important, and economic-development rate and participation are only modestly related, particularly in comparison to participation's association with communication and industrialization rates.

As Table 7-4 shows, these same two variables are most closely associated with variations in public liberties, with beta weights of −1.82 and 3.16. Yet the two independent rates of change variables are virtually interchangeable. Over half (52.9%) of the variation in liberties is statistically explained by the five rates of mobilization. Finally, the composite index of liberal democracy has a large negative beta weight with communication rate ($\beta = -1.64$) and a large positive beta weight with industrialization ($\beta = 3.07$). Of lesser but still noticeable importance in producing fluctuations in liberal democracy is economic-development rate, with a negative beta weight of −0.73. Just over half (50.6%) of liberal democracy's variation is accounted for by rates of mobilization.

Next we examine whether it is overall level or rate of change of mobilization that has the greater impact on liberal democracy in the Near and Far Eastern nations.

Relative Influence of Levels and Rates of Social Mobilization

Table 7-5 presents the results of multiple regression of all 10 mobilization variables on liberal democracy measures in column 3; it also includes in columns 4 and 5 the multiple-partial-correlation coefficients measuring the impact of level of mobilization on democratic practices while holding constant the influence of rate of mobilization, and a similar partial coefficient for the influence of rate of mobilization when level is held constant. In addition,

Table 7-5
Multiple and Multiple-Partial-Correlation Coefficients for Levels and Rates of Social Mobilization and Liberal Democracy for the Near and Far East

	Multiple-Correlation Coefficients			Multiple-Partial-Correlation Coefficients	
	1	2	3	4	5
	Levels	Rates	Levels and Rates	Levels w/ Rates Constant	Rates w/ Levels Constant
Competitiveness	0.89	0.74	0.89	0.74	0.04
Participation	0.69	0.50	0.70	0.57	−0.17
Liberties	0.79	0.73	0.80	0.50	0.24
Liberal democracy	0.84	0.71	0.84	0.65	−0.04

columns 1 and 2 repeat the multiple-correlation coefficients for levels and rates from the two immediately preceding tables.

Examination of column 3 in Table 7-5 reveals that all 10 social mobilization variables account for little or no additional variation in the dependent variables over that already explained by either levels or rates of mobilization alone. However, this finding is not unexpected, in view of the fact that levels of mobilization, for example, already accounted for such a high proportion of the dependent variable's variation.

More important are the results listed in columns 4 and 5. When the influence of rate of mobilization is partialled out, level of mobilization still retains large coefficients, as column 4 shows. Regardless of the rate of social mobilization in the Near and Far East, the level of mobilization strongly appears to be the controlling influence on liberal democracy. This is particularly true with regard to political competitiveness, where level of mobilization still produces a coefficient of 0.74 even when rate of mobilization is held constant. In stark contrast, rate of mobilization coefficients are reduced practically to nothing when level of mobilization is controlled for. A comparison of columns 5 and 2 reveals the degree of reduction in size of the coefficients. In fact, rate of change of social mobilization actually produces a negative coefficient (–0.17) with mass participation when level of mobilization is held constant. The same is true, to a lesser extent, for the composite indicator of liberal democracy as well. This pattern of results is the opposite of that found when data from all 85 nations is similarly analyzed. In the global model, rate of mobilization retained much of its explanatory usefulness when level of mobilization was held constant, but the converse was not the case. And in the global analysis, none of the coefficients was as large as had been found in the Near and Far Eastern model.

Social mobilization seems to be, by way of summary, largely responsible for variations in liberal democracy in the Near and Far East; the relationship is strong but not always positive when one considers individual mobilization variables. It appears to be level, and not rate of change, of social mobilization that so strongly anchors liberal-democratic practices in these 16 nations. Rate of change has produced only a small positive or negative effect on the sustenance of liberal democracy.

Unexplained Variation and the Deviant Cases

Since the regression equations employing social-mobilization variables to explain the three dimensions of democracy and the composite indicator of liberal democracy produce such large correlation coefficients, there is more to be gained from an effort to explain the close association than from an effort to explain why there are deviant cases. But before a discussion of Near and Far

Eastern political traditions is introduced to account for the strong relationships between mobilization and democracy, a brief look at the position of each of the nations about the regression line is informative. Figure 7-1 is a scattergram of the regression of social-mobilization variables on the composite index of liberal democracy, the multiple-correlation coefficient of which is $R = 0.84$.

In the context of the overall relationship between social mobilization and democracy in the Near and Far East, there are three nations that are clearly over-democratized, and two nations that are under-democratized. The standard error of the estimate is 6.6. Table 7-6 contains each list of deviant cases.

Reference to Figure 7-1 places the deviance of these five nations in the proper context. The distribution of the 16 cases about the regression line in that figure is gourd-shaped, with the large end of the gourd in the lower left corner of the

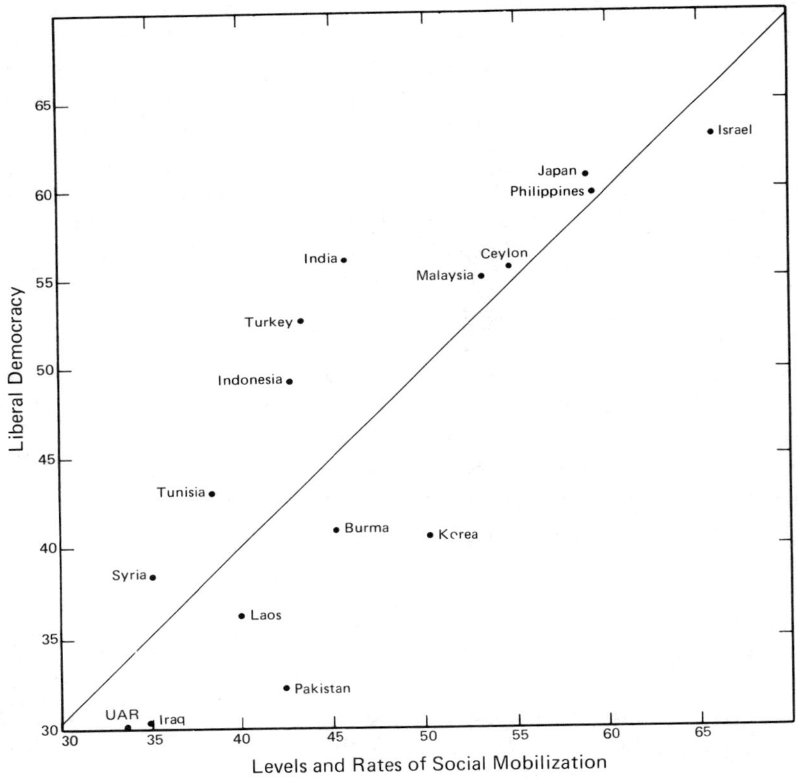

Figure 7-1. Scattergram of Levels and Rates of Social Mobilization with Liberal Democracy for the Near and Far Eastern Nations ($R = 0.84$)

Table 7-6
Under-Democratized and Over-Democratized Nations in the Near and Far East

Over-Democratized		Under-Democratized	
India	+10.3	Pakistan	−10.1
Indonesia	+ 6.7	Korea	− 9.6
Turkey	+ 9.4		

scattergram. Less socially mobilized nations in the Near and Far East generally tend to experience a more remote relationship between mobilization and democracy. As their mobilization level and rate increases, there is a tendency for mobilization variables to begin to have more profound and direct political consequences. Of the six nations that have mobilization scores of 50.0 or greater, five are extremely close to the regression line (Israel, Japan, Philippines, Ceylon, and Malaysia), denoting a close relationship between mobilization and democracy. Korea is evidently a deviant case. The large portion of the gourd consists mainly of nations whose distance from the line is greater and whose mobilization-democracy relationship is, therefore, weaker. It contains four of the five deviant cases. Although a larger number of cases would be necessary before such a statement could be made with assurance, the threshold for really close association between social mobilization and liberal democracy in the Near and Far East appears to be at a mobilization score of about 50.0.

The Near and Far Eastern Political Traditions: Communalism/Secularism

As suggested earlier, when the coefficients of multiple correlation and determination for the relationship between social mobilization and measures of liberal democracy are uniformly large, the task is not one of seeking an explanation of why the theory does not apply. Rather the task is to identify basic elements in the political traditions, shared by the nation states of the geocultural region, which appear to permit or even to facilitate and strengthen the predicted relationship between mobilization and democracy. Since the coefficients of association are so high for this region, it is apparent that at the very least no social or cultural forces are seriously inhibiting the expected political consequences of social mobilization. Moreover, the social and cultural forces and concomitant political tradition that characterize the region actually provide a context in which the predicted relationships are quite strong. Although social mobilization theory supplies its own explanation when and where it works as predicted, it is nonetheless useful to identify the facilitating aspects of the region's political tradition.

Initially, it is not enough simply to assert that the 16 nations listed under the title Near and Far East are, in fact, a geocultural region, especially since they cover such a wide and apparently diverse area of the globe.[5] It is evident that the nations of this region are more similar to each other than they are to any other geocultural region. But in addition there is compelling empirical evidence that not only strongly suggests that these nations are part of a geocultural region but also indicates some of the aspects of the political culture and structure common to those nations.

Bruce M. Russett's factor analyses[6] of 54 variables from the *World Handbook of Political and Social Indicators*[7] produced five sociocultural factors that he labeled "economic development, communism, intensive agriculture, size, and Catholic culture."[8] The five factors together explained approximately 60 percent of the variance in the variables. This initial factor analysis produced loadings or scores for each nation for each factor, and these scores can be used to measure cultural differences or distances between nations on a given factor and for all factors. Through a factor analysis of the matrix of differences on each factor,[9] Russett produced a second set of factors that clusters cases, or nation-states, in terms of cultural distance, rather than clusters variables in terms of linear correlation. This second factor analysis produced five clusters of nations, each of which was formed on the basis of a tendency toward cultural homogeneity among the nations in the cluster. All five clusters are basically geographical regions, with some few exceptions. One of the regions contains 19 nations and is labeled by Russett as "Asia" and elsewhere called "Asia and the Arab States." This designation and the nations contained within it are quite similar to the one presently undertaken.[10] A third factor analysis computed factor loadings for each nation on each of the four sociocultural factors.[11] The tendencies of the nations labeled "Asia and the Arab States" (or the Near and Far East) on each of the four factors are unmistakably clear and strong. The 16 nations under study were, in Russett's third factor analysis, very low on socioeconomic development, moderately noncommunist, medium high on intensive agriculture, and decidedly not Catholic in culture. Their factor scores were generally in the same direction (either all positive or all negative) and approximately the same size.[12] These 16 nations do strongly tend to cohere in terms of a large number of the 54 *World Handbook* variables as they cluster in four underlying factors, and these variables as clustered comprise a substantial proportion of the Near and Far Eastern sociocultural tradition. Russett's factor analysis of 54 social, economic, and cultural variables is quite consistent with the social-mobilization levels and rates used in the present study, and it indicates that these 16 nations tend to be socioculturally coherent as a region.

However, establishing the political coherence of the nations in this geocultural region requires another step in the reasoning process and additional evidence, and the analysis becomes slightly more complicated. Again, it is factor analysis that provides the evidence. However, in this instance, the evidence suggests that although the nations of the Near and Far East share a common sociocultural tradition, in post-colonial times a bifurcated political tradition has emerged. Two major kinds of political tradition, one old and changing slowly and one new and changing more rapidly, exist and function side by side in this geocultural region. These two sets of political culture and structure correspond fairly closely to the conventional terms used in political development analysis, "traditional" and "transitional." Although both sets of nations were, at some earlier period in their histories, firmly traditionalistic in terms of political development, one set has tended to remain so and the other set has tended to change. The key to an understanding of the absence of a relationship between social mobilization and democratic practices in African nations is communalism. The traditionalistic set of nations in the Near and Far East still experiences considerable communalism and primordial loyalty. The transitional set of nations has at least partially escaped from the inhibiting qualities of communalism.[13]

Systematic evidence suggesting the bifurcation of political culture and structure in the Near and Far East is available in the *Q*-type factor analysis by Arthur S. Banks and Phillip M. Gregg[14] of 68 primarily political variables from *A Cross-Polity Survey.*[15] *Q*-type factor analysis groups cases or polities in terms of relationships of variables, rather than variables in terms of cases. Thus, the Banks and Gregg analysis produced five factors, each of which is composed of a cluster of political systems. With respect to the nature of the political systems which cluster together, Banks and Gregg label their five factors or clusters of polities "polyarchic, elitist, centrist, personalist, and traditional." When the 16 nations of the present analysis are identified with respect to the sizes of their factor loadings in each factor, it is quite obvious that there are two distinct political tendencies in the Near and Far East region–polyarchic and elitist. A political profile of each set of nations provides a substantive description of the main elements in each political tradition, one old and one new.

Nine of the 16 nations receive high factor scores on what Banks and Gregg call the "elitist" dimension (Burma, Indonesia, Pakistan, Tunisia, Laos, UAR, South Korea, Syria, and Iraq).[16] But the term elitist is used not so much to describe the society and polity generally, but to emphasize the relative smallness of the leadership group of " 'modernizing elites' [that] are attempting to bring about rapid and radical social change in the face of impressive cultural resistance of an essentially 'parochial' character that remains as a carry-over from the colonial period."[17] In addition to this elitist character, these nine nations also tend to have strong secondary centrist or personalist features as major aspects of the absence of differentiation of their political structures and secularization of their political cultures. For example, the United Arab Republic loads high on centrist factor, which groups this strongly authoritarian polity with a number of Communist states. Laos, South Korea, Syria, and Iraq have strong personalist characteristics, that is, a high degree of political personalism. Finally, Laos has a strong traditional component. These nine nations, in comparison with the other seven, tend to be considerably more under-developed or less developed in social and economic terms. Using the measure of economic development employed in this study as one indicator of social mobilization, the nine elitist nations of the Near and Far East have an average economic development score of 42.9, compared with 46.4 for the seven polyarchic nations. The nine elitist polities tend to be less Westernized, more communal, to have a higher degree of political sectionalism, less political consensus, more cultural resistance to social, economic, and political modernization, and to be rather new polities.[18] The communal and cultural resistance to change is strong and has, apparently, served effectively to inhibit both economic growth and modernization as well as any nascent tendency toward democratization of the political systems.[19] These nations are at a low level of economic development and democratization.

The seven polyarchic polities of the Near and Far East are Ceylon, India, Israel, Japan, Malaysia, Philippines, and Turkey. They are all comparatively more developed economically, more Westernized, less communal, have less political sectionalism, more consensus, less cultural resistance to both economic and political change, and are more democratic.[20] Their average score on the composite index of liberal democracy used in this study is 57.5, compared with the average of 37.8 for the nine elitist nations. The spread of the world culture, or Westernization, has impinged more heavily on these seven polyarchies and their receptivity to change has been greater. Their escape from communalism and the forces of tradition are incomplete, to be sure; several of them have strong secondary elitist, personalistic, and/or traditional tendencies. For example, the Philippines, Israel, and India reveal slightly elitist tendencies in the *Q*-type factor analysis of Banks and Gregg. Malaysia has both elitist and traditionalist secondary tendencies, and although Ceylon's highest factor loading is on the polyarchy factor, there are noticeably high elitist, personalist, and traditional loadings of Ceylon's polity in the factor analysis.

It is interesting to note three common features of the seven polyarchic nations. First, all but Israel are slightly to vastly over-democratized in the regression analysis of social-mobilization/liberal-democracy as displayed in Figure 7-1. Second, as already mentioned, they all score high on the Banks and Gregg polyarchy factor. Third, an analysis of the colonial experience of each of these seven nations reveals that the duration and intensity of Westernization were especially great and more or less unique among Third World nations. Although it would be inappropriate to discuss the unique colonial experiences of these nations here, especially since that has been done in rich historical detail elsewhere, a brief statement of the manner in which the world culture from the West was so strongly introduced in these countries is in order. These brief descriptions are hardly intended to be original or novel interpretations or explanations; in fact they are already well known in several disciplines. Rather, they are simply suggested as a partial explanation for the polyarchic character of these seven polities. The inference is that they resemble the other nine elitist-personalist-traditional polities of the Near and Far East more than they resemble polyarchy, except for their unique colonial experiences, which began the erosion of communalism and the development of democracy. The legacy of the British civil service in India is well known. At the beginning of independence in 1947, India already had an impressively well-educated, competent, and democratic civil service mostly of native Indians.[21] The same tends to be true of Ceylon, perhaps slightly more so.[22] Probably no other colonies were as well prepared for democratic self-government at the time of their independence as were these two. A third country, Israel, is largely European in ethnic stock and political orientations and represents a transplanted European political culture that, since independence in 1947, has simply become increasingly Westernized and modernized and economically developed.[23] A fourth nation-state, Japan, suffered devastating defeat and unconditional surrender in World War II. To the victors, the Western powers, went the spoils of writing a new Japanese constitution and restructuring Japanese politics, obviously along the lines of Western, parliamentary, party-oriented democracy. Japan had little choice in the matter.[24] Malaysia is similar to India and Ceylon in the sense that she inherited at independence a remarkably stable, democratic, and well-trained group of indigenous civil servants.[25] The Philippines benefited from a lengthy United States tutelage in democratic practices and, although democracy has been less stable there than in, say, India, the Philippines has been relatively democratic along Western and particularly American lines.[26] Finally, Turkey experienced profound and revolutionary change under the leadership of Kemal Ataturk. He used a decidedly Western model to modernize his country and produce a new Turkey; his success was outstanding.[27]

In summary, each of the seven polyarchies in the Near and Far East experienced an unusual colonial or tutelary period or at least underwent Westernization in a different and more profound way than the other nine states of the area. Although these unique characteristics might well be called accidents of history, their effect on these seven countries is nonetheless clear and strong. They are unusual countries in the Near and Far East; they tend to be less communal and more polyarchic. Yet they are, as a group, not experiencing dissynchronization of social-mobilization and democratic practices. They are, in their geocultural regional context, both democratic and mobilized. The other nine elitist polities are both considerably more authoritarian and less mobilized. In short, the 16 nations of the Near and Far East are about as democratic, on the whole, as they ought to be with respect to their level and rate of social mobilization.

8 Geocultural Regionalism, Political Traditions, and Cross-National Political Analysis

It is now time to return to the initial hypothesis that social mobilization produces liberal democracy and to the arguments about the complexity of liberal democracy, the nature and relationships among aspects of social mobilization, and the political meaning of geocultural regionalism. This discussion will, therefore, proceed on two different levels: the first pertains to the substantive findings of the study and the nature of social mobilization and liberal democracy in the world today; the second pertains to several of the more intractable methodological problems of macroquantitative political analysis.

On the whole the evidence examined in this analysis confirms the basic hypothesis that social mobilization tends to result in liberal-democratic practices. However, what the data in this study suggest even more strongly is that the statement and evidence in support of this hypothesis at the global level are inadequate, insufficiently qualified, imprecise, too simplistic, and therefore misleading and probably inaccurate.[1] It should be clear by this point that liberal democracy is not, in point of fact, a single, unitary, coherent political phenomenon. It consists of at least three aspects or variables, and, moreover, these three aspects are not only not always mutually supportive but sometimes actually are mutually counteractive. The extent of democracy is made up of levels of political competitiveness, popular participation, and public liberties, and in given situations certain pairs of these three may be antagonistic. The phenomenon of liberal democracy is considerably more complex and complicated than previous macroquantitative research has assumed.

In addition, liberal democracy and its three separate dimensions are affected (more or less strongly) by both levels and rates of social mobilization, and sometimes they are affected differently by levels and rates. And although some mobilization variables can be substituted for some others without loss of explanatory utility, some variables cannot be substituted for others at all. Within the broad two-step phenomenon of social mobilization are social, economic, and cultural forces, some of which are highly positively intercorrelated, some of which are not intercorrelated, and some of which are negatively intercorrelated. Like liberal democracy, social mobilization is a potentially contradictory phenomenon; it can contain within itself certain contradictory tendencies. These hostile tendencies may occur between levels and rates of social mobilization, or among individual processes (urbanization, industrialization, etc.), within levels or within rates of mobilization. Previous chapters have dealt in detail with these characteristics of both democracy and mobilization, so there is no need to describe again the kinds of contradictions that the evidence documents. Suffice it to say that three not necessarily supportive dimensions of democracy and their combination are differentially influenced by five separate and sometimes conflicting processes of social-mobilization levels and rates of change in the 85 nations of the world included in the analysis.

As if such findings are not complicated enough, one must also take into account the further complicating influences of geocultural regionalism. Different dimensions of democracy are differentially related to different processes of social mobilization levels and rates of change not only in global analysis but in different geocultural regions of the world as well. Chapters 3 through 7 spelled out in detail the substance of the differences and sought to provide explanations for them. However, it seems evident that the discovery of the necessity to qualify the basic hypothesis in terms of what aspect of liberal democracy, whether level or rate of mobilization or both, which processes of level or rate or both, and whether in the world at-large or in which geocultural region, renders the authority of the hypothesis less than overwhelming. The findings of this research strongly suggest either that the hypothesis relating social mobilization and liberal democracy is not empirically applicable at the global level, or that the results of its global application can be understood only in terms of subapplications at the geocultural regional level. It is to a discussion of some of the implications of the proposition that we now turn. The purpose in such a concluding statement is to examine theory, methodology, and findings simultaneously with the intention of improving the precision but also the parsimony of the theory; determining where the methodology succeeds and where it fails; and where it is more and less effective, and why; and to evaluate the substantive findings with respect to their validity and generalizability.

Globalism versus Regionalism

The analyses clearly suggest that generalizations about dimensions of democracy and their antecedent social-mobilization conditions at the global or universal level may conceal more or as much as they reveal. Statements about relational regularities at the aggregate level of data at the global level of analysis may be an artifact of the techniques of analysis and result from the averaging of some sets of extreme regularities and some sets of moderate, weak, or nonregularities. And these separate sets of relationships may be extremely, moderately, weakly, or not at all regular, each set for a different kind of reason. Geocultural region, as employed in the present analyses, appears to provide such a way of dividing the nations of the globe into meaningful sets of regularities with regard to social mobilization and liberal-democratic practices. As has been demonstrated in previous chapters, the nature of the relationships between certain variables in several of the geocultural regions differs substantially from that of the universal analysis. It is with a description of the nature and extent of these differences that we are presently concerned. The analysis of two kinds of evidence, both of which have been presented in earlier chapters in identical or quite similar form, is adequate to make the point: first, a comparison of the relationships of mass participation with both political competitiveness and public liberties in the global and regional models; second, a comparison of the strength or slope and direction of the relationships between social mobilization variables and liberal democracy variables among the global and regional models.

It is with regionalism as a configurative phenomenon, rather than with geographic regionalism or sociological regionalism, that the present analysis is concerned.[2] For example, in the case of geographic regionalism, the nations of a region have similar or virtually identical values on a particular variable or variables; for example, the Netherlands has a relatively high gross national product per capita because it is in Anglo-Europa, and Anglo-Europa means having a higher GNP per capita than, say, Africa. Or the Netherlands is highly urbanized, because it is in Anglo-Europa, and Anglo-Europa means having a high level of urbanization. *Geographic regionalism* means a clustering of geographically proximate states at or around a certain value of a variable. *Sociological regionalism*, on the other hand, involves explanation of the regional clusterings of data of the geographic approach in terms of generalized cultural, sociological, political, or economic variables that correlate with the regional groupings. Region is viewed as a composite index of variables of a nonregional sort, and these nonregional variables describe the incidence and extent of properties common to all political systems; they are viewed as global sociological properties. For example, domestic unrest in Brazil is accounted for not by anything unique to the Iberic-Latin region but by such conditions as the degree of concentration of land ownership, or the extent of a sense of relative deprivation, or the level of political and economic development. These three latter variables are nonregional in nature, and serve an explanation of Brazil's level of domestic strife, or that of any Iberic-Latin nation, or that of any nation.

Finally, *configurative regionalism* assumes the possibility of three kinds of differences by region. Among regions, there can be differences in the meaning of a social process or event,[3] differences in the degree and kind of association between two or more social processes or events, and there can be differences in the meaning of the association between social processes or events. Important for the present analysis, configurative regionalism assumes that the nature of the relationships between variables may be different for data from different geocultural regions or contexts *because* the meaning of the variables and their relationships differ from region to region.

A geocultural region is a set of conditions and can, as an intervening influence on a global relationship, produce at least five kinds of conditional relationships—discriminating, directional, associational, threshold, and causal conditions.[4] A *discriminating condition* is one which two or more regions differ from each other in terms of the level of the dependent variable that is associated with a particular range of the independent variable. For example, in region 1, low values of the independent variable are closely correlated with medium values of the dependent variable, and in region 2, low values of the independent variable are strongly associated with high values of the dependent variable. When the relationship between the two variables is analyzed for the nations of both regions together, only a weak relationship appears; when the two regions are separately analyzed, the discriminating condition (region) affects the relationship. Second, a *directional condition* is one that actually changes or reverses the sign, positive or negative, or slope of a relationship. In a regression equation, the sign of the regression coefficient(s) would change from positive to negative or the reverse. Third, when the introduction of region into the analysis changes not the direction but the degree of association between variables, for example, from weak to strong or from strong to moderate, it is an *associational condition.* For instance, if two variables are only weakly associated in a global analysis but strongly associated in regional analyses, the regions represent associational conditions. Fourth, *threshold conditions* are a special mixture of directional and discriminating conditions that serve to change both the slopes or signs and the levels of association between two variables, but only once, and that from a situation of no relationship to one of a positive or negative relationship. Finally, *causal conditions*, unlike independent causes or discriminating conditions or variables, produce irreducible directional changes in a relationship.

The next portion of this final chapter deals principally with geocultural region as a conditioner of the relationship between social-mobilization and liberal-democratic practices, and to a lesser extent with the association of mass participation with political competitiveness and with public liberties. Maintaining a balance or parity between level of participation and levels of either competitiveness or liberties appears to be an extremely difficult task under certain conditions. Table 8-1 presents simple-correlation coefficients between participation and the other two democracy variables for four regions and the

Table 8-1
Simple-Correlation Coefficients of Participation with Competitiveness and Liberties for Regions and the Global Model

	Participation with Competitiveness	Participation with Liberties
Global analysis	0.20	0.19
Anglo-Europa	−0.69	−0.70
Iberic-Latin region	0.24	0.00
Africa	−0.37	−0.01
Near and Far East	0.54	0.72

global model. The differences among regions and between each region and the global analysis in the size and direction of the coefficients are stark.

On the basis of the global analysis, it is plausible to infer that there is only a weak positive relationship between each of these two pairs of liberal democracy variables. It is possible, moreover, to develop an elaborate theoretical explanation of why there is only a small positive association. One might even construct a persuasive normative argument in support of or opposition to the explanatory theory. However, all of these endeavors run the serious risk of inductively erecting a plausible theory on the basis of perfidious statistical findings. An inspection of the coefficients in Table 8-1 supports the claim that things are not always what they seem. Among the Anglo-European nations, there is a strong *negative* correlation between both pairs of variables. In the Near and Far Eastern region, there is a strong *positive* correlation between both pairs of variables. In the Iberic-Latin region, participation is moderately related to competitiveness in a negative direction but totally unrelated to liberties. African nations show only a weak positive relationship between participation and competitiveness, and virtually no relationship between participation and liberties. It is obvious that dividing the nations into geocultural regional sets permits much more precision in predicting one variable from another. It is also obvious that analysis of regional patterns permits the identification of varying degrees of strength of relationship that are regionally distributed. Consideration of the influence of the intervening variable of geocultural region is neglected at great peril.

Similar results accrue in an examination of relationships between social mobilization and liberal democracy. Table 8-2 provides the constants, that is, the *a*'s or *Y*-intercepts and slopes or regression coefficients, of the regression equations for the global and four regional analyses of the relationship between both level (b_1) and rate (b_2) of mobilization and political competitiveness. The multiple-correlation coefficients are also included.

The *Y*-intercept or *a* is the predicted value of *Y*, the dependent variable, when

Table 8-2
Regression Equations for Levels and Rates of Social Mobilization with Political Competitiveness for the Global and Regional Analyses

		Y-Intercept		Level of Mobilization		Rate of Mobilization	Multiple Correlation Coefficient (*R*)
Y'	=	(a)	+	$(b_1)X_1$	+	$(b_2)X_2$	
Global analysis		6.9		0.25		0.81	0.75
Anglo-Europa		−2.0		0.15		0.88	0.95
Iberic-Latin region		−53.1		1.03		1.04	0.39
Africa		− 2.5		0.82		0.23	0.85
Near and Far East		− 0.7		0.97		0.04	0.89

both X_1 and X_2, the two independent variables, equal zero. The Y-intercept in the global analysis is +6.9, meaning that some competitiveness tends to exist even in the absence of any social mobilization. In the four regional models, such is not the case. A low threshold of mobilization must be reached in three of the regions before competitiveness is affected (the a is "pulled up" to a positive number) and a substantially higher threshold of mobilization must be reached in the Latin-Iberic region before mobilization has consequences for political competitiveness.

The b_1 coefficients indicate the absolute amount of change in the level of competitiveness for an incremental amount of change in the level of social mobilization. Or, alternatively, the b_1 coefficients indicate the slope of the line or function in a plane parallel to the plane formed by the Y and X_1 axes.[5] Similar interpretations apply to the b_2 coefficients or rates of mobilization. The size of the multiple-correlation coefficient (R) produced by a given regression equation should be kept in mind when analyzing and comparing the size and sign of regression coefficients within and between regression equations. In spite of the fact that all of the regression coefficients in the five equations in Table 8-2 are positive, there are some interesting differences. Geocultural region acts as an associational condition with respect to the relationship between social mobilization and political competitiveness; it changes the degree of association between these variables as one performs the analysis for the global model and then for the regional models. In terms of slope of level of mobilization, only Anglo-Europa ($b_1 = 0.15$) bears resemblance to the global slope ($b_1 = 0.25$); the other three regional regression coefficients for level of mobilization are much larger. On the other hand, both Anglo-Europa and the Iberic-Latin region have slopes for rate of mobilization ($b_2 = 0.88$ and 1.04 respectively) similar in size (large) to the global coefficient ($b_2 = 0.81$). And in this case, Africa and the Near and Far East reveal very small coefficients.

In addition, whereas the global coefficient of multiple correlation is fairly large ($R = 0.75$), indicating a strong relationship, the Iberic-Latin R is only 0.39, revealing a rather weak relationship. The other three regions have multiple-correlation coefficients that are appreciably larger than the global coefficient. It is clear that the Iberic-Latin region is, as an associational condition, very strong indeed. A final characteristic of global-regional comparison of competitiveness in Table 8-2 concerns the relative size of b_1 and b_2 within each equation. In the global model, clearly the rate of mobilization (x_2) predominates with respect to influence on competitiveness; such is also the case in Anglo-Europa. In contrast, the two coefficients are about the same in the Iberic-Latin analysis, and level of mobilization (b_1) is obviously the larger in the African and Near and Far Eastern analyses.

An examination of the regression equations that describe the participation functions provides similar kinds of conclusions regarding globalism and regionalism. The results of such analysis are incorporated in Table 8-3.

Table 8-3
Regression Equations for Levels and Rates of Social Mobilization with Mass Participation for the Global and Regional Analyses

Y'	=	Y-Intercept (a)	+	Level of Mobilization $(b_1)X_1$	+	Rate of Mobilization $(b_2)X_2$	Multiple-Correlation Coefficient (R)
Global analysis		– 5.4		0.27		0.84	0.58
Anglo-Europa		– 8.0		0.44		0.70	0.79
Iberic-Latin region		–19.3		0.67		0.75	0.66
Africa		0.6		1.04		–0.05	0.82
Near and Far East		8.1		1.26		–0.44	0.70

The regression line in the global analysis crosses the Y axis at –5.4, indicating a low threshold before which increases in social mobilization have no impact on participation. Likewise, the Anglo-European function is characterized by the same sort of low-level threshold. However, the Iberic-Latin equation has a considerably greater threshold below which increasing levels and rates of mobilization have no mass participational effects. Africa, in contrast, has a very slight amount of participation even with no social mobilization, and the Near and Far Eastern nations also have an even greater degree of participation (8.1) under such hypothetical circumstances.

Examining the b_1 regression coefficients in Table 8-3 that document the change in participation associated with an incremental change in the value of level of social mobilization, the global coefficient is fairly small and positive (0.27). The Anglo-European coefficient is about twice as large, but still not to be considered a large regression coefficient. However, the Iberic-Latin coefficient is about three times the size of the global coefficient. The African and Near and Far Eastern equations provide mobilization-level coefficients that are, respectively, five and six times the size of that of the global model. At least three of the regions, therefore, introduce strong associational conditions into the basic relationship between social mobilization and participation, since the degree of association is radically changed from global to regional analyses. The change in the slope of the function produced by an incremental change in the rate of mobilization (b_2) is approximately the same for the Anglo-European and Iberic-Latin models as it is for the global model; all are positive and fairly large. However, that same regression coefficient for Africa and for the Near and Far East are negative; the African coefficient is, however, quite small (–0.05), but the Near and Far Eastern coefficient is moderate in size (–0.44). Therefore, Africa and the Near and Far East also represent, as geocultural regions, directional conditions that reverse the sign or slope of the relationship between rate of social mobilization and mass political participation from positive to negative.

The coefficients of multiple correlation in Table 8-3 are all moderate to large in size. However, the smallest is the global coefficient ($R = 0.58$). When region is introduced as an intervening variable that can, possibly, condition that relationship, the coefficients are all increased in size, particularly the Anglo-European ($R = 0.79$), African ($R = 0.82$), and Near and Far Eastern ($R = 0.82$). Although the Iberic-Latin coefficient of multiple correlation is larger than that of the global model, it is the smallest of the four regions at $R = 0.66$. Finally, the Anglo-European model resembles the global model in that rate of mobilization is a stronger influence on participation than level. In the Iberic-Latin region, the two are approximately even, and in Africa and the Near and Far East, it is level of mobilization, not rate, which has the apparent predominance.

With regard to analysis of the 85 nations included in the global model, even if there is no social mobilization as measured in this study, there is still some degree of public liberties; the regression line for the global model crosses the Y axis in its positive section at 7.8. (See Table 8-4.) This is not the case in any of the four geocultural regions; all have negative values for the a constants in their respective regression equations. In the case of Anglo-Europa and the Near and Far East, the a's are small, indicating that the regression line crosses the Y axis only slightly below zero. But the Y-intercepts in the Iberic-Latin and African equations are noticeably large and negative at −19.7 and −20.7 respectively. A considerable build-up of social mobilization processes is required in these two regions before they begin to have an effect on the degree of public liberties characteristic of polities in those regions.

Again, the b_1 coefficient for level of mobilization in the global equation is small (0.09), and again it is approximated by that of the Anglo-European model (0.12). And a third time, as in the analysis of the previous two dimensions of liberal democracy, the b_1 coefficients for the Iberic-Latin, African, and Near and Far Eastern regions are large, and provide additional evidence in support of the argument that geocultural region is an associational condition that changes the extent of relationship between mobilization and liberal democracy.

Table 8-4
Regression Equations for Levels and Rates of Social Mobilization with Public Liberties for the Global and Regional Analyses

		Y-Intercept		Level of Mobilization		Rate of Mobilization	Multiple-Correlation Coefficient (R)
Y'	=	(a)	+	$(b_1)X_1$	+	$(b_2)X_2$	
Global analysis		7.8		0.09		0.95	0.67
Anglo-Europa		− 2.1		0.12		0.91	0.94
Iberic-Latin region		−19.7		0.91		0.49	0.70
Africa		−20.7		0.59		0.85	0.30
Near and Far East		− 4.9		0.72		0.38	0.80

The degree to which two regions, Anglo-European and African, introduce associational conditions into the relationship between rate of mobilization (b_2) and public liberties is really quite negligible. In that relationship, the global coefficient is 0.95; that of Anglo-Europa is 0.91; and that of Africa is 0.85. However, the associational conditions introduced by the regions Iberic-Latin and Near and Far East are substantial, since their coefficients are reduced to 0.49 and 0.38 respectively. The relative size of the coefficients within each regression equation differs in some respect from that of the two previous analyses of competitiveness and participation. For public liberties, the rate coefficient (b_2) is by far the larger of the two mobilization constants; the Anglo-European equation is similar in this regard, as it was in the previous two analyses. However, the mobilization level coefficient (b_1) is about twice as large as the rate coefficient. The African rate coefficient is appreciably larger than its level coefficient and that makes the African liberties function different from the African competitiveness and participation functions. Also, the Near and Far Eastern level coefficient is over twice as large as its rate coefficient, and that makes it similar to the other two Near and Far Eastern equations.

Final evidence of the strength of the associational conditions introduced by region as an intervening variable is found in the size of the coefficients of multiple correlation. For the global model, the R is a moderately large 0.67; and for the first time, the Iberic-Latin multiple coefficient is similar in size ($R = 0.70$) rather than substantially smaller; social mobilization and public liberties are related to about the same degree in both the global and Iberic-Latin models. However, this relationship is much stronger among the nations of Anglo-Europa than it is among all 85 nations. It is only about one-half as large in the African analysis as it is in the global model, and the Near and Far Eastern coefficient is noticeably larger than that for the global analysis. Again, a moderate to strong associational condition is operative with regard to region and the relationship between social mobilization and public liberties.

Finally, we see in Table 8-5 a display of the Y-intercepts and both slopes in

Table 8-5
Regression Equations for Levels and Rates of Social Mobilization with Liberal Democracy for the Global and Regional Analyses

		Y-Intercept		Level of Mobilization		Rate of Mobilization	Multiple Correlation Coefficient (R)
Y'	=	(a)	+	$(b_1)X_1$	+	$(b_2)X_2$	
Global analysis		− 2.8		0.44		0.61	0.73
Anglo-Europa		− 2.7		0.17		0.87	0.93
Iberic-Latin region		−60.4		1.14		1.13	0.53
Africa		−10.2		0.65		0.58	0.44
Near and Far East		+ 7.2		1.04		−0.05	0.84

the five multiple-regression equations and their respective multiple-correlation coefficients. It should be kept in mind when interpreting the data in this table that the composite index of liberal democracy weights equally each of the three measures of democracy. In addition, it should be remembered that the nature of the interrelationships between democracy variables differs from one region to another and from global to regional models. In spite of these empirical inconsistencies, the computations in Table 8-5 provide an excellent overall summary of (a) the relationships between social mobilization and liberal democracy, and (b) the changes in the regression slopes and correlation coefficients produced when geocultural region is introduced as a condition.

As is evident in Table 8-5, there are only two major differences in the value of the Y-intercept caused by the introduction of the regional condition. The Near and Far Eastern Y-intercept is positive (+7.2) and therefore different from that global constant, and the Iberic-Latin a is extremely large at −60.4. It should be added that in the global and three regional models (the three with negative Y-intercepts) there are thresholds below which increases in social mobilization produce no measurable liberal democratic effects, particularly in the case of the Iberic-Latin analysis and to a lesser extent in the African model. However, there is a prior portion of liberal democracy in the Near and Far East ($a = +7.2$) that thrives in the absence of causal influence by social-mobilization variables.

All five of the b_1 slopes of the lines in the planes parallel to the planes formed by the Y and X_1 axes are positive; each of these regression coefficients indicates that a positive change in the value of level of mobilization in each equation produces a positive change or increase in the dependent variable, liberal democracy. But the sizes of the regression coefficients are substantially different. The global-analysis coefficient ($b_1 = 0.44$) is of moderate size. The Anglo-European slope is considerably less steep ($b_1 = 0.17$), while those of the Iberic-Latin and Near and Far Eastern models are considerably greater. The African coefficient is about the same size as the global coefficient. When liberal democracy is the dependent variable, the impact of social mobilization in geocultural regions is different from that in the global analysis. In all cases it has a positive effect, but the degree of impact differs considerably.

Rate of social mobilization seems to have a similar kind of effect. It is positively related to liberal democracy in all cases except the Near and Far East, where the coefficient is negative but negligible ($b_2 = -0.05$). In the global analysis, the slopes are approximately equal and moderate in size ($b = 0.44$ and 0.61 respectively). The same characterization holds also for the African equation. Although the Iberic-Latin coefficients are about equal in size, they are the largest in any of the regression equations in Table 8-5. In the case of Anglo-Europa, the level coefficient is much smaller than that of rate of mobilization, whereas in the Near and Far Eastern analysis, the coefficient for level is much larger than that for rate of change, and the latter is negative. Thus for the Near and Far East, region is a slightly directional condition. In all the other cases in Table 8-5, the regional condition is associational. Of course, a multiple-correlation coefficient can reveal only associational and none of the other kinds of conditions. The associational impact of region is again evident in the last column of Table 8-5. For the global analysis, $R = 0.73$; but the introduction of region changes the size of this summary coefficient substantially. Both Anglo-Europa and the Near and Far East permit a higher extent of association between social mobilization and liberal democracy than is evident in the entire group of 85 nations. Introducing the Iberic-Latin region and the African region appreciably depresses the size of the coefficient. This summary is completely in agreement with the more detailed findings in previous chapters that deal with the global and regional models separately.

The Importance of Regionalism

Literally hundreds of individual conclusions might be drawn about aspects of the relationships between dimensions of democracy (or the composite index of liberal democracy) and any of the 10 indicators of social mobilization (or levels or rate of mobilization) in the world at large of in any of four geocultural regions. However, since these findings have been discussed in detail in earlier chapters, only the principal conclusion, with the most importance and relevance to the development of an empirical theory of social mobilization and liberal democracy in the post-war world, will be discussed. The mix of substantive, theoretical, and methodological issues is complicated in such a conclusion; the discussion might use any one of these as a lens through which to put a final interpretation on the myriad findings. An attempt to untangle each individual issue systematically is beyond the scope of the present discussion. The central conclusion, which contains substantive, theoretical, and methodological aspects and problems, is that although social mobilization may be related to liberal democratic practices in the post-war world, the nature and meaning of the conditions under which, and the areas in which, the relationship prevails (or does not prevail) are of supreme theoretical importance.

Perhaps the most important social process at work in the world today is social mobilization. Yet given the empirical findings of this study, one might well argue with equal validity and relevance that corporatism and communalism are two of the most significant social processes extant today. And both of them existed in their current areas before social mobilization as we think of that latter concept in Karl W. Deutsch's terms. Corporatism and communalism are important because they are two kinds of social systems and political traditions that predominate in many nation-states of the world. Although they operate in different ways, their effect on social mobilization is about the same. Where it predominates, each tends to operate as a geocultural regional set of intervening conditions between social mobilization and its expected political consequences, particularly liberal-democratic practices. Relatively modern social processes like social mobilization may, in fact, be inhibited or prevented for long periods by corporatism or communalism. As was discussed in Chapters 6 and 7, corporatism and communalism have almost incredible capabilities with respect to the absorption, distortion, transformation, dispersion, and recycling of modern social-mobilization processes in a way that is not evident in noncorporatist and noncommunal societies.

These two types of society and polity should not be viewed as opposite ends of a continuum. It is tempting, however, to theorize that they are and to try to make the necessary substantive and logical connections. For example, one might hypothesize that corporatism and communalism are, for the purposes under consideration, polar opposites on a continuum of centralization of pluralistic tendencies in a society. In this perspective, corporatism represents an extreme statist form of over-centralization of social pluralism, while corporatism represents an extreme substatist form of over-decentralization of pluralistic tendencies. An imaginative and clever social scientist could, no doubt, argue this position rather persuasively with historical and contemporary evidence. Further, such an endeavor might well involve an attempt to measure variation on the centralization continuum so that each nation-state in the present analysis could be assigned a score on such a scale. However, that is decidedly not the position taken here. Communalism and corporatism, as societal conditions and political traditions in two different geocultural regions of the world, are radically different phenomena. Geocultural regions are nominal polychotomies which differ in kind and quality, not just in degree or quantity. They are attributes, not variables. Inclusion of a measure of corporatism or communalism or both along with social-mobilization variables in a multiple-regression equation would probably not increase the size of the multiple-correlation coefficient. The reason is because it is the *kind* or *quality* of the condition that operates to inhibit or encourage social mobilization's political effects that is important. In fact, by computing multiple-regression analyses by geocultural region, corporatism and communalism were, in effect, held constant in the two relevant analyses, Iberic-Latin and African. Such analyses produced generally small coefficients of relationship. Geocultural region is unique; it involves the historical manifestation and operation of the collective subjective meaning attached to the political tradition of a society by its inhabitants. It cannot be measured cross-regionally. It may vary among societies within regions; Portugal may be more corporatist than Chile, and Uganda may be more communalistic than Tanzania. But at this point it seems unlikely that anyone can successfully identify, substantively define, untangle, operationalize, measure, and interrelate the numerous and super-complex sets of variables that comprise corporatism and communalism as one or more cross-regional continuua.

Geocultural regionalism, or area studies as it is more commonly known in the academic programs of political and other social science departments, must be studied on its own terms in its own area or countries as a complex set of conditions, especially directional, associational, and causal. It very well may prove to be impossible to convert configurative regionalism to sociological regionalism—to explain, measure, and use geocultural regional variables as composite indicators of variables more or less present in and characteristic of each of the nations of the globe.

Thus we return to the fundamental problem of political science originally posed by Aristotle in about 335 B.C., quoted in the preface of this book:

> . . . politics has to consider what sort of constitution suits what sort of civic body. The attainment of the best constitution is likely to be impossible for the general run of states; and the good lawgiver and the true statesman must therefore have their eyes open not only for what is the absolute best, but also to what is the best in relation to actual conditions.[6]

The research reported in this book is based on an attempt to determine empirically what kinds of regimes, more or less liberal democratic, are best suited to what kinds of actual conditions of social mobilization and modernization. The three-part answer that has resulted is neither simple nor without exceptions. First, the political properties of constitutions are complicated and occasionally internally inconsistent, contradictory, and counteractive. Second, the processes of "actual conditions" are likewise complicated and occasionally internally inconsistent, contradictory, and counteractive. Finally, the political traditions of different geocultural regions of the world include different kinds, strengths, and meanings of the relationship between actual conditions and constitutions. But Aristotle probably knew that best of all.

One of the major points in this book is that communalism and corporatism have distinct relationships with social mobilization. Communalism tends to prevent altogether the modernization that produces social mobilization, and very seriously tends to inhibit or even to prevent the anticipated political consequences of social mobilization when it does occur. Corporatism, on the other hand, permits and in some ways even encourages some kinds of modernization and allows some of what we usually think of as social mobilization. But, through its adaptive, co-optative, and assimilationist capacities, the corporatist state allows only limited social mobilization to occur while precluding its anticipated political effects. Communalism tends to inhibit nation- and state-building, while corporatism protects the existing nation-state from the forces of change. Both kinds of polities are resistant to change and its implications, especially social and political change. As the accelerative thrust of change continues to increase in the modernized West as the world moves toward the twenty-first century, the gap between the modernized Westernized nations and the primitive and traditional countries grows even wider.[7]

Emerging from the quantitative analyses of the relationships between social mobilization and liberal democracy in the global and geocultural regional models and the theoretical explanations offered to account for those relationships (political traditions) are the elements of a strategy of political change. Open to the communal countries of Africa and the Near and Far East is the corporatist strategy. Available to the nation-states of the Iberic-Latin region is the tutelary liberalist-socialist strategy. Tanzania provides an actual example of an African country that has begun to adopt the corporatist strategy as a means whereby to undertake sociopolitical change and reorganization, to try to achieve modernization as it is known in the twentieth century. Peru serves as an empirical example of an Iberic-Latin nation-state that has adopted the tutelary liberalist-socialist strategy for encouraging and productively managing sociopolitical change, modernization, and social mobilization. An examination of recent politics in these two countries will demonstrate concretely the strategy that each has adopted and the distinct possibilities for sociopolitical change that each represents for communal and corporatist political systems respectively. Underlying these points is an implicit statment of the processes of nation- and state-building and modernization with its concomitant social mobilization: the processual linkage between communalism and corporatism and between corporatism and its potential successors.

Before these two cases and their theoretical importance are discussed, a series of disclaimers is in order. The countries of Africa and the Near and Far East (particularly those not so deeply affected by Western colonial practices) may never and perhaps should never successfully adopt the institutions of liberal or socialist democracy. Certainly these variants of democracy represent neither an inevitable stage nor an endpoint in political development at the nation-state level. Similarly, it is quite conceivable that modernization and the processes of social mobilization, even in limited degrees, may never occur in the countries of Africa and the Near and Far East. Or if the processes of social mobilization do begin, they may become stuck for a substantial period of time between erosion of old and induction into new values and behaviors. Or real social mobilization may not get underway in many of these countries for about 500 years. The point is, the future of these countries is uncertain. Even if modernization and both steps of social mobilization do occur, it is not known whether the political consequences will produce liberal democracy, radical socialism (Marxist-Leninist, Maoist, indigenous nationalist, etc.), some hybrid or some yet unperceived kind of political system. And finally, it may be foolish even to think about the future development of some of these countries, particularly some of those in Africa, since they are "paper" states whose political, economic, social, cultural, and even physical viability is highly questionable.[8] Similarly, some Iberic-Latin nations may remain unchanging, traditional-corporatists states virtually forever.

However, whatever the uncertainties, improbabilities, and impossibilities in the short run, what is being suggested here is that both communal and corporatist societies have long-term solutions of sociopolitical change open to them. No sense of inevitability should be inferred. All that is being suggested is that if communal countries want to become modernizing nation-states, then they should first corporatize; if corporatist nation-states want to become modern, then they should adopt tutelary liberal-socialism. A discussion of recent Tanzanian and Peruvian politics will clarify these points and their theoretical importance.

Tanzania: The Corporatization of Communalism

Politics in many African and Near and Far Eastern countries is profoundly characterized by diffuseness, parochialism, primitivism, traditionalism, little or no structural differentiation or cultural secularization, and quite limited system versatility with respect to political capabilities. As argued in previous chapters, the strength of primordial sentiments, of political communalism, has barred the creation of modernizing nation-states throughout most of Africa and the Near and Far East. However, Tanzania definitely appears to be corporatizing its communalism and showing promise of building a nation-state. An inspection of seven serendipitous conditions and the many deliberate efforts of President Julius Nyerere and his political party, the Tanzania African National Union (TANU), to transform Tanzanian political institutions and culture, clearly reveals the advantages of corporatism as an avenue of escape from communalism.

Among the serendipitous circumstances facilitating the corporatization of Tanzanian communalism are the population distribution, ethnic composition, the location of the national capital, the brevity and levity of colonialism, the emergence of a politically adroit charismatic leader, the existence of more or less functionally based bribes, and the widespread knowledge of the Swahili language.[9] First, the population is mainly peripherally concentrated in Tanganyika because of the existence of a large mainland plateau of 3,000 to 4,000 feet in height that has too little rainfall for viable cultivation. The population is located mainly in the highland areas of the northeast and southwest and in areas near lakes or the sea where there is enough rainfall. About two-thirds of the population are concentrated in one-tenth of the land area, rather than being spread out all over the country. Second, Tanzania has incredible ethnic diversity with fully 120 separate tribes, almost all of which are classified as Bantu, but none of which is large or strong enough to dominate. The Sukuma comprise about one million or 10 percent of the population and are the largest tribe; the next largest tribe is the Nyamwezi with only about 350,000 members. Thus none of the tribes is able realistically to contemplate a separate political existence. The Sukuma are unified enough to do this, but they are not economically viable and have too few educated leaders. Both the Chagga and the Haya are more economically and educationally developed and have a modern, educated leadership, but each is relatively small in number.[10] Third, the capital city, Dar es Salaam, is not located in the area of the largest and most developed tribe or people. Therefore, the location of the capital has not provoked fear of or facilitated the possible domination of the national political leadership by one ethnic group. Fourth, the Swahili language was the lingua franca for the huge majority of Tanzanians, at least as a second or third language. This linguistic similarity greatly facilitated national elite-mass communication and the ability of the government and TANU to send officials to any part of the country. As a culture and a language, Swahili is urban-based and exercises a homogenizing influence.[11] In the towns, the dominant culture is associated with the ordinary man in the street, rather than with the mission-educated, up-country elite.

A fifth serendipitous condition concerns the length and nature of colonial rule in Tanzania. Both the Germans and British stayed in Tanzania for relatively short periods and ruled the colony in a comparatively gentle manner, thus minimizing the impact of a distinct colonial culture. German and British rule was later tempered by a League of Nation's mandate and a United Nation's trusteeship. The uncertainty over the territory's future discouraged many Europeans from coming there to settle, and thus there was a smaller and less homogeneous immigrant community in colonial Tanganyika. As a result, Tanganyika was less closely administered and economically aided than other African colonies such as Kenya. Similarly, when the Tanganyikan Nationalist movement began, it encountered less internal resistance and more international stimulation and support.[12] Also, finally, in 1953 during the initial stages of the Nationalist movement, all civil servants were banned from membership in any political party. Since most educated persons were civil servants, and since very few educated Africans were employed outside government and therefore available for political roles, membership in TANU was not restricted to a small educated elite but was forced to cater to the needs of the masses. In addition, since each branch of TANU had to register with the government, all local parts of TANU kept in frequent touch with the center.

Sixth, Julius Nyerere is an unusual political figure in that he combines charisma with genuine political skill and intellectual ability. Leader of the Tanganyikan nationalist liberation, post-independence leader, author of several major books,[13] Nyerere is described as charismatic, admired, idolized, and emulated in dress and speech by other leaders and citizens alike.[14] He is an extraordinary person. Incidentally, he came from a relatively small and insignificant tribe in the northeast, the Zaneki. Seventh, many tribes in Tanzania are, though culturally and linguistically distinct, functionally specialized with regard to their occupational activities in agriculture; some tribes are hunters and gatherers, some subsistence agriculturalists, some cash crop agriculturalists, some are pastoral and semi-pastoral people, etc.[15] This existing tendency toward functional specialization made possible a natural interdependence, a socioeconomic relationship of mutual dependence.

For these seven reasons, efforts to achieve political integration and nation-

and state-building have had a better-than-average chance to succeed in Tanzania. However, it was incumbent on one man, President Nyerere, and one organization, TANU, to identify these latent properties of Tanzanian society, to maximize their utility, to overcome the many primordial and disintegrative tendencies, and to centralize the Tanzanian polity. Nyerere may not be a self-conscious corporatist, but many of his political techniques, especially those that show most promise for success, are thoroughly corporatist in nature. With regard to the sociopolitical order, the tactics that Nyerere and TANU have used include centralization, functionalization, vertical segmentalization, consolidation, neutralization, absorption, co-optation, infiltration, bureaucratization, fusion, and homogenization vis-à-vis groups in Tanzania. With regard to changing Tanzanian political culture, Nyerere has developed his own brand of African socialism, *ujamaa*; its values, philosophy, ideology, and mass-party aspects make it singularly organicist in effect. In other words, Nyerere is employing a corporatist strategy to transform Tanzanian sociopolitical institutions and political culture. A brief examination of some of his specific policies clearly demonstrates a picture of change, movement, transition from communalism to corporatism and perhaps beyond.

In terms of sociopolitical transformation, the following points are paramount: the organization of TANU and the one-party state, detribalization, the creation and manipulation of functional groups, and the fusion of TANU and formal government. TANU was born as an anticolonialist, nationalist, liberationist mass movement.[16] Upon the establishment of Tanganyikan independence, TANU became a political party and very quickly a ruling party. Tanganyika soon became a constitutional one-party state.[17] Members of other political parties can neither compete in elections nor sit in the national legislature. Candidates for Parliament are chosen by and from TANU from among TANU members who offer themselves. The party chooses one presidential candidate who runs in a plebiscite. Nyerere has always been that candidate and has always run TANU. Although it is not without problems of center-periphery relations, TANU is the only party in Tanganyika, de facto and de jure, and it is hierarchically organized and led by a charismatic leader.[18]

Government and TANU policies designed to detribalize Tanzania include Africanization and linguistic homogenization. The government, through its Africanization policy, has made available many positions in many occupational areas to Africans; formerly, prior to independence, these positions were filled with Asians and Europeans. Also, beginning with the September 1965 elections, all candidates for office were ordered by TANU to campaign only in Swahili. In 1967 the government made Swahili the only official language. These measures have substantially encouraged a detribalization process whereby Africans have relinquished their traditional patterns of values, habits, customs, and have become committed to a more modernized way of life. This government/TANU sponsored process usually involves entrance into the wage economy, conversion to Christianity or Islam, changes in style of dress, and a general erosion of a variety of tribal customs.[19]

Perhaps most effective of all corporatist techniques has been creation and manipulation of functional groups. President Nyerere, through the vehicle of TANU, continues to exercise an increasing degree of monolithic control and to consolidate and centralize political power through the creation and domination of a vertically segmented hierarchy of functional groupings. Both potential and expressed dissatisfaction and dissent are either co-opted, neutralized, or repressed by the government. Groups that do not find recognition within TANU do not find recognition in Tanzania. The government has corporatized the potentially pluralistic group structure in a three-tiered, bureaucratized system: departments, affiliates, and clients. The three groups that comprise formal departments of TANU are women (the Union of Women of Tanzania, UWT), elders (the Elder's Section), and youth (the TANU Youth League, TYL). Through their formal linkage with its organization, TANU exercises tight control over these groups.[20] The second tier of TANU affiliates includes trade unions (National Union of Tanganyikan Workers, NUTA), agricultural cooperative societies (the Cooperative Union of Tanzania, CUT), supply (the Cooperative Supply Association of Tanzania, CSAT), and parents (Tanganyikan African Parents Association, TAPA). In 1958 the Tanganyikan Federation of Labor was formally associated with TANU. When a TANU government was established committed to pursuit of economic development, tensions soon arose between government (TANU) and labor. Union demands were not always compatible with the government's priorities of economic modernization, and the federation of unions was viewed by government as merely one of many groups. In 1964, in an attempt to take advantage of the unrest and chaos in the aftermath of an army mutiny, the leaders of the Tanganyikan Federation of Labor threatened to call a general strike in support of the mutineers. The government promptly dissolved the unions, detained about 200 of the leaders and members up to two years, and later reconstituted the trade movement into a single, centralized body renamed NUTA. The new national labor organization, which represents *all* laborers, is closely and organically affiliated with TANU, and is controlled much more closely by the government. For example, the government has considerable financial control and appoints the two top NUTA officials. However, recently the government has been lobbying to make NUTA a department.

A second affiliate of TANU is the agricultural movement, which was brought under the single umbrella of the Co-operative Union of Tanzania (CUT). For this reason, and since the government creates the co-ops, farmers are well controlled. In addition, the Cooperative Supply Association of Tanganyika and the Tanganyikan African Parents Association are also well controlled, and efforts to exercise more stringent control over all four affiliates are being made by the government.[21]

Informal but nonetheless controlled groups that have clientelistic relationships with the government are local government, the civil service, and the armed services. Regarding local government, the government has created Village Development Corporations (VCDs), and TANU has created local cells (in addition to being heavily involved in planning and managing the VCDs). These VCDs are organs of local government as well as machinery for economic development and planning. It might also be mentioned that Tanzania is divided into 20 regions with regional commissioners responsible for coordinating the business of the central government ministries in their respective regions and supervising regional development. The regions are also divided into 60 districts with area officers whose functions are similar to those of the commissioners, but on a district scale. Local councils are, therefore, under the constant purview of national officials in all matters of interest to central government. The TANU cells were established in late 1964 to build a grass-roots organization on the basis of every 10 houses. The cells serve as a channel of political communication and as a means of mass mobilization. The party cells have usurped numerous functions of local government, including judicial, police, and economic development.[22]

The techniques by which Nyerere and TANU gained control of the civil service and military were mainly infiltration of these two groups by TANU people and fusion of the TANU structure with the group structure.[23] It was done subtly with the civil bureaucracy. Because of the 1953 civil service regulation banning party membership for bureaucrats, none of them participated in the independence struggle. Consequently, there developed appreciable suspicion and distrust between civil servants and politicians in the post-colonial period. Both were inexperienced and insecure at governing, but TANU was relatively well-organized, dynamic, respected, and legitimate. When the provincial administration was Africanized, it was staffed mainly with TANU members, who replaced all of the colonial Regional and Area Commissioners. Then TANU made the new Regional and Area Commissioners regional and area secretaries of TANU. The distinction between civil servant and TANU official soon lost all meaning. In 1964 civil servants were allowed to join TANU, and the central government bureaucracy was increasingly integrated with the party regime, and TANU was able to infuse its own values throughout the administrative structure.[24] Party and state, legitimacy and authority, became one through this infiltration, integration, and fusion process.

Nyerere's effort to get control of the army for TANU was less subtle and more dramatic.[25] After the January 1964 mutiny, all noncommissioned soldiers were dismissed and for a time all new recruits were drawn from the TANU Youth League. The party also supplied many of the new officers, both those who were responsible for traditional military duties and those in charge of political education. Also, both the military and police are allowed and encouraged to join TANU. The army was the last major group to come under government/TANU control.

As a part of the functionalization program, according to the Tanzanian Constitution, seven national institutions or functional groups are allowed to nominate a pool of candidates for Parliament, and the regularly elected members of Parliament then elect fifteen of these nominees. The national institutions are labor, agriculture, parents, women, youth—all acting through their closely controlled national organizations, University College at Dar es Salaam, and the Association of Chambers of Commerce.[26]

Because of the success of its corporatization program, the central government does not have a significant internal security problem and only rarely finds repressive measures necessary. Mention was made earlier of the detention of many labor leaders and members and the firing of many soldiers and officers after the mutiny. But there are still those who seek in some way to dissent from TANU policies, mainly because of alleged slowness of the government to implement policies, not because of policy content. One example is provided by the secretary of the TANU Youth League, who was unhappy with the slowness with which foreign bank nationalization policy was being implemented. He tore down the portrait of Queen Juliana in a former Dutch bank in Dar es Salaam. For this, he was dismissed from his position by President Nyerere. Later the former TYL secretary and four other people were detained by the government for allegedly trying to involve the army in a coup d'etat against the president. In another incident, the National Executive Council of TANU dismissed seven members of Parliament from TANU membership and their seats in Parliament on the grounds of "anti-TANU and unprincipled attitudes."[27]

Although repression is a tactic that the government and TANU are prepared to use if necessary, their increasing overlap of both membership and functions in numerous sectoral groups has increasingly produced a single, bureaucratized, hierarchical, segmented, stratified administrative-political unit. Not unexpectedly, this corporatization process has resulted in many of the problems perennially associated with the traditionally corporatist states of the Iberic-Latin region. The bureaucratization of the agricultural cooperative societies in CUT provides an important example. According to one official committee of enquiry, governmental agricultural organization in Tanzania is unfair, dishonest, and corrupt, lacks adequately trained manpower, is too bureaucratic, undemocratic, and inefficient as a result of its political motivation.[28] Other close, first-hand observers of the Tanzanian cooperative system confirm these complaints as more or less accurate.[29]

Efforts on the part of Nyerere and TANU to transform the political culture of Tanzania can best be understood in terms of Nyerere's own version of African socialism, *ujamaa.*[30] The Swahili term *ujamaa* means "brotherhood" or "familyhood," and is based on the traditional Tanzanian village concepts of love or mutual respect, common property including food, and the obligation to work. Its author describes it best; President Nyerere said:[31]

The foundation, and the objective, of African socialism is the extended family. The true African socialist does not look on one class of men as his bretheren and another as his natural enemies. He does not form an alliance with the "bretheren" for the extermination of the "non-brethren." He regards all men as his bretheren—as members of his ever-extending family. . . .

"Ujamaa" then, or "familyhood," describes our socialism. It is opposed to capitalism, which seeks to build a happy society on the basis of the exploitation of man by man, and it is equally opposed to doctrinaire socialism which seeks to build its happy society on a philosophy of inevitable conflict between man and man.. . . .

Modern African socialism can draw from its traditional heritage the recognition of "society" as an extension of the basic family unit. But it can no longer confine the idea of the social family within the limits of the tribe. . . .

Ujamaa implies social consciousness of the organic family or brotherhood, the sense of obligation that people have for the welfare of their fellowmen. The theme of organic solidarity is a recurrent one in Tanzanian political thought. President Nyerere put ujamaa and African socialism in perspective when he stated, "What we are attempting is a telescoped evolution of our society and our economy. . . . The *natural growth* of our country can be telescoped and still remain *organic.*" [italics added].[32] Ujamaa insists on adherence or at least acquiescence to a single organicist-cultural value system—familyhood, brotherhood, extended family, mutual obligation—in the framework of a strong, one-party system binding all people and all groups in an organicist-corporatist hierarchy.

There may be some differences between the strategies adopted by Nyerere in pursuit of political integration in Tanzania and the archtypical system-maintenance functions of the corporatist polity in the Iberic-Latin tradition. But the similarities are clearly overwhelming. What has been going on in Tanzania in the past decade is the corporatization of communalism. Tanzania is in corporatist transition from communalism to some variant of modernization; the corporatist strategy seems to be the best means to move up from communalism.

In other words, the path to modernization for many, perhaps most, African and Near and Far Eastern countries is neither liberal democracy of the Western variant nor some variant of socialism or communism from Moscow or Peking. Both of these are clearly developmentally oriented, though in radically different perspectives, of course. But both are distinctly alien to the indigenous cultural, social, and political forces, whether dormant, latent, or manifest, most characteristic of communalism. Rather, the path to modernization for these countries is some variant of corporatism as has been practiced in the Iberic-Latin countries. The strategies and properties of corporatism as we have described them in Chapter 6 certainly seem to fit the political traditions of African and many Near and Far Eastern countries better than Western political ideas, although even corporatism demands substantial cultural change. It is a fact that the corporatist nations of the Iberic-Latin area have reached greater levels of industrialization and economic productivity than African and most Near and Far Eastern nations. This is in part true because the institutionalization of corporatism meant the eradication or overcoming of the divisiveness of communal and other kinds of primordial sentiments.[33] When this fact is grasped, African and some Near and Far Eastern leaders may, with considerable deliberate effort, much good fortune, and a long period of time, be able to guide their countries into the processes of twentieth century modernization. It should be realized that such a transformation may be viewed as altogether undesirable and therefore it may never occur. It is simply proposed here as one attractive kind of option for development that promises to work effectively and stably in Africa and the Near and Far East.

Peru: The Liberalist-Socialist Democratization of Corporatism

But presuming that the countries of Africa and the Near and Far East were able, through corporatist strategies, to overcome the divisive primordial forces of communalism, create nation-states via processes of assimilation or through the achievement of unity in diversity,[34] and establish a position of strength and versatility[35] vis-à-vis the processes of social mobilization, would they not still remain impervious to the expected political consequences of social mobilization, as have most Iberic-Latin nations? Yes, for awhile, but just as there is a potential corporatist path out of communalism, there is also a path out of corporatism leading eventually to a more fully participant society with high levels of political versatility and economic development. That path can be called tutelary liberalist-socialist democracy. It is a corporatism that is both liberalizing and socializing its political practices and at the same time institutionalizing these increasingly liberal and socialistic practices. Just how this process might work to transform a corporatist polity into a liberal-socialist-democratic polity is demonstrated with remarkable precision by Peru since 1968.

Again, it should be recalled that a variety of the properties of corporatism work to stifle social mobilization and its possible political consequences. Peru before 1968 was a more or less typical corporatist polity and society in the Iberic-Latin tradition. However, since 1968 Peru represents a significant exception to that corporatist tradition.

On October 3, 1968 a group of military officers led by General Juan Velasco Alvardo carried out a successful coup d'etat and overthrew the incumbent Peruvian chief executive, President Fernando Belaunde Terry. In the years since 1968, President Velasco has proved to be a remarkably atypical Iberic-Latin military-political leader, and his regime has been truly exceptional in the Iberic-Latin corporatist context. The regime and its leader have been characterized by the following kinds of adjectives, for example: tutelary, bureaucratic, military-populistic, technocratic, revolutionary, radical, leftist, modernizing, authoritarian, secularizing, nationalistic, reformist, and etatist.[36] Again, an examination of some serendipitous conditions and Velasco's deliberate policies will demonstrate the strategy by which corporatism can be converted to a different kind of regime through the route of tutelary liberalist-socialism.

Mainly six societal conditions in Peru not only made the 1968 coup likely but also almost guaranteed its success.. First, Peru, like many Latin American countries but more so, has a history of effecting the transfer of executive political power through the coup d'etat. This process is viewed by many Latin American scholars as the functional equivalent of elections. During the period 1947-67, Peru had averaged a military coup every five years. That General Velasco staged a coup was neither wholly unexpected nor surprising. Second, and also pertaining to General Velasco and his associates, is the new concept of military social responsibility that has developed in the Centro De Altos Estudios Militares (CAEM) in Lima. The CAEM, Peru's war college, is staffed by the most radical professors in the country. Its curriculum is rather uncommon in that it vastly transcends classical military subjects, drawing on the concept that true national security must spring from social justice as well as military power. The course of study at CAEM included social science training and work on the Peruvian political system and on national problems, potential, and planning.[37]

In addition, Peru's military officers come mainly from the lower and middle classes and are well-traveled enough in Peru and other countries to know the appalling conditions of poverty that exist in their own country. All of these conditions combined to produce a new professionalism among Peruvian military officers whose view of development and modernization includes not only economic growth but social and political change, and internal economic redistribution. Not every corporatist polity has a CAEM.

Like many less developed countries, however, Peru did have an oligarchic elite that was probably more oppressive than most. The Forty Families of Lima, as the traditional elite is called, refused to allow agrarian reforms. Since this condition is characteristic of most less developed nations, it is probably a necessary but not sufficient condition to permit a coup by radical reformist military officers. A fourth serendipitous condition is related to the existence of an oppressive economic oligarchy of landed elites; it pertains to rising expectations and frustrations on the part of a large number of Peruvian citizens. This condition reflected the inability of the Belaunde government to curb inflation, which was running at 20 percent in 1968. Using 1967 as a base year of 100, the consumer price index in early 1968 was approaching 150. Belaunde, the leader of the minority Accion Popular party, was consistently defeated in budget requests to Congress. Institutionally, he was blocked because of a lack of presidential veto power. To keep his government solvent, Belaunde borrowed heavily from foreign banks, opening his administration to charges of selling out his nation. Belaunde's borrowing policy finally forced him to devaluate the sol in September 1967.

The devaluation itself, which fell within the executive power of the president, was belatedly decreed on September 1, 1967. The political haggling over the budget cost three cabinets, alienated the military and deprived the president of any semblance of political independence.[38]

As a result, Belaunde's economic policy did not strengthen the economy; rather, it moved Peru into economic insecurity and recession.

Combined with the declining viability of economic life of the average Peruvian citizen was a fifth condition which further conditioned Peru's future—government corruption. Although there were many incidents and charges of dishonesty and corruption on the part of President Belaunde and members of his administration, the precipitating and perhaps most dramatic revelation of official corruption concerned Belaunde's handling of the expropriation of the United States-owned International Petroleum Company (IPC). Peru had presumably expropriated IPC, but the terms of payments had never been arranged. The Belaunde compromise promised to make a relatively small payment to a central fund from which the United States would pay off all outstanding claims. In 1968 the director of the national petroleum company complained that the eleventh and last page of the agreement was missing. This page supposedly established the price which Peru would pay IPC for oil. Belaunde was again accused of selling Peru to the United States, and the Accion Popular declined him further support.[39] However, Jaquette maintains that[40]

> [T]he crisis developed . . . not because the Belaunde government was corrupt, but because it failed to fulfill its promise to generate peaceful social change. The lesson of this failure was that reformist civilian governments are too weak to "change the structures."

In any case, the rising discontent brought on by economic stagnation, inflation, and government corruption seriously eroded the legitimacy accorded to Belaunde's government and the civilian regime by Peruvian citizens in general. This sixth serendipitous condition, loss of legitimacy, was perhaps the most serious and final blow to the central features of Peruvian politics—ineffective rule and public policies of a conservative civilian regime, oligarchic control by the Forty Families, and the absence of productive programs of social, economic, and political change.

These six conditions facilitated the military coup as well as the new president's policies, which aim at order through change and egalitarianism: radical socioeconomic policy reforms, amnesty for political prisoners, radical foreign economic-policy reforms, and both institutionalized and noninstitutionalized citizen participation in the Peruvian economy and polity. An examination of the details of the Velasco programs reveals that they are coherently aimed at little less than the complete transformation of Peru from a corporatist to a liberalist-socialist polity.

The sociopolitical reform program involved radical changes in numerous sectors of Peruvian society: agrarian, industrial, mining, fisheries, communication, and education.[41] The Agrarian Reform law took effect on June 24, 1969, quite obviously at the severe expense of the oligarchic landed elite. It limited the size of land holdings to about 375 acres on the coast and 112 acres in the highlands. Land holdings in excess of the maximum allowed size were expropriated and paid for in cash up to about $25,000 per property and the balance in government bonds. Further, the expropriated lands were sold to cooperatives, peasant communities, and agricultural societies or to qualified peasants. In March, 1973 President Velasco decreed the waiver of all payments by small tenant farmers for land acquired under the Agrarian Reform law.[42] In a society where 0.8 percent of the people owned 82.6 percent of the land,[43] this reform law was unthinkably revolutionary.

The General Industrial law, put into effect on July 28, 1970, established the participation of workers in company management and ownership. Each company with five or more employees and a gross annual income of $230,000 or more must distribute to its work force 10 percent of the net, pretax income and transfer 15 percent of the net, pretax income in shareholdings to the industrial community, a legal entity which represents the company's workers. In addition, the General Industrial law provides considerable inducement for industrialists to reinvest their profits. This law also radically altered Peruvian society by redistributing wealth and participation in economic and industrial decisions.

On March 29, 1971 President Velasco instituted a new law regulating the very important Peruvian fisheries industry. The law involved the establishment of a fisherman's community in each company to represent the employees and to administer the monetary and stock benefits provided by the firm. Also, a fisherman's compensation community was set up to represent the workers in fisheries and to redistribute a percent of all industry profits to the fisherman's communities according to the number of workers in each community. Fishery firms must pay 4 percent of their net income to the fisherman's community and 4 percent to the compensation community. In addition, companies must buy stocks for their workers' community until the community holds 50 percent of the shares. The stocks are bought with 12 percent of the yearly net income.

A similarly radical General Telecommunications law was effectuated on November 10, 1971. Television and radio stations were brought under government control through expropriation of 51 percent of the television stock and 25 percent of the radio stock. The law also placed the stations in worker communities providing employees with 25 percent of the profits in cash and stock annually. These changes in the structure of the communications industry were consistent with the Velasco regime's radical reforms in other sectors of the economy. Similar kinds of reforms were imposed on the mining industry.

Two revolutionary changes in the Peruvian educational system were also effected. The first, the New University law which began in February, 1969, made a complete college education free for all those who could not pay. However, the main educational reform was introduced with the March 1972 Educational Reform law that mandated five principal changes: bilingual education—Spanish and the various Indian dialects (estimates of the Indian percentage of Peruvian population run as high as 67 percent); equal opportunity for women; student participation in university government; provisions for preschool education; and obligatory vocational training for all pupils from age 15 on, for two to three years.

These six radical sociopolitical reform programs have had profound impact on all aspects of Peruvian life. Another small but significant part of the Velasco revolution was a distinctly political act. In December 1971 the President granted amnesty for all (approximately 100) political prisoners and cancelled all political trials. Moreover, after their release there was no restriction placed on their movements or activities. What is perhaps most remarkable about the amnesty decree is that it emanated from a group of generals who had been fighting those same prisoners just about five years earlier. The granting of amnesty also symbolized the increasingly preponderant influence of the liberal wing over the conservative wing in the Velasco cabinet and in the upper echelons of the armed services.

A third policy with which Velasco is transforming Peru's corporatist structure involved expropriation and nationalization of foreign concerns and the regulation of terms of credit for such firms. Unlike Belaunde, Velasco actually expropriated the International Petroleum Company. Also he nationalized the Peruvian Telephone Company of the International Telephone and Telegraph (ITT). Third, in June 1971 a law was passed which limited access of all firms with less than 80 percent Peruvian participation to local bank and credit facilities. These three and other similar measures served not only to limit foreign control of Peru's economy but to Peruvianize important sectors of it, particularly in conjunction with the reforms in agriculture, industry, fishing, etc.

Obviously, the socioeconomic reforms have placed considerable participation, influence, and control over the economy in the hands of the workers of Peru. This economic power, exercised through local, functional sectors, is directly translatable into political power. But beyond the direct political implications of the socioeconomic reforms, the Velasco regime has also undertaken a program of direct encouragement and stimulation of widespread citizen participation in politics.[44] On June 24, 1971 Velasco announced the creation of the National Social Mobilization Support System (SINAMOS).[45] The purpose of this institution is to create conditions for the direct, effective, and permanent participation of all Peruvians in the development of the revolution. The president maintains that SINAMOS is not an official part of his regime, but it appears to be the government's substitute for political parties, which Velasco has criticized for allegedly serving only the interests of the former Peruvian oligarchy. SINAMOS is charged with seeking out and building cadres that can educate the masses, explain the modernizing aims of the regime, and integrate the Indians into Peruvian life. In 1971-72 SINAMOS had 4,500 personnel and an annual budget of $92,000,000.[46]

Social mobilization was defined in the Peruvian national plan in July 1971: it is

the process by which the emerging groups come to exercise a basic or structural participation by gaining access to the control of the society's key resources. (These key resources) are basically the ownership of the means of production and the making of the central decisions which affect the most important aspects of society as a whole. (It is the state's responsibility to) stimulate, channel, and consolidate (the participation of the people because our) people are relatively untrained and incapable of assuming fully and in the short run (their) responsibilities under the present dynamic of change.[47]

Thus SINAMOS is the agency which is responsible for creating, institutionalizing, optimizing, and rendering effective citizen participation in all realms of society, especially politics and government. But in addition to these efforts, the government also undertakes a number of noninstitutionalized programs to stimulate an effective bond between the military elite and the general population, and to erode the old institutional loyalties to political party and union. These noninstitutionalized mechanisms include expropriation of IPC, a barrage of speeches throughout Peru by the president and his ministers, weekly food handouts to the residents of Lima's squatter settlements by the president, personal removal of an official for not doing his job, direct repression (for example, deportations and jailings without due process), and the use of legitimate violence by the police or troops to break up strikes, demonstrations, etc.[48] The program of direct relationships with citizens adds up to military populism.

President Velasco has developed an elaborate and coherent ideology of the Peruvian revolution, which he articulated precisely in a formal speech marking the Susquicentennial of Peruvian independence on July 28, 1971:

. . . [O]ur position is defined in terms of a revolutionary humanism. . . . This position picks the best of the legacies of the Christian, libertarian, and socialist traditions . . . [and] represents the confluence of the most illustrious streams of revolutionary thought of our own historic tradition. It constitutes the basis for a new socio-political conceptualization in Peru . . . which has as its object the construction of a fully participatory social democracy . . . a system based on a moral order of solidarity, not individualism . . . [In such a system] the means of production are predominantly social property, under the direct control of those who generate the wealth from their work. [Within the] political order [of such a system] the power of decision . . . is diffuse and rests essentially in social, economic, and political institutions which are conducted by the men and women who make them up, with a minimum of intermediaries, or with no intermediaries whatsoever. . . .[49]

It is clear that Valesco's goal is not simply increasing economic growth and productivity, as was apparently the goal of his predecessor, but an egalitarian distribution of the wealth produced. SINAMOS was created to effectuate the goal and its ideology, rather than using a political party system. And of course SINAMOS is designed to serve as a mechanism for the reception, expression, transmission, and resolution of the concerns of Peruvian citizens. Yet there is a distinct flavor of tutelary guidance in the ideology and practice of Velasco's program. The citizens are to learn while doing; they must learn to walk before they can (are allowed to) run. Because the military regime has a deep concern for its own survival and for internal security, full participatory freedom cannot be immediately granted; rather, Velasco emphasizes a form of decreasingly constrained freedom.

Yet it is just this military interest in internal security that apparently underlies the regime's very explicit concern with the careful institutionalization and organization of participation as a means to achieve and safeguard orderly processes of development, a societal order that they feel can be achieved and maintained only through social, economic, and political change. In Velasco's initial rejection of both the Marxist alternative of class solidarity and overthrow of authority and the Western democratic alternative of pluralism reconciled through interest groups and political parties,[50] his tutelary emphasis on the stimulation but control of participation, his policy of gradualism, and his realization that Peruvian order can be preserved only through fundamental change, the president has sought to make his regime compatible with and to draw upon Peru's corporatist political tradition. For example, participation is to begin in local functional groups.

The changes instituted by the Velasco regime will invariably produce many basic short- and long-term repercussions throughout Peru. If present trends continue, that is, as participation, gross national product, gross national product per capita, and the egalitarian distribution of Peru's wealth continue to increase, Peru will eventually be thoroughly transformed. David Scott Palmer summarizes the portent for change and suggests the likely outcome in this way:

As citizens gain competence through the experience of participating at the local level in the local participation units, they should expect to be granted increased responsibilities to affect the course of decision-making at the national level. One way for this to occur is through truly representational associations based on functional criteria of workplace or residence. While the model suggests that ultimate control will remain centralized and concentrated, citizens organized in associations and represented through them to the departmental and national levels would presumably have an increased role in the determination of policy within their own functional areas, if not society as a whole. If these representatives should come to actually and effectively determine the naming of the central authorities themselves in a climate of routinized and regular turnover, the character of the corporate model takes on a dimension of responsiveness and hence ultimate responsibility to the citizens themselves. Thus the training in participation originally available only at the local level becomes the school for socialization into a new value framework *which eventually undermines the Hispanic (or Iberic-Latin) tradition.* [italics added][51]

The present military regime is borrowing on Peru's very own corporatist tradition to decorporatize; Velasco is instituting and gradually institutionalizing a form of tutelary liberalist-socialist democracy largely *within* the framework of the Iberic-Latin corporatist culture and institutions. Barring cataclysm, Peru will likely become a participatory, democratic, pluralistic, liberalist-socialist political system, with a responsible and responsive set of political institutions anchored in a more or less secular political culture. General Velasco is leading his nation up from corporatism.

Postscript: Common Elements of a Strategy of Political Change

There are at least eight important points common to the experience of both Tanzania and Peru as they continue their separate attempts at political modernization. With the proper exercise of judgement and caution, these elements of the Tanzanian and Peruvian strategies of political change could be generalized to apply to all or most primarily communal or primarily corporatist regimes. These elements should not, however, be taken as exhaustive. Rather they form a core of interrelated tactics that, in terms of the spread of a world culture *and* the existence of vastly different regional cultures, seem essential if political change is to be real, continuous, and minimally disruptive. They are probably necessary but probably not sufficient in themselves to move countries from communalism to corporatism and beyond.

1. Countries must possess numerous serendipitous conditions that make the other tactics effective. This point sounds facetious, but it is apparent that some countries not only lack such favorable circumstances but have characteristics that severely militate against conversion of the piece of territory and its peoples into a modernizing nation-state where human suffering and malaise can ever be minimized. In any event, the greater the number and intensity of serendipitous conditions, of the sort mentioned in the earlier discussion of Tanzania and Peru, the better the chances of success in political modernization.

2. Political leadership must assume the full responsibility for designing, implementing, and safeguarding the modernization enterprise. Political leaders must take the initiative to mold and remold polity, society, economy, culture, personality, and all other dimensions of human existence. The polity cannot simply be a reflection of the economy, society, and culture, as it is often argued that Western, particularly North American, polities are. It seems to be helpful if the political leader can, at least to some extent call upon more than one source to justify his claim to leadership, such as charisma, tradition, and bureaucratic or rational-legal sources. The leader will vary the source he calls upon in terms of the time, place, and sector of the public or subelite with which he is dealing.

3. Programs designed to produce modernization should be anchored in and

harness the forces of indigenous sociopolitical traditions. Nyerere modernizes Tanzania by invoking the power of ancient Tanzanian village traditions of ujamaa. Velasco modernizes Peru by invoking the power of Hispanic (or Iberic-Latin) corporatist organization of all-encompassing functional units. Both leaders depend on indigenous traditions as a basis for changing their societies and emphasize nationalism as a contemporary force to unify those traditions. The only way to modernize is to capitalize on the indigenous traditions of the past in order to identify and shape the possible alternatives in the future.

4. Change or modernization should be societal, holistic, or configurative in nature. That is, not only should the modernization programs aim to change political, economic, cultural, social, and personality variables, but they should specify the kind of relationships among these variables that are to be achieved. A communal polity probably ought to become a corporatist society; a corporatist state probably ought to become a socialist society. If one of the sectors of a country is insufficiently transformed, or if modernization occurs unevenly among them, disequilibrating forces may cause a setback.

5. Modernization should be gradual. Leaders and followers should expect, or at least accept, that change will be slow and deliberate. Politics by fits and starts, the coup and revolution syndrome characteristic of so many less developed polities, does not produce permanent and continuing modernization. Gains must be protected, nurtured, pyramided—but gradually.

6. Modernization should be institutionalized, and institutionalization of new habits, practices, values, and so forth is a gradual process. Suddenly increasing the electorate by several million new voters makes institutionalization difficult or even impossible—similarly, with completely freeing a press that has a long tradition of state censorship, or suddenly creating and placing heavy responsibility on a national legislature.

7. Political change from one kind of regime to another ought to take place under tutelary guidance. It is fortunate if the modernizing elite and its government are "naturally" accorded considerable authority and legitimacy by a large majority of the citizens, even as the elite uses its governing institutions to produce some unfamiliar and painful changes. But good fortune needs to be bolstered by a primarily benign monopoly over the legitimate (or illegitimate) use of violence, force, and coercion in the society. It helps to control loyal and reasonably effective military and police establishments. This coercive potential should decrease, however, in proportion to the gradual institutionalization of some form of democracy. President Velasco has ordered Peruvians to practice participatory democracy, and he is in a position to punish disobedient citizens severely. Successful incremental modernization tends to make possible a transfer of the source of authority and legitimacy from a monopoly over technological violence to the entire citizenry of the sovereign nation state.

8. Finally, Marx and Locke, representing the two important Western traditions of liberalism and socialism (or capitalism and communism), should be

subjected to thorough interpolation before they are applied in a country to produce modernization. Unadulterated radical socialism of the Marxist-Leninist variety, stemming as it does from the European experience, has not been notably successful in less developed countries in producing manageable and permanent modernization. Lockean liberalism has not worked either, and for some of the same reasons. Political leadership must seek out the relevant implications, suggestions, and possibilities in these and other Western philosophies and ideologies, blend their various normative dimensions, tactics, goals, and incentives in appropriate ways, infuse the hybrid with neotraditional meaning and nationalism, and only then will modernization programs, based on such Western ideas, stand a chance of success. Nyerere's socialism is based on African ujamaa; Velasco's socialism is based on Peruvian local, vertically functionalized units. They stand a much better than average chance of succeeding.

Notes

Notes

Preface

1. The annual United Nations *Statistical Yearbook* and *Demographic Yearbook* are only two of the many data compendia, produced by the U.N. and various of its agencies, that are invaluable to cross-national social science research.

2. See Arthur S. Banks and Robert B. Textor, *A Cross-Polity Survey* (Cambridge, Mass., The M.I.T. Press, 1963); and Arthur Banks, *Cross-Polity Time Series Data* (Cambridge, Mass., The M.I.T. Press, 1971).

3. See Bruce R. Russett, et al., eds., *World Handbook of Political and Social Indicators*, 1st ed. (New Haven: Yale University Press, 1963). See also Charles Lewis Taylor, ed., *Aggregate Data Analysis, Political and Social Indicators in Cross-National Research* (Paris: Mouton and Company, 1968) for a bibliography of 129 articles based on data from Russett's *World Handbook* written between publication of the *Handbook* in 1964 and 1968.

4. See Charles Lewis Taylor and Michael C. Hudson, *World Handbook of Political and Social Indicators*, 2nd ed. (New Haven: Yale University Press, 1972).

5. Ernest Barker, trans. *The Politics of Aristotle* (New York: Oxford University Press, 1958), pp. xxxiii-xxxiv.

6. Ibid., p. xxxiv.

7. Ibid., ch. 2.

8. Ibid., pp. 386-87.

9. Ibid., pp. 155.

10. One of the severest critics of attempts at comparative political analysis is Peter Winch, *The Idea of a Social Science* (London: Routledge and Kegan Paul, 1958). See also the two essays by Alasdair MacIntyre in his *Against the Self-Images of the Age* (New York: Schoken Books, 1971), entitled "Is a Science of Comparative Politics Possible?" pp. 260-79 and "The Idea of a Social Science," pp. 311-29.

Chapter 1
Framework for Analysis: Theory and Research Design

1. For a very perceptive interpretation of the historical sequence of liberalization and democratization of the state in the West, cf. C.B. McPherson, *The Real World of Democracy* (London: Oxford University Press, 1966), pp. 3-11.

2. It describes the legal relationship of individuals to the state, the political system, and government in the formal sense. It does not refer to social, economic, or industrial democracy, which generally apply to types of human equality in context other than juridico-legal equality, for example, "leveling," equal income, equal power with regard to control of the means of production and distribution, social justice, collective ownership of the means of production, etc. Nor is democracy as used here meant to imply equality of power relationships in firms, factories, families, educational institutions, or other similar social structures. It is meant to refer only to the nature of political relations in the system of government of a nation-state, not to other kinds of relations in other types of social structures.

Admittedly, the employer-employee relationship in the context of an industrial plant, for example, has both indirect and direct political relevance and implications. This point could be defended as true on the basis of at least two arguments. First, politics can be defined as any set of power relationships characterizing an aggregate of persons. Cf. Harold Lasswell, *Politics* (New York: Whittlesey House, 1936), and *Power and Personality* (New York: Norton and Company, Inc.) p. 10 ff. Second, the activities of industries and corporations are so heavily involved and implicated in the distributions of burdens and benefits in a "modern" society and are so powerful in terms of defining the "public interest" that they are directly part of the government. Both of these arguments must be acknowledged. However, defining all power relationships and all activities that allocate burdens and benefits for society as politics quickly leads to a definition of politics that includes virtually everything. Although this kind of definition is defensible from the point of view of certain normative preferences, it is certainly beyond the realm of empirical cross-national comparison.

3. Sartori identifies the essential problem and dynamic of liberal democracy as the balancing and integrating of the sometimes contradictory values of liberty and equality: "To isolate liberalism from democracy, we say that liberalism calls for liberty and democracy for equality. To unite them, we say that it is the task of liberal-democratic systems to combine liberty with equality." Giovanni Sartori, *Democratic Theory* (Detroit: Wayne State University Press, 1962), p. 386.

4. For a discussion of the essentials of contemporary liberal democracy as they developed out of classical liberalism, the process of that historical development, and the political ideational context in which the development occurred, see David G. Smith, "Liberalism," *International Encyclopedia of the Social Sciences* (New York: The Macmillan Company and the Free Press, 1968), vol. 9, pp. 276-82. See also, M. Rejai, *Democracy: The Contemporary Theories* (New York: Atherton Press, 1967), pp. 88-173; Sartori, *Democratic Theory*, pp. 207-374; J.R. Lewis, *Democracy, The Theory and Practice* (London: Allman and Son, 1963), pp. 41-87; Dorothy Pickles, *Democracy* (New York: Basic

Books, 1970), pp. 42-75, 79-87, and 115-69; and Jean Blondel, *Comparing Political Systems* (New York: Praeger Publishers, 1972), pp. 167-86.

5. There are at least four reasons for cross-national, comparative examination of liberal democracy. First, the West does in fact stand as a prominent model of political development for all the developing Third World (and even the developed Second World led by the USSR) to see and possibly to emulate. It is difficult, if not impossible for any country in the Third World to ignore the economic, technological, and political influence of either the First World (led by the United States) or the Second World (led by the USSR). The Third World nations are demanding economic development and are looking to available political models for guidance in this process; they are borrowing bits and pieces of political institutions, practices, ideologies, norms, laws, etc. from both major sources in their own attempts to develop the right hybrid polity to manage economic transformation. The point is, some aspects of the West's brand of liberal democracy are accepted as one major model for the rest of the world. A second reason why liberal democracy is important is because it is the predominant form of politics practiced more or less precariously by about 25 nations of the world, encompassing approximately 700,000,000 people.

A third argument concerns the practices of new dictators. Upon the assumption of power by whatever means (for example, coup d'etat), a new dictator or other authoritarian leader almost invariably begins the new regime by abolishing some or all of the institutional bases and expressions of liberal democracy. (New authoritarian regimes often come into being because of the overthrow and abolition of liberal democratic practices.) Apparently, the leaders of authoritarian regimes feel rather strongly that liberal-democratic institutions and practices are important; otherwise they would not so consistently act to eliminate them. Wherever an authoritarian regime takes power, it dismisses parliament, outlaws political parties and other potential oppositions, bans freedoms of press and assembly, promises but seldom or never actually holds free elections, and employs the army and/or police to remain in power.

A fourth argument is that many of the countries of the West were (and in some ways still are) major colonial powers for a century or more. Nations such as Great Britain, France, the Netherlands, Belgium, and the United States were substantial influences on the formation of polities in many (but not all) of the nations that they colonized. The decisive British colonial legacy in India is the prime example. It is not uncommon for the oppressed to adopt at least some of the methods and philosophies of their (former) oppressors.

For these four reasons, it can be concluded that the features of liberal democracy are important variables, the incidence and intensity of which can and should be studied comparatively among nations of the world.

6. Phillips Cutright, "National Political Development: Social and Economic Correlates," in Nelson Polsby, et al., eds., *Politics and Social Life* (Boston: Houghton Mifflin Company, 1963), p. 574.

7. Naturally there are many other important kinds of participation in national elections, such as contributing money, distributing leaflets, providing physical labor, or persuading others to vote a certain way. Similarly, there are other important kinds of elections in which the population might participate—state, or provincial, or local. And finally, there are numerous other important kinds of mass participation other than electoral, such as writing to a political figure such as a parliamentarian and organizing or participating in a formal interest group, organizing or participating in an informal interest group such as a riot or a strike, organizing or participating in a meat boycott, responding to a Gallup interviewer, following certain religious principles (such as Muslim, Christian, Zionist) or even being counted (or not counted) in a national census. Needless to say, the problems involved in measuring the level of these kinds of participation across many nations are surmountable at this time only in principle, not in practice.

8. Arthur S. Banks and Robert B. Textor, *A Cross-Polity Survey* (Cambridge: The M.I.T. Press, 1963), pp. 67-68, p. 87, pp. 113-14, and pp. 187.

9. T-scoring is a nonlinear transformation of a set of data that involves both standardization and normalization. T-scored data are transformed so that they have a mean of 50 and a standard deviation of 10. The purpose of such a transformation is to ensure minimum distortion of a correlation or other measure of association between variables due to the extreme skewness of the distribution of either variable. For a discussion of the logic and procedure of T-scores see John T. Roscoe, *Fundamental Research Statistics for the Behavioral Sciences* (New York: Holt, Rinehart and Winston, Inc., 1969), ch. 11.

10. To the statistically minded, it might at first glance seem that there are 36 theoretically possible types: $[N(N-1)]$. However, one kind of competitiveness cannot be combined with another kind of competitiveness, one kind of public liberties cannot be combined with another kind of public liberties, etc. For any one of the nine classifications, two others are automatically eliminated. The ranges of the three categories for each dimension of democracy are as follows: for competitiveness, 39.1 - 47.4 is monopolistic, 47.5 - 55.8 is moderate, and 55.9 - 63.5 is pluralistic; for participation, 29.6 to 40.7 is exclusive, 40.8 - 51.9 is moderate, and 50.2 - 63.1 is inclusive; for public liberties, 33.4 - 42.5 is coercive, 42.6 - 51.7 is moderate, and 51.8 - 60.7 is libertarian. These ranges are arrived at by breaking each continuum into three equal-sized categories.

11. All 17 of these liberal democracies are included by Dahl in his list of 26 "polyarchies." In addition, he includes Costa Rica, France, India, Italy, Lebanon, Philippines, Trinidad and Tobago, and Uruguay. See Robert A. Dahl, *Polyarchy* (New Haven: Yale University Press, 1971), p. 248. An examination of the scores of the eight nations on each of the three dimensions of democracy in Table 1-1 reveals why they are not categorized as liberal democracies in this study.

12. Ibid., pp. 34-48. Dahl's historical analysis also suggests that there may be

either close association or wide discrepancy between liberalization of a regime (public contestation) and inclusiveness (participation), his two elements of polyarchy.

13. Karl W. Deutsch, "Social Mobilization and Political Development," *American Political Science Review* 55 (September 1961): 494-95.

14. Ibid., p. 496.

15. Ibid.

16. The original discussion of the characteristics of social mobilization from which this list is derived is found in Deutsch, "Social Mobilization," pp. 494-95.

17. S.N. Eisenstadt, *Modernization: Protest and Change.* (Englewood Cliffs: Prentice-Hall, Inc., 1966), pp. 4, 34-35.

18. Ibid.

19. Ibid.

20. Seymour Martin Lipset, "Some Social Requisites of Democracy," *American Political Science Review*" (March 1959): 69-105.

21. Daniel Lerner, *The Passing of Traditional Society* (Glencoe: The Free Press, 1958).

22. Empirical applications of the theory of social mobilization and democratic political development include the following: Phillips Cutright, "National Political Development: Measurement and Analysis," *American Sociological Review* 28 (April 1963): 253-64; _______ "National Political Development," in Nelson W. Polsby, et al., eds., *Politics and Social Life* (Boston: Houghton Mifflin Co., 1965), pp. 569-82; _______ "Political Structure, Economic Development, and National Social Security Programs," *American Journal of Sociology* 70 (March 1965): 537-50; William Flanigan and Edwin Fogelman, "Patterns of Democratic Development and Democratization: A Quantitative Analysis," and "Patterns of Democratic Development: An Historical Comparative Analysis," in John V. Gillespie and Betty A. Nesvold, eds., *Macro-Quantitative Analysis: Conflict, Development, and Democratization* (Beverly Hills: Sage Publications, 1971), chs. 20 and 21. Phillips Cutright, "Inequality: A Cross-National Analysis," *American Sociological Review* 32 (August 1967): 562-78; Donald J. McCrone and Charles F. Cnudde, "Toward a Communications Theory of Political Development: A Causal Model," *American Political Science Review* 61 (March 1967): 72-79; Dean E. Neubauer, "Some Conditions of Democracy," *American Political Science Review* 61 (December 1967): 1002-1009; Gilbert R. Winham, "Political Development and Lerner's Theory: Further Test of a Causal Model," *American Political Science Review* 64 (September 1970): 810-19; Jack Sawyer, "Dimensions of Nations: Size, Wealth, and Politics," *American Journal of Sociology* 72 (September 1967): 145-73; Marie R. Haug, "Social and Cultural Pluralism as a Concept in Social System Analysis," *American Journal of Sociology* 72 (November 1967): 294-305; Philip Coulter, "Democratic Political Development: A Systemic Model Based on Regulative Policy," *Development and Change* 3 (Fall 1971): 25-62; _______ "National Socioeconomic Development

and Democracy: A Note on the Political Role of the Police," *International Journal of Comparative Sociology* 13 (March 1972): 65-72; Arthur K. Smith, Jr., "Socioeconomic Development and Political Development: A Causal Analysis," *Midwest Journal of Political Science* 13 (February 1969): 95-125; Arthur S. Banks, "Correlates of Democratic Performance," *Comparative Politics* 4 (January 1972): 217-31; and Harold D. Clarke and Allan Kornburg, "A Note on Social Cleavages and Democratic Performance," *Comparative Political Studies* 4 (October 1971): 349-61.

23. Lerner, *The Passing of Traditional Society*, p. 60.

24. Ibid.

25. Coulter, "Democratic Political Development," pp. 26-28 discusses Lerner's work.

26. Lucian W. Pye, *Aspects of Political Development* (Boston: Little, Brown and Co., 1966), pp. 10-11.

27. Ibid., p. 8.

28. Ibid., pp. 9-11.

29. For a discussion of some of the methodological difficulties involved in this kind of analysis, cf. Philip Coulter, "Political Development and Political Theory: Methodological and Technological Problems in the Comparative Study of Political Development," *Polity* V (Winter 1972): 233-43.

Chapter 2
The Global Model of Liberal Democracy

1. For a discussion of the numerous measures produced by multiple-regression analysis as well as a technical discussion of the logic and computational procedures, cf. Mordecai Ezekiel and Karl A. Fox, *Methods of Correlation and Regression Analysis* (New York: John Wiley and Sons, 1967), especially ch. 12.

2. Daniel Lerner, *The Passing of Traditional Society* (Glencoe: The Free Press, 1958); and Donald J. McCrone and Charles F. Cnudde, "Toward a Communications Theory of Political Development: A Causal Model," *American Political Science Review* 61 (March 1967): 1002-1009.

3. For a similar conclusion, see David R. Cameron, J. Stephen Hendricks, and Richard I. Hofferbert, "Urbanization, Social Structure, and Mass Politics," *Comparative Political Studies* 5 (October 1972): 259-91.

4. By and large, previous studies that have investigated social mobilization and liberal democracy (such as those cited in note 29, Chapter 1) have not used rates of social mobilization, only levels.

5. Occasionally, the term "increase" is used instead of "change" when referring to rates of social mobilization. In all but a few cases, the change was an increase and not a decrease in any of the indicators of social-mobilization variables.

6. In the computation of the multiple-partial-regression coefficients, a single surrogate variable was used for all five level of mobilization variables and a single surrogate variable was used for all five rate of change variables. In the former instance, the surrogate was the predicted value of a democracy variable produced in the regression equation including five level variables, and in the second instance, the surrogate was the predicted value for a dependent democracy variable produced in a regression equation including all five rates of change variables. Virtually no change in the results was obtained by employing these substitutes. The standard errors of the estimate, regression coefficients, and correlation coefficients remained practically the same, whether one surrogate variable was used for five independent variables, or all five independent variables were used. The use of just two (surrogate) independent variables simplifies analysis considerably without distorting the results.

7. It should be remembered that over-democratized, under-democratized and optimally democratized nations refer to the degree to which they fall above or below the regression line, and how far above or below. Where a nation falls depends entirely upon the nature of the relationship between its social mobilization and liberal democratic features, that is, the extent to which they are congruent. If all nations had perfectly congruent mobilization and liberal democracy, for example if all were perfectly optimally democratic, they would all fall exactly on the diagonal regression line, because the prediction equation would precisely predict their liberal democracy scores.

When individual social-mobilization variables were used to explain the four separate measures of liberal democracy, substantial nonlinearity was indicated in only five cases; only five correlation coefficients computed with the use of a second-order or quadratic polynomial ($Y = a + bX + cX^2$) were appreciably higher than the coefficients computed from the first-order or linear equation ($Y = a + bX$). They are:

Variables	Linear	Quadratic
Education with participation	0.40	0.51
Economic development with participation	0.41	0.60
Industrialization rate with competitiveness	0.26	0.40
Industrialization rate with liberties	0.15	0.33
Industrialization rate with liberal democracy	0.41	0.58

In these cases, use of the quadratic polynomial (a curve with one bend) rather than the linear polynomial (a straight line) improves the predictive ability of the regression equation, in spite of the fact that all values were first *T*-scored.

Chapter 3
Geocultural Regions and Political Traditions

1. The 29 nations included in the Anglo-European region are the following: Albania, Australia, Austria, Belgium, Bulgaria, Canada, Czechoslovakia, Den-

mark, Eastern Germany, Finland, France, Greece, Hungary, Iceland, Ireland, Italy, Luxembourg, Netherlands, New Zealand, Norway, Poland, Rumania, Sweden, Switzerland, United Kingdom, United States, Union of Soviet Socialist Republics, Western Germany, and Yugoslavia.

2. The 24 Iberic-Latin American nations are Argentina, Bolivia, Brazil, Chile, Colombia, Costa Rica, Cuba, Dominican Republic, Ecuador, El Salvador, Guatemala, Haiti, Honduras, Jamaica, Mexico, Nicaragua, Panama, Paraguay, Peru, Portugal, Spain, Trinidad and Tobago, Uruguay, and Venezuela.

3. The 16 African nations, all south of the Sahara, are Cameroun, Dahomey, Gabon, Ghana, Guinea, Ivory Coast, Kenya, Liberia, Malagasy Republic, Malawi, Nigeria, Sierra Leone, South Africa, Sudan, Tanzania, and Uganda.

4. The 16 nations of the Near and Far Eastern region are Burma, India, Indonesia, Iraq, Israel, Japan, Laos, Malaysia, Pakistan, Philippines, South Korea, Sri Lanka (formerly Ceylon), Syria, Tunisia, Turkey, and United Arab Republic.

5. For example, with regard to arguments over the placement of a given country in one region or another, some claim that Italy (at least southern Italy) has more in common with Spain or even northern Africa than with the nations of central and northern Europe, and therefore Italy should be classified with the Iberic-Latin American countries. Or that the Iberic-Latin geocultural region should be slightly expanded to become the Iberic-Latin-Mediterranean region. Others maintain that the proper region in which to classify Italy is western and central Europe. Neither side of the argument is without merit. When constructing such a classificatory scheme, one simply does the best that one can and judges the wisdom of a particular set of national allocations among regions on the basis of the results it produces.

A similar argument pertains to the fact that even though a nation may be characterized as 60 percent urban or 77 percent literate, the internal distribution of urbanization and literacy may be very uneven. Again, the contrast between northern and southern Italy is illustrative of vast inequalities or unevenness of economic development and modernization. Linz and de Miguel have described fully eight separate subcultural regions in Spain; cf. Juan J. Linz and Amando de Miguel, "Within-Nation Differences and Comparisons: The Eight Spains," in Richard Lawrence Merrit and Stein Rokkan, eds., *Comparing Nations* (New Haven: Yale University Press, 1966) pp. 267-319. See also Juan J. Linz, "An Authoritarian Regime: Spain," in Erik Allardt and Yrjo Littunen, eds., *Cleavages, Ideologies and Party Systems* (Helsinki: Academic Bookstore, 1964), pp. 291-341.

6. The importance that political scientists place on regional area foci is aptly demonstrated by inspection of the curriculum of any political science department; there are invariably numerous courses dealing with the government and politics of particular regions of the world. But for a contrary view, cf. Dankwart A. Rustow, "Modernization and Comparative Politics: Prospects in Research and Theory," *Comparative Politics* 1 (October 1968): 45-47. See also Arend

Lijphart, "Comparative Politics and the Comparative Method," *American Political Science Review* 65 (September 1971): 682-94.

7. There are, however, several instances of attempts to define or delineate regions empirically on the basis of a very large number of variables measured across all the nations for which data were available: cf. Phillip M. Gregg and Arthur S. Banks, "Dimensions of Political Systems: Factor Analysis of A Cross-Polity Survey," *American Political Science Review* 59 (September 1965): 555-78; Arthur S. Banks and Phillip M. Gregg, "Grouping Political Systems: Q-Factor Analysis of a Cross-Polity Survey," *The American Behavioral Scientist* 9 (November 1965): 3-5; Bruce M. Russett, "Delineating International Regions," in J. David Singer, ed., *Quantitative International Politics: Insights and Evidence* (New York: The Free Press, 1968), pp. 317-52; and Bruce M. Russett, *International Regions and the International System* (Chicago: Rand McNally, 1967).

8. Admittedly, "political tradition," like the term "political culture," has various conceptual meanings and operational definitions in the literature of political science, and the literature is enormous and growing. Some of the more illustrative and valuable works are: Gabriel A. Almond and Sidney Verba, *The Civic Culture* (Princeton: Princeton University Press, 1963); Edward Banfield and Laura Banfield, *The Moral Basis of a Backward Society* (New York: The Free Press, 1967); Lucian W. Pye, *Politics, Personality, and Nation-Building* (New Haven: Yale University Press, 1962); Lucian W. Pye and Sydney Verba, eds., *Political Culture and Political Development* (Princeton: Princeton University Press, 1966); and Gabriel A. Almond, "Comparative Political Systems," *Journal of Politics* 18 (August 1956): 391-409.

9. This use of the term "political culture" is suggestive of an earlier concept in political science, "national character." This latter concept has been more or less discredited by those who pursue a more precise and microquantitative conception of political culture. One early and perceptive use of the term "national character" is Alex Inkeles, "National Character and Modern Political Systems," in Francis L. Hsu, ed., *Psychological Anthropology: Approaches to Culture and Personality* (Homewood, Ill.: Dorsey Press, 1961), pp. 172-202.

10. Lucian W. Pye, *Politics, Personality, and Nation-Building*, p. 38.

11. It should be remembered that the "world culture," in Pye's terms, which is spreading throughout the world, began in Europe. The values of the world culture are, therefore, oldest in Europe and likely to be strongest and most advanced in Europe (and Anglo-Europe) as well. This characteristic should certainly distinguish the Anglo-European political tradition from that of the other geocultural regions.

12. The contrasts between England and Ireland, for example, demonstrate such wide intraregion variation. Another example from the Far East is the contrast between Japan and Indonesia. The point is that while the countries of a given geocultural region tend to be more similar to each other than they are

similar to another geocultural region, no geocultural region is actually homogeneous with regard to any important variable.

13. One has only to examine the extremely important bicultural pluralism and cleavage in Belgium (Flemings versus Walloons), Canada (French versus English), South Africa (black versus white), or Italy (north versus south) to understand intranational subcultural pluralism. Cf. Cynthia Enloe, *Ethnic Conflict and Political Development* (Boston: Little, Brown and Co., 1973).

14. Not only does the political tradition or political culture vary within single nations but the degree to which formally similar or identical structures perform similar or identical functions varies tremendously. For an analysis of this problem in the United States, cf. Malcolm E. Jewell, *The State Legislature, Politics and Practice* (New York: Random House, 1962), and Daniel J. Elazar, *American Federalism: A View From the States* (New York: Thomas Y. Crowell Co.).

15. Here the reference is not just to relative levels of violence that might occur in a military takeover, but to fundamental orientations toward basic and important regime change. The 1972 military coup in Ghana led by Colonel I.K. Acheampong was greeted with mixed reactions by people in Ghana. Many people, particularly those in the middle class, felt that on the whole the coup was not a bad thing. In any case, within 24 hours after the takeover, the streets of the capital city were calm, people were going about their lives in a more or less ordinary way, and polity, society, and economy continued to function pretty much as if nothing had happened. In the 1973 coup in Chile, a great many Chileans felt that disaster had occurred, but many also felt that Chile would be better off under the rule of General Ugarte. The turmoil of the takeover did last about a week, but when the smoke cleared, many close analysts called the coup "typical" in Latin American terms and refused to get excited about it. However, if Canada were to experience a military coup—if Prime Minister Trudeau and parliamentary democracy were overthrown by a cabal of army generals—Canadians and the Western world would probably view it as total, unadulterated cataclysm, even if GNP per capita went up, and taxes, inflation, and cost of living down. In other words, the coup d'etat takes on much of its meaning in terms of the political tradition of the nation in which it occurs.

16. For other purposes of inquiry, precisely the opposite position might be taken, that is, a random selection of countries is superior to a regional selection, because the former reveals more variation of certain important variables. And in this way, it allows for a more effective test of the hypotheses that posit a relationship between the variation of pairs of variables, because in a random selection the widest possible variation on each variable is more likely. Cf. Dell G. Hitchner and Carol Levine, *Comparative Government and Politics* (New York: Dodd, Mead Co., 1967), pp. 7-8.

17. Lucian W. Pye, *Aspects of Political Development* (Boston: Little, Brown and Co., 1966), pp. 9-11.

18. The general political culture of the political elite may be in harmony or conflict with that of the members of the polity. And naturally, the political elite tends to have a more elaborated set of values than does the bulk of the mass, most of the time. When elite and mass culture are in conflict or when the political elite does have an orientation toward some aspect of politics and the bulk of the mass has little or none, the elite culture would be the important factor that would likely determine the behavior of the polity. Cf. Pye and Verba, *Political Culture and Political Development*, pp. 15-17. See also, Robert D. Putnam, "Studying Elite Political Culture: The Case of Ideology," *American Political Science Review* 65 (September 1971): 651-82.

19. For a discussion of the logic and procedures of computation of the coefficient of relative variability, see Dennis J. Palumbo *Statistics in Behavioral and Political Science* (New York: Appleton-Century-Crofts, 1969), p. 51.

Chapter 4
The Anglo-European Model of Liberal Democracy

1. Karl Deutsch, "Social Mobilization and Political Development," *American Political Science Review* 55 (September 1961): 496 ff.

2. Daniel Lerner, *The Passing of Traditional Society* (Glencoe: The Free Press, 1958).

3. In the global model, the equivalent multiple-determination coefficients recorded in Table 3-1 are as follows: competitiveness, 43%; participation, 21%; liberties, 25%; liberal democracy, 48%.

4. This finding is certainly consistent with the global model.

5. This finding is not consistent with the global model. In the global model, although only 21 percent of the variation in participation was accounted for, the education beta was 0.28 and the primary influence, with lesser influence on the part of urbanization ($\beta = 0.16$) and communication ($\beta = 0.17$).

6. For discussion of this kind of feature of post-industrial society cf. M. Rejai, ed., *Decline of Ideology* (Chicago: Aldine Atherton, 1971); Samuel H. Beer, et al., *Patterns of Government* (New York: Random House, 1973), pp. 1-9; Donald M. Hancock and Gideon Sjoberg, *Politics in the Post-Welfare State: Responses to the New Individualism* (New York: Columbia University Press, 1972); Alan Touraine, *The Post-Industrial Society*. (New York: Random House, Inc., 1971); and Donald M. Hancock, *Sweden: The Politics of Post-Industrial Change* (Hinsdale, Illinois: Dryden Press, 1972).

7. Compare this Anglo-European pattern with the relationship between measures of social mobilization and political participation in Japan; cf. Roger W. Benjamin, *Patterns of Political Development* (New York: David McKay Co., 1972), ch. 4; and Bradley M. Richardson, "Urbanization and Political Participation: "The Case of Japan," *American Political Science Review*" 67 (June 1973):

433-53. In Japan, the pattern of relationship is apparently the opposite. India's pattern of relationship between urbanization and democracy is similar to the Anglo-European model, and Israel's experience shows no relationship at all. See Benjamin, *Patterns of Political Development*, chs. 2 and 3.

8. This resembles the global model.

9. This finding is similar to that of the global model.

10. This result conforms to that of the global model.

11. The United States was the first society in which more than half the total nonagricultural labor force was engaged in ancillary service occupations, since about 1956. Since then, several European nations, especially Sweden, Britain, Belgium, Canada, and the Netherlands, are moving rapidly in that direction. See Albin Toffler, *Future Shock* (New York: Bantam Books, Inc. 1970), pp. 12-18.

12. This pattern is in conformity to the global model where industrial rate is predominant and economic development has considerably less influence.

13. This finding resembles the global model.

14. This relationship is in conformity to the global model.

15. The conventional wisdom of political science suggests that eastern European nations are considerably less democratic than is their natural impulse, mainly because of Soviet imperialism and Communist party ideological controls. The evidence discussed here seems clearly to contradict this assumption. Although all but two eastern European nations (Czechoslovakia and Rumania) are below the regression line, all nine of these nations are quite close to the line. It would seem that neither Soviet oppression nor Communist ideology is completely responsible for the nature of eastern European political regimes. See Irving Louis Horowitz, *Three Worlds of Development* (New York: Oxford University Press, 1972), pp. 163-204.

16. The only nation that appears on both the Anglo-European list of 11 under-democratized polities in the global model (Table 3-5) is the United States. In both global terms and the context of Anglo-Europa, the United States is under-democratized. The only nation that appears on the list of 14 over-democratized nations in the global model (Table 3-6) and the Anglo-European list of four over-democratized polities is Ireland. Thus, Ireland is over-democratized in terms of both models. It should be remembered that the standard error of the estimate is 7.03 for the global model and 3.1 for the Anglo-European model.

17. Numerous explanations of why a given nation is over-democratized or under-democratized in terms of the Anglo-European model might be attempted, although such is not the purpose here. Switzerland, for example, is under-democratized, at least in part, because during the period of this study, women were denied suffrage in national elections. Such a situation has drastic and obvious consequences for political participation. Only in 1971 did Switzerland adopt adult, as opposed to male adult, suffrage in national elections. Similarly, the United States deviance could be explained in terms of its extremely high levels and rates of social mobilization. Both are so incredibly high, by any set of

standards, that it may well be unrealistic to expect democracy as measured here to reflect these levels and rates. It could easily be argued that the United States is over-developed with regard to social mobilization. In addition, the United States is notoriously well-known for its low levels of participation in presidential elections. The United States is second lowest among the 29 Anglo-European nations; Switzerland is lowest. Students of American voting behavior offer many reaons for this extremely low turnout rate in American national elections: apathy; too many elections; satisfaction with the status quo; a sense of powerlessness, anomie, or alienation, low sense of political efficacy; intimidation (especially of black Americans), state restrictions, and registration requirements. It is estimated that if people met the state requirements defining suffrage (such as minimum voting ages before 1972, residence requirements, poll taxes, literacy tests), or if there were no such requirements and if they registered, the United States turnout rate would range from 72 percent to 80 percent. See Frank Sorauf, *Party Politics in America* (Boston: Little, Brown and Company, 1972), pp. 179-93; Hugh A. Bone and Austin Ranney, *Politics and Voters* (New York: McGraw-Hill Book Co., 1971), pp. 4-6; Angus Campbell, et al., *The American Voter* (New York: John Wiley and Sons, 1960); and Bernard R. Berelson, et al., *Voting* (Chicago: The University of Chicago Press, 1954).

Ireland's over-democratization might be accounted for by referring to the very heavy British (Parliamentary democratic) influence on a nation that is still largely a developing country in many ways. Ireland ranks considerably below the Anglo-European mean on seven of the 10 social mobilization variables. See Basil Chubb, *The Government and Politics of Ireland* (Stanford: Stanford University Press, 1970), pp. 43-61. Italy is similar and ranks considerably below the Anglo-European mean on six of the 10 social mobilization indicators. Italy is often pathetically referred to as the "sick man of Europe" in Common Market circles. Although Italy has had probably more than its share of instability, tension, and changes of government, it has maintained a relatively liberal democratic regime since World War II. However, as Stephen Holt points out, it has not been easy. For example, he reports that the United States intervened both to ensure pluralism and to help defeat communism through threats to terminate both United States economic aid to Italy and the awarding of defense contracts to Italian contractors. Nonetheless, the Italian Communist party has remained the second largest party in Italy in electoral support and parliamentary membership. See Stephen Holt, *Six European States* (London: Hamish Hamilton, 1970), ch. 3, esp. pp. 195-96. And because of the similarities of the Mediterranean political culture to that of the Iberic-Latin American nations, Italy's political tradition is less secular and more fragmented than most of Anglo-Europa. See Gabriel A. Almond and G. Bingham Powell, Jr., *Comparative Politics, A Developmental Approach* (Boston: Little, Brown and Co., 1966), pp. 111-12.

18. This approach to Anglo-European political tradition is largely drawn from

the works of Gabriel A. Almond and his collaborators. Cf. Almond and Powell, *Comparative Politics*, ch. 10; Gabriel A. Almond, "Comparative Political Systems," *Journal of Politics* 18 (August 1956): 391-409; Gabriel A. Almond and Sidney Verba, *The Civic Culture* (Princeton: Princeton University Press, 1963); and Lucian W. Pye and Sidney Verba, eds., *Political Culture and Political Development* (Princeton: Princeton University Press, 1966).

19. Almond and Verba, *The Civic Culture.*

20. The theoretical and empirical aspects of this accommodative technique of overcoming fairly serious subcultural pluralism and conflict are examined in Arend Lijphart, *The Politics of Accommodation* (Berkeley: University of California Press, 1967); Arend Lijphart, "Consociational Democracy," *World Politics* 21 (January 1969): 207-25; Hans Daalder, "On Building Consociational Democracy: The Cases of the Netherlands and Switzerland," *International Social Science Journal* 3 (1971): 355-70; and Gordon L. Weil, *The Benelux Nations* (New York: Holt, Rinehart and Winston, Inc., 1970), pp. 83-128.

21. Weil, *The Benelux Nations*; Val Lorwin, "Segmented Pluralism: Ideological Cleavages and Political Cohesion in the Smaller European Democracies," *Comparative Politics* 3 (January 1971): 141-77; and Frank E. Huggett, *Modern Belgium* (New York: Frederick A. Praeger, Publishers, 1969), chs. 4-7.

22. This discussion of the main elements of the European democratic developmental experience is drawn from Reinhold Neibuhr and Paul E. Sigmund, *The Democratic Experience* (New York: Frederick A. Praeger, Publishers, 1969), ch. 5. It is conventional wisdom that the eastern European nations have nonsecularized ideological-communist political cultures and undifferentiated though technologically modern political structures. However, as Almond and Powell, *Comparative Politics*, pp. 274 ff., argue, the evidence suggests that

> They are political systems which have come into existence after the industrial revolution, after some urbanization has actually taken place or after the impact of Western industrialized society has been felt through the diffusion of the ideas, aspirations, and some of the practices of Western society and politics. . . . We are dealing with regimes which came into existence in societies which were already in the process of industrialization and urbanization and in which some political infrastructure of political parties, associational interest groups, and media of mass communication had already emerged.

See also T.H. Rigby, "Crypto-Politics," *Survey* (January 1964): ch. 10, for a discussion of 12 categories of competitive conflict in Soviet and eastern European politics.

23. What is implicit but uncertain here is the possibility of a transition from increasing liberal democratization to the development of social, economic, industrial, and other forms of democratization. The quality is different. The latter are not just more liberal democracy, but different kinds and conceptions of democracy.

Chapter 5
The Iberic-Latin Model of Liberal Democracy

1. All of these Iberic-Latin nations are either contiguous or close and separated only by water, except Spain and Portugal, the European powers that colonized Latin America. These latter two European nations were included in two separate regression analyses, the Anglo-European and the Iberic-Latin. In the former, they were both wildly deviant in terms of social mobilization and liberal democracy; thus they are included with the Latin American nations.

2. In the global model, the simple-correlation coefficient between communication rate and economic-development rate is $r = 0.84$.

3. The results that can accrue in cases of imbalance among sectors of society are explored in Andrew J. Sofranko and Robert C. Bealer, "Modernization, Balance, Imbalance, and Domestic Instability," *Economic Development and Cultural Change* 22 (October 1973): 52-73; Dick Simpson, "The Congruence of the Political, Social and Economic Aspects of Development," *International Development Review* 6 (June 1964): 21-25; Arnold S. Feldman, "Violence and Volatility: the Likelihood of Revolution," in Harry Eckstein, ed., *Internal War* (New York: Macmillan Co., 1961), pp. 111-29; Wilbert E. Moore, "Predicting Discontinuities in Social Change," *American Sociological Review* 29 (June 1964): 331-38; and Wilbert E. Moore, "Problems of Timing, Balance and Priorities in Development," *Economic Development and Cultural Change* 2 (January 1954): 239-48.

4. The proportion of explained variation in the global model is $R^2 = 0.43\%$.

5. The proportion of explained variation in the global model is $R^2 = 0.21\%$.

6. The proportion of explained variation in the global model is $R^2 = 0.25\%$.

7. The proportion of explained variation in the global model is $R^2 = 0.48\%$.

8. Martin C. Needler, "Political Development and Military Intervention in Latin America," *American Political Science Review* 60 (September 1966): 616-27; Ernest A. Duff and John F. McCamant, "Measuring Social and Political Requirements for System Stability in Latin America," *American Political Science Review* 62 (December 1968): 1125-44; and Martin C. Needler, "Political Development and Socioeconomic Development; The Case of Latin America," *American Political Science Review* 62 (December 1968): 889-897.

9. The equivalent coefficients of multiple determination in the global model are as follows: competitiveness, $R^2 = 52\%$; participation, $R^2 = 31\%$; public liberties, $R^2 = 40\%$; and liberal democracy, $R^2 = 50\%$.

10. Compare these findings for Iberic-Latin nations with those of the global model: competitiveness, $R^2 = 56.2\%$; participation, $R^2 = 33.7\%$; public liberties, $R^2 = 44.9\%$; and liberal democracy, $R^2 = 53.3\%$.

11. These two terms, "organicist-corporatist," and "patrimonialist-corporatist," and their explication with regard to the Iberic-Latin political tradition are drawn largely from two authors: Howard J. Wiarda, "Toward a Framework for

the Study of Political Change in the Iberic-Latin Tradition: the Corporative Model," *World Politics* 25 (January 1973): 206-35; _______ , "Corporatism and Development in the Iberic-Latin World, Persistent Strains and New Variations," *Political Science Quarterly* forthcoming, 1974; and Philippe C. Schmitter, "Paths to Political Development in Latin America," *Proceedings of The Academy of Political Science* 30 (August 1972): 83-105. See also, Howard J. Wiarda, *Politics and Social Change in Latin America: The Distinct Tradition* (Amherst: University of Massachusetts Press, 1974); John Mander, *The Unrevolutionary Society: The Power of Latin American Conservatism in a Changing World* (New York: Alfred A. Knopf, 1969); Louis Hartz, et al., *The Founding of New Societies* (New York: Harcourt, Brace and World, 1964); Kalman H. Silvert, *Expectant Peoples: Nationalism and Development* (New York: Random House, 1967); Kalman H. Silvert, *The Conflict Society: Reaction and Revolution in Latin America* (New York: American Universities Field Staff, 1966); and Gabriel A. Almond and G. Bingham Powell, Jr., *Comparative Politics: A Developmental Approach* (Boston: Little, Brown and Co., 1966), pp. 134-47, 223-32, and 303-304.

12. Wiarda, "Corporatism and Development in the Iberic-Latin World."

13. Ibid. The early Roman influences on the development of corporatism in the Iberic-Latin tradition are also treated in Rafael Altamira, *A History of Spain*, trans. Muna Lee (New York: D. Van Nostrand, 1949), ch. 3; Brian Chapman, *The Profession of Government* (London: George Allen and Unwin, 1959), ch. 1; and John H. Merryman, *The Civil Law Tradition: An Introduction to the Legal Systems of Western Europe and Latin America* (Stanford: Stanford University Press, 1969).

14. The four schools of corporatist philosophy are developed fully in Philippe C. Schmitter, "Corporatist Interest Representation and Public Policy-Making in Portugal," paper presented at the 1972 Annual Meeting of the American Political Science Association, Washington, D.C., September 5-9.

15. Wiarda, "Toward a Framework for the Study of Political Change in the Iberic-Latin Tradition," pp. 206-35.

16. Almost everyone has known someone who underwent some rather radical changes, such as becoming wealthy or famous, but who himself or herself was not changed. The person who underwent such changes maintained the same old friends, continued wearing the same kinds of clothes, continued living in the same modest or middle-class home, kept the same personal habits, likes, and dislikes, political attitudes, etc. The kind of personality structure that assimilates changes without itself being transformed and without resulting in seriously altered patterns of behavior performs in a manner similar to the corporatist polity.

17. Wiarda, "Corporatism and Development in the Iberic-Latin World." A somewhat similar and wholly compatible definition of corporatism is found in Gabriel A. Almond and G. Bingham Powell, Jr., *Comparative Politics, A*

Developmental Approach (Boston: Little, Brown and Co., 1966); they also suggest as prime examples of corporatist polities Pharohnic Egypt and the Ouagadougou of Upper Volta. Cf. pp. 223-32.

18. Wiarda, "Corporatism and Development."

19. Schmitter, "Corporatist Interest Representation," pp. 91-94.

20. Latin Americanists frequently assert that the Western notion of "civil-military" relations or of "civilian control of the military" is largely unknown in or irrelevant to politics in the Iberic-Latin nations. No matter who is in power, the military rules. Although this may be a slight exaggeration, the point seems valid in the light of the Iberic-Latin political experience. As evidence that the military is not shy about openly assuming direct control of the polity, consider that since 1960, there have been 24 successful coups d'etat in 12 Latin American nations.

21. Howard J. Wiarda, "Corporatist Theory and Ideology: The Latin American Development Paradigm," unpublished paper, University of Massachusetts, Amherst, Mass. n.d. For a similar argument, see also Ronald L. Rogowski and Lois Wasserspring, *Does Political Development Exist? Corporatism in Old and New Societies* (Beverly Hills: Sage Publications, Sage Professional Papers in Comparative Politics, series # 01-024, vol. 2, 1971).

Chapter 6
The African Model of Liberal Democracy

1. Complete data on all variables were available for only 16 nations of sub-Saharan Africa. Included are both black and white states, former colonies of France, Great Britain, and others (as well as Liberia, which was never a colony), and nations from all regions, geographical sizes, and population sizes. Although the data were collected before the publication of Donald G. Morrison, et al., *Black Africa, A Comparative Handbook* (New York: The Free Press, 1972), a comparison of the data with that of Morrison et al. suggests no changes or additions.

2. One major type of African political regime is exactly represented by six of the nations in the sample of 16 (Cameroun, Dahomey, Gabon, Ivory Coast, Guinea, and Liberia) with very low levels of competitiveness and very high levels of mass participation, for example, one- or no-party regimes that produce high turnouts in national elections. Just the opposite situation, however, prevails in South Africa. Most of the African states approximate the low competitiveness-high participation regime in varying degrees. The global model, with its simple-correlation coefficient of +0.20 between competitiveness and participation, contains a substantially lower proportion of such regimes.

3. Compare the four African coefficients of multiple determination for levels in Table 6-3 with those of the global model: competitiveness, 43%;

participation, 21%; liberties, 25%; and liberal democracy, 48%. Obviously the behavior of African nations is in large part responsible for depressing the size of the three low coefficients in the global model results.

4. Compare these coefficients with the equivalent ones in the global model: competitiveness, 52%; participation, 31%; public liberties, 40%; and liberal democracy, 50%.

5. There are a few African nations that have some high rates of mobilization by global standards. Cameroun's rate of communication is 57.7. Urbanization rates in Dahomey and Malawi are 59.1 and 72.4 respectively. The other high rates are all in education: Ghana, 74.8; Ivory Coast, 55.6; and Sudan, 67.7. The mean for all 85 nations on each of these variables is 50.0. South Africa is the only state with any level of mobilization variable over the mean.

6. Uganda has moved down to the regression line since the end of the period covered by these data. In late 1966 Prime Minister Milton Obote led a preemptive coup against the president, the Kebaka of Buganda. In 1969 he banned all political parties. In 1971 Obote's government was overthrown by the Ugandan army led by Major General Idi Amin, who promptly decreed a ban on political activities for two years and increased powers of detention against antigovernment elements.

7. Not only are the means for all 10 measures of social mobilization lower in Africa than in the other geocultural regions or in the global analysis, but the standard deviations and coefficients of relative variability are also the lowest, except for urbanization level. This suggests that the low African means are comparatively more representative of the countries' actual values than is the case in other regions.

8. This discussion of African political culture follows the distinctions and descriptions of Gabriel A. Almond and G. Bingham Powell, Jr., *Comparative Politics: A Developmental Approach* (Boston: Little, Brown and Company, 1966), pp. 50-73; Gabriel A. Almond, "Comparative Political Systems," *Journal of Politics* 18 (August 1956): 391-409; and Gabriel A. Almond and Sidney Verba, *The Civic Culture* (Princeton: Princeton University Press, 1963).

9. Almond and Powell, *Comparative Politics*, pp. 213-23.

10. Ibid., p. 286.

11. Ibid., pp. 284-98.

12. Almond, "Comparative Political Systems," pp. 391-409; Irma Adelman and Cynthia Taft Morris, *Society, Politics and Economic Development* (Baltimore: Johns Hopkins University Press, 1967), p. 163, find in their analysis that African countries are "characterized by the predominance of preliterate communities. As emphasized by Gerschenkron and others, an essential prerequisite for the initiation of a process of economic growth is a social transformation characterized by the breakdown of traditionalism, the spread of literacy, increased communication, and greater receptivity to modern ideas and techniques. The results of the regional analysis underscore the fact that most of the

African nations are still at a stage of development in which traditional social structures create critical barriers to growth. . . . [M]ost African nations have not yet established the basic social prerequisites for the evolution of participant political institutions; literacy rates and receptivity to change, for example, are still extremely low and attitudes toward political life as yet are strongly conditioned by the relatively static norms of traditional social organization."

13. The coinage and development of this concept is the responsibility of Clifford Geertz, ed. "The Integrative Revolution: Primordian Sentiments and Civic Politics in the New States," *Old Societies and New States: The Quest for Modernity in Asia and Africa* (Glencoe: The Free Press, 1963), pp. 105-57.

14. It should be noted, too, that these communal cultural forces also inhibit social and economic development and integration as well as political. Ivor Jennings captured the essence of this important result of communalism when he wrote, "the people cannot decide until somebody decides who are the people." In *The Approach to Self-Government* (Cambridge: Cambridge University Press, 1956), p. 56.

15. It is well known that British, French, and other national officials who originally decided on the drawing of the national boundaries of their African colonies often did so with little knowledge or understanding of Africa. Such unenlightened drawing of boundaries has created states described as "artificial" and "unnatural." See Rupert Emerson, "Nation-Building in Africa," in Karl W. Deutsch and William J. Foltz, *Nation-Building* (Chicago: Aldine Atherton Press, 1963), pp. 95-117; George P. Murdock, *Africa: Its Peoples and Their Cultural History* (New York: McGraw-Hill, 1959), and S.B. Jones, *Boundary-Making: A Handbook for Statesmen, Treaty Editors and Boundary Commissioners* (Washington: Carnegie Endowment for International Peace, 1945).

16. The following discussion of the politically disruptive results of social mobilization in African communal societies follows closely the arguments of the excellent article by Robert Melson and Howard Wolpe, "Modernization and the Politics of Communalism: A Theoretical Perspective," *American Political Science Review* 64 (December 1970): 1112-31.

17. The term "complimentarity of communications," refers to "the ability to communicate more effectively and over a wider range of subjects with members of one large group than with outsiders"; see Karl W. Deutsch, *Nationalism and Social Communication* (Cambridge: M.I.T. Press, 1953), p. 71.

18. Milton Gordon, *Assimilation in American Life* (New York: Oxford University Press, 1964), p. 39.

19. Fred G. Burke, *Africa's Quest for Order* (Englewood Cliffs, New Jersey: Prentice-Hall, Inc., 1964), p. 19.

20. Geertz, "The Integrative Revolution," p. 111.

21. Ibid.

22. Ibid.

23. Almond and Powell, *Comparative Politics*, p. 314. See also the essays on nation-building in Deutsch and Foltz, *Nation-Building*.

24. Myron Weiner, "Political Integration and Political Development," *The Annals of the American Academy of Political and Social Science* 358 (March 1965): 52-64. See also Leonard Binder, "National Integration and Political Development," *American Political Science Review* 58 (September 1964): 622-31; James S. Coleman and Carl G. Rosberg, Jr., eds., *Political Parties and National Integration in Africa* (Berkeley: University of California Press, 1964); Willard R. Johnson, *The Cameroon Federation: Political Integration in a Fragmentary Society* (Princeton: Princeton University Press, 1970); Astride R. Zolberg, "Mass Parties and National Integration: the Case of the Ivory Coast," *Journal of Politics* 25 (February 1963): 36-48; Rupert Emerson, "Nationalism and Political Development," *Journal of Politics* 22 (February 1960): 3-28; and _______, *From Empire to Nation: The Rise to Self-Assertion of Asian and African Peoples* (Cambridge: Harvard University Press, 1960).

25. Adelman and Taft Morris, *Society, Politics, and Economic Development*, p. 45, state: "In countries where the ties of most of the population are still 'primordial,' such as those of kin, tribe, and race, the creation of a national government is likely, for a time at least, to result in parallel and nonintegrated structures of authority: that is, on the one hand, a multiplicity of purely local traditional (often tribal) authorities and, on the other hand, a national political structure that lacks grass roots mechanisms for the articulation of local interests." In their factor analysis of the data for 27 African nations, they find that the loadings of two items, degree of ethnic and cultural homogeneity, and degree of national integration and sense of national unity, in factor four are both high and positive (0.84 and 0.79 respectively), p. 160.

In their listings of nations by types of cultural pluralism, Charles W. Anderson, et al., *Issues of Political Development* (Englewood Cliffs, New Jersey: Prentice-Hall, Inc., 1967), pp. 80-82, list nations by degree of cultural pluralism from "1" (homogeneous state) through "4" (multiplicity of culture). Eleven of the African nations in the present study rank "4"; three of them rank "3"; and two rank "2".

Similarly, Adelman and Taft Morris, *Society, Politics, and Economic Development*, pp. 41-44 and 54-56, list nine of the 16 nations in the lowest category of cultural and ethnic homogeneity. On their scale of degree of national integration and sense of national unity, which reflects degree of cultural and ethnic heterogeneity and communalism, they classify 11 of the 16 countries in the most extreme category of "marked absence" of national integration and unity.

26. David E. Apter, *Some Conceptual Approaches to the Study of Modernization* (Englewood Cliffs, New Jersey: Prentice-Hall, Inc., 1968), pp. 114-17 and passim. See also David E. Apter, *The Politics of Modernization* (Chicago: University of Chicago Press, 1965), ch. 3.

27. Apter, *Some Conceptual Approaches*, pp. 115-16.

28. Ibid., p. 117.

29. Ibid., p. 116.
30. Ibid., p. 117.
31. Melson and Wolpe, "Modernization and the Politics of Communalism," pp. 1114-15.
32. Anderson et al., *Issues of Political Development*, pp. 29-33; and Burke, *Africa's Quest for Order*, pp. 46-51.
33. Melson and Wolpe, "Modernization and the Politics of Communalism," pp. 1115-17.
34. The "need to achieve," a psychocultural concept, is offered by some as the reason for creating a receptivity to change on the part of those with such a need. Cf. David C. McClelland, *The Achieving Society* (Princeton: Van Nostrand, 1961); Everett E. Hagen, *On the Theory of Social Change* (Homewood, Illinois: Dorsey Press, 1962); Adelman and Taft Morris, *Society, Politics, and Economic Development*, pp. 49-51; and Robert A. LeVine, *Dreams and Deeds: Achievement Motivation in Nigeria* (Chicago: University of Chicago Press, 1965).
35. On the importance of "legitimacy" for the survival and success of a political system, see Seymour Martin Lipset, "Some Social Requisites of Democracy: Economic Development and Political Legitimacy," *American Political Science Review* 53 (March 1959): 69-105.
36. Melson and Wolpe, "Modernization and the Politics of Communalism," pp. 1120-21.
37. See Samuel P. Huntington, *Political Order in Changing Societies* (New Haven: Yale University Press, 1968), pp. 8-32.
38. Melson and Wolpe, "Modernization and the Politics of Communalism," p. 1122; and Huntington, *Political Order in Changing Societies*, pp. 32-72.
39. Weiner, "Political Integration and Political Development," p. 64.
40. Herbert J. Spiro, ed., *Africa, The Primacy of Politics* (New York: Random House, 1966), pp. 150-71, argues that what is most interesting and crucial in Africa is not the "politics of development," but the "development of politics," by which he means "the process by which a community deals with common problems that its members face and recognize . . . (and) an enlargement in the capacity of a political system to generate new goals and to expand and improve the formulation, deliberation, and resolution of issues," pp. 153-54.
41. Reinhold Niebuhr and Paul E. Sigmund, *The Democratic Experience* (New York: Frederick A. Praeger, Publishers, 1969), p. 107.

Chapter 7
The Near and Far Eastern Model of Liberal Democracy

1. This group of 16 nations does not, at first glance, appear to form as cohesive a geocultural region as the other three regions treated in this study.

However, there is substantial evidence to suggest that they do form a coherent region when compared to the rest of the nations of the world; that evidence is presented below.

2. Particularly noticeable in the Near and Far Eastern analysis is the contrast in the size of simple-correlation coefficients and beta coefficients for the relationships between urbanization and each of the four measures of liberal democracy. When the influence of the other four independent variables is held constant, and the impact of urbanization on liberal-democratic variables is measured in standardized terms, fairly large beta weights are produced.

3. This finding is clearly inconsistent with Lerner's assertion about the relationship between urbanization and education in the Middle East:

> Sheer density of population, without countervailing urbanization, operates in turn as an anti-literacy force in most societies. Education is cheaper when pupils live close together and hence, other things being equal, density should be associated with greater literacy. But, without urbanization, other things are *not* equal—i.e., the production, distribution, and consumption of wealth are much lower. This has a direct depressing effect on all public services, notably free public education. Dense nonurban societies, where national income is relatively small, tend to maintain relatively fewer schools by public funds; also, since per capita income is lower and less widely distributed, fewer individuals can afford to attend school.

Daniel Lerner, *The Passing of Traditional Society* (Glencoe: The Free Press, 1958), pp. 65-66.

4. Robert A. Dahl, *Polyarchy, Participation and Opposition* (New Haven: Yale University Press, 1971), pp. 53-56, explains the difference between a relatively undemocratic traditional peasant society and a relatively democratic free farmer society. The latter type of agrarian democracy is democratic because it has more widespread beliefs in equality, a greater degree of equality in the distribution of land, and a greater equality in the distribution of instruments of coercion (for example, guns), particularly with respect to an organized military with technological capabilities.

5. Irma Adelman and Cynthia Taft Morris, *Society, Politics and Economic Development* (Baltimore: Johns Hopkins Press, 1967), pp. 161 and 165-66, also concentrate on the Near and Far East as a cohesive geocultural region, and in fact their factor analysis results of economic development for this region markedly differ from the other regions they examine.

6. Bruce M. Russett, *International Regions and the International System* (Chicago: Rand McNally, 1967). See also Bruce M. Russett, "Homogeneous Regions," *Seadag Papers*, no. 4 (December 29, 1966).

7. Bruce Russett, et al., *World Handbook of Political and Social Indicators* (New Haven: Yale University Press, 1964).

8. Fully 25 variables are correlated with the economic-development factor at 0.50 or higher, many above 0.80. Among the higher positive loadings are GNP

per capita, newspapers per 1,000 population, nonagricultural workers as a percent of wage and salary earners, life expectancy, and radios per 1,000 population. Among the higher negative loadings are percent of labor force in agriculture, percent of GNP from agriculture, and inhabitants per hospital bed and per physician. Russett states: "It is remarkable, in fact, how high these correlations are for so many variables. Virtually any one of them would, by itself, form a reasonable measure of economic development. Together in this factor they account for 31% of the total variance of the table." Russett, "Homogeneous Regions," p. 4.

Loading high and negative on the second factor, communist influence, are the following variables: votes for communist parties, government expenditure as a percent of GNP, government revenue as a percent of GNP, GNP per capita annual increase, and votes as a percent of voting age population. Loading high and negative on this factor was noncommunist secular votes as a percent of all votes.

Factor three is called *in*tensive agriculture to contrast it with *ex*tensive agriculture, that is, it represents the method of cultivating the land designed to increase the productivity of a given area by the expenditure of more capital and labor upon it. Population density, population per hectare of agricultural land, and the ratio of foreign mail sent to foreign mail received load high and positive on this factor. Loading high and negative is inequality of farm land distribution. Russett explains the importance of this factor in the following manner: "One might call the dimension simply 'density' except for the fact that inequality of land distribution . . . is rather negatively correlated with it, emphasizing that in sparsely settled countries there are not only small family farms but a number of great estates as well. Though it is hard to find a perfect label, it is clear that a pattern of agriculture is the dimension at issue here, a pattern that may have important roots and consequences in the general structure of a society." Russett, "Homogeneous Regions."

The fourth factor, size, was considered not to be a cultural attribute of a nation-state and was therefore omitted from further analysis. Factor five is called Catholic culture, and the following variables were highly positively correlated with it: Roman Catholics as a percent of the population, and all Christians as a percent of the population. Among the higher negative correlates were socialist vote as a percent of all votes, Moslems as a percent of the population, television sets per 1,000 population, speakers of the dominant language as a percent of the population, and inequality of farm land distribution. About this factor, Russett says: "The dimension 'Catholic culture' is *not* identical with 'percentage Catholic' (the variable loading most highly on it). The correlation between the two is .87 which, though high, yields an r^2 of .76—thus the marker variable in this case explains only three quarters of the variance in the factor. The factor score is a *composite indicator* built up from a number of variables, in the tradition of a social science which seeks complex indices to measure complex phenomena. . . . 'Catholic culture' is a useful and descriptive label, but nevertheless an imperfect label for the underlying cultural dimensions being measured." Russett, "Homogeneous Regions," pp. 12-13.

9. Russett computed the matrix of sociocultural differences in the following manner. Each country has a standardized factor score on each factor or dimension, representing its value for each of the variables and their relative contribution to the dimension. For example, the United States had a +2.03 on the economic-development dimension, and Pakistan had a –2.06. Using these factor scores, Russett computed a matrix of "distance" of each country from each other country on each factor. The economic-development distance of the United States from Pakistan was 4.09. The combined distance for the four factors is the differences on each of the four factors summed. The formula for computing the index of cultural distance is: $Dij = \sqrt{\sum_{p=1}^{k} (Xip - Xjp)^2}$ where i and j are two nations, x_p the factor scores on factor p, and there are k factors. Russett, "Homogeneous Regions," p. 6.

10. Russett's Asia factor contains 14 of the nations of the Near and Far East as designated in the present study, plus Thailand, Morocco, Jordan, Iran, Haiti, Jamaica, Mauritius, and Algeria at or above a factor loading of 0.50. Egypt and Israel narrowly fall below this cutoff point.

11. The fourth factor, size, was dropped because it was not considered to be a *cultural* attribute of a nation-state.

12. On the economic-development factor, only Japan and Israel could be considered deviant cases, because they have moderate to high *positive* scores, indicating higher levels of economic development. Burma, Indonesia, and Israel are exceptions on the communism factor; they load moderately positively, rather than negatively. Burma, Tunisia, Iraq, and Syria are slightly deviant (negatively correlated) with regard to the intensive agriculture factor. The Philippines and Egypt are positive on the Catholic culture dimension and therefore exceptional cases.

13. For a discussion of the causes and consequences of communalism in the Asian context with reference to case material on specific countries, see Rene Peritz, *Changing Politics of Modern Asia* (New York: D. Van Nostrand Co., 1973), pp. 31-48.

14. Arthur S. Banks and Phillip M. Gregg, "Grouping Political Systems: Q-Factor Analysis of a Cross-Polity Survey," *American Behavioral Scientist* 9 (November 1965): 3-5. See also Phillip M. Gregg and Arthur S. Banks, "Dimensions of Political Systems: Factor Analysis of A Cross-Polity Survey," *American Political Science Review* 59 (September 1965): 555-78.

15. Arthur S. Banks and Robert B. Textor, *A Cross-Polity Survey* (Cambridge: MIT Press, 1963).

16. In fact, 24 of the 30 nations that loaded high on the elitist factor were

Black African nations where communalism is among the strongest social and cultural forces in politics.

17. Banks and Gregg, "Grouping Political Systems," p. 3.

18. Ibid., pp. 3-4.

19. Adelman and Taft Morris, *Society, Politics, and Economic Development*, p. 166, specifically discuss the nature of cultural resistance to various kinds of change in this geocultural region and, on the basis of their factor analyses, conclude that "in the Near and Far East economic growth is less critically hindered by traditional social structures than it is in Africa."

20. Banks and Gregg, "Grouping Political Systems."

21. The British legacy in India of parliamentary democracy and an effective civil service is treated in Krishan Bhatia, *The Ordeal of Nationhood, A Social Study of India Since Independence, 1947-1970* (New York: Atheneum, 1971), pp. 165-77; Vera Micheles Dean, *New Patterns of Democracy in India* (Cambridge: Harvard University Press, 1959); Sir Percival Griffiths, *Modern India* (New York: Frederick A. Praeger, Publishers, 1957), pp. 45-97; A.H. Hanson and Janet Douglas, *India's Democracy* (New York: W.W. Norton and Company, Inc., 1972), ch. 2; and Sidney D. Bailey, *Parliamentary Government in Southern Asia* (London: Hansard Society, 1953).

22. Ceylon inherited virtually the same kind of political apparatus from Britain as did India. For a description of the use of this political legacy early in Ceylonese independence, see W. Howard Wriggins, *Ceylon, Dilemmas of a New Nation* (Princeton: Princeton University Press, 1960), pp. 11-51 and 458-70; W. Howard Wriggins, "Development and Protest in Ceylon and South Asia," Occasional Paper Series, no. 1, Centre for Developing-Area Studies, McGill University, Toronto, 1968; S. Arasaratnam, *Ceylon* (Englewood Cliffs, N.J.: Prentice-Hall, 1964), pp. 124-73; and Sidney D. Bailey, *Ceylon* (London: University Library Series, 1952).

23. Israel's European bases are discussed in Leonard J. Fein, *Politics in Israel* (Boston: Little, Brown and Co., 1967), pp. 32-67; Lester G. Seligman, *Leadership in a New Nation, Political Development in Israel* (New York: Atherton Press, 1964), p. 38; and Gerald E. Caiden, *Israel's Administrative Culture* (Berkeley: Institute of Governmental Studies, 1970), pp. 10-20.

24. The discontinuity in Japanese political institutions in pre- and post-war times is documented in John M. Maki, *Government and Politics in Japan, The Road to Democracy* (New York: Frederick A. Praeger, Publishers, 1962), pp. 3-59; Robert A. Scalapino, "Environmental and Foreign Contributions, Japan," in Robert E. Ward and Dankwart A. Rustow, eds., *Political Modernization in Japan and Turkey* (Princeton: Princeton University Press, 1964), pp. 64-91; William W. Lockwood, "Economic and Political Modernization, Japan," in Ward and Rustow, *Political Modernization in Japan and Turkey*, pp. 146-76; Niranjan Bhuinya, *Parliamentary Democracy in Japan* (New Delhi: Harper and Row, Publishers, 1972), pp. 1-7; and Robert E. Ward, "Reflections on the Allied

Occupation and Planned Political Change in Japan," in Robert E. Ward, ed., *Political Development in Modern Japan* (Princeton: Princeton University Press, 1968), pp. 477-537.

25. The continuation of British colonial practices of parliamentary democracy in Malaysia is described in Richard Allen, *Malaysia, Prospect and Retrospect: The Impact and Aftermath of Colonial Rule* (London: Oxford University Press, 1968), pp. 6-79 and 274-86; Gordon P. Means, *Malaysian Politics* (London: University of London Press, 1970), pp. 42-68; and Robert O. Tilman, *Bureaucratic Transition in Malaya* (Durham: Duke University Press, 1964).

26. For a discussion of these influences in the Philippines, see Charles Burke Elliot, *The Philippines, A Study in Tropical Democracy* (New York: Greenwood Press, Publishers, 1968); David Wurfel, "The Philippines," in George McTurnan Kahin, ed., *Governments and Politics of Southeast Asia* (Ithaca: Cornell University Press, 1959), pp. 421-502; and Jean Grossholtz, *Politics in the Philippines* (Boston: Little, Brown and Co., 1964), ch. 7.

27. Turkey's rapid leap into modernization and Ataturk's role in it are described in Firouz Bahrampour, *Turkey: Political and Social Transformation* (Brooklyn: Theo. Gaus' Sons, Inc., 1967); Lord Kinross, *Ataturk* (New York: William Morrow and Co., 1965); Niyazi Berkes, *The Development of Secularism in Turkey* (Montreal: McGill University Press, 1964), pp. 431-507; and Kemal H. Karpat, *Turkey's Politics* (Princeton: Princeton University Press, 1959), ch. 3.

Chapter 8
Geocultural Regionalism, Political Traditions, and Cross-National Political Analysis

1. As will be discussed later in this concluding chapter, the basic Lerner and Lipset model of social mobilization and liberal democracy maximized parsimony and generality and minimized accuracy and causality. See Adam Przeworski and Henry Teune, *The Logic of Comparative Social Inquiry* (New York: John Wiley and Sons, 1970), pp. 17-23.

2. Hayward Alker, Jr., "Regionalism versus Universalism in Comparing Nations," in Bruce M. Russett, et al., eds., *World Handbook of Political and Social Indicators* (New Haven: Yale University Press, 1954), pp. 322-23. See also W.S. Robinson, "Ecological Correlations and the Behavior of Individuals," *American Sociological Review* 15 (June 1950): 351-57; Erwin K. Scheuch, "Cross-National Comparisons Using Aggregate Data: Substantive and Methodological Problems," in Richard L. Merritt and Stein Rokkan, eds., *Comparing Nations: The Use of Quantitative Data in Cross-National Research* (New Haven: Yale University Press, 1966); and Richard L. Merritt, *Systematic Approaches to Comparative Politics* (Chicago: Rand McNally and Company, 1970), pp. 13-16.

3. This conception of regionalism is particularly relevant to the problem of

"functional equivalence" of meanings in cross-national survey research. Cf. Merritt, *Systematic Approaches to Comparative Politics*, pp. 140-92; and Przeworski and Teune, *The Logic of Comparative Social Inquiry*, pp. 113-32.

4. Alker, "Regionalism versus Universalism," p. 336. See also Merritt, *Systematic Approaches to Comparative Politics*, pp. 51-56.

5. This interpretation of beta weights is closer to the traditional calculus interpretation than to that of statistics. See Robert L. Childress, *Calculus for Business and Economics* (Englewood Cliffs, N.J.: Prentice-Hall, 1972), pp. 88-135.

6. Ernest Barker, trans., *The Politics of Aristotle* (New York: Oxford University Press, 1958), p. 155.

7. In a report issued on April 16, 1974, the World Bank concluded that the gap between have and have-not countries will become even more exaggerated because of several new elements: the explosion of energy prices, the high prices of grains, the jump in the cost of fertilizer together with a shortage of supply, high prices of nonfood raw materials, and the prospect of a slowdown in the economies of the industrial countries in 1974-75. The World Bank estimated that $9 billion more is needed during 1974 just to maintain current levels of growth.

8. The African area known as the Sahel contains six countries whose futures are most certainly dismal and that simply may not be viable countries: Mauritania, Mali, Upper Volta, Niger, Chad, and Senegal (the Sudan might also be included). There drought and famine kill thousands annually.

9. The discussion of these fortunate conditions in Tanzania is drawn mainly from Lionel Cliffe, "The Political System," in Lionel Cliffe, ed., *One Party Democracy. The 1965 Tanzanian General Elections* (Nairobi: East African Publishing House, 1967), pp. 1-19; and Allison Butler Herrick, et al., *Area Handbook for Tanzania* (Washington, D.C.: United States Government Printing Office, 1968), pp. 1-89 and 93.

10. Herrick, *Area Handbook for Tanzania*, pp. 87-104.

11. Henry Bienen, *Tanzania. Party Transformation and Economic Development* (Princeton: Princeton University Press, 1970), pp. 43-48; Herrick, *Area Handbook for Tanzania*, pp. 90-92; and W.H. Whitely, "Swahili: The National Language of Tanzania," in K.E. Svendsen and Merete Teisen, eds., *Self-Reliant Tanzania* (Dar Es Salaam: Tanzanian Publishing House, 1969), pp. 111-19.

12. Bienen, *Tanzania*, pp. 21-22.

13. Cf. the following books by President Nyerere: *Ujamaa: The Basis of African Socialism* (Dar Es Salaam: Tanganyikan Standard, 1962); *Democracy and the Party System* (Dar Es Salaam: Tanganyikan Standard, 1963); *Freedom and Unity/Uhuru Na Ujamaa* (Dar Es Salaam: Oxford University Press, 1966); and *Freedom and Socialism/Uhuru Na Ujamaa* (Dar Es Salaam: Oxford University Press, 1968).

14. Herrick, *Area Handbook for Tanzania*, pp. 164-65; and Bienen, *Tanzania*, passim.

15. Herrick, *Area Handbook for Tanzania*, pp. 88-89.

16. For a discussion of early TANU development, see Bienen, *Tanzania*, pp. 50-73.

17. Bienen, *Tanzania*, pp. 73-259; _______, "The Ruling Party in a One-Party State: TANU in Tanzania" *Journal of Commonwealth Political Studies* V (November 1967): 214-30; Lionel Cliffe, "Socialist Transformation and Party Development," *African Political Review* 1 (October 1969); and Herrick, *Area Handbook for Tanzania*, pp. 217-30.

18. Bienen, *Tanzania*, pp. 3-19.

19. Herrick, *Area Handbook for Tanzania*, pp. 107 and 244. It might also be mentioned that TANU ordered all its candidates not to mention race, tribe, or religion, or to organize groups of supporters in the campaign for the 1956 general elections; they complied with that order. See Bienen, *Tanzania*, pp. 112-58.

20. Cliffe, "The Political System"; and Herrick, *Area Handbook for Tanzania*, p. 221.

21. Cliffe, "The Political System"; Herrick, *Area Handbook for Tanzania*, pp. 221-22; and Bienen, *Tanzania*, passim.

22. Cliffe, "The Political System"; Herrick, *Area Handbook for Tanzania*, p. 213; and Bienen, *Tanzania*, pp. 307-61.

23. Andrew J. Perry, "Politics in Tanzania," in Gabriel A. Almond, ed., *Comparative Politics Today. A World View* (Boston: Little, Brown and Company, 1974), pp. 426-28.

24. Cliffe, "The Political System."

25. Bienen, *Tanzania*, pp. 363-82.

26. Whitely, "Swahili," pp. 111-19.

27. K.E. Svendsen, "Problems and Conflicts of Political Life," in Svendsen and Teisen, *Self-Reliant Tanzania*, pp. 154-56.

28. Committee of Enquiry, "Official Report on the Co-operative Movement," in Svendsen and Teisen, *Self-Reliant Tanzania*, pp. 281-85.

29. Professor Michael Ford of the University of Massachusetts, who spent two years setting up several co-ops, has in personal conversations with the author generally confirmed these charges against the co-operative movement.

30. See Nyerere, *Ujamaa; Democracy and the Party System; Freedom and Unity; Freedom and Socialism.*

31. Julius K. Nyerere, "Ujamaa—The Basis of African Socialism," in Svendsen and Teisen, *Self-Reliant Tanzania*, p. 165. See also Nyerere, "Socialism and Rural Development," in Svendsen and Teisen, *Self-Reliant Tanzania*, pp. 246-47; and Bienen, *Tanzania*, pp. 203-59.

32. Julius K. Nyerere, quoted by Roger Lewin and Griffiths Cunningham, "The Prospects for Ujamaa Villages," in Svendsen and Teisen, *Self-Reliant Tanzania*, p. 273.

33. Several Latin American nations have overcome the divisiveness of com-

munalism partly through simply ignoring and isolating a substantial Indian population. Peru is an example.

34. Charles F. Andrain, *Political Life and Social Change* (Belmont, California: Duxbury Press, 1974), pp. 64-94.

35. Gabriel A. Almond and G. Bingham Powell, Jr., *Comparative Politics, A Developmental Approach* (Boston: Little, Brown and Company, 1967), pp. 207.

36. These are descriptive adjectives used in the world press as recorded by *Deadline Data.* In addition, the main features of the various reform policies and programs adopted by President Velasco are drawn from descriptions in press articles quoted in *Deadline Data* since 1968.

37. Alfred C. Stepan, *Authoritarian Brazil: Origins, Policies, and Future* (Princeton: Princeton University Press, 1973), pp. 47-57; Lyle N. McAlister, et al., *The Military in Latin American Socio-Political Evolution* (Washington: American Institute for Research, 1970), p. 7; and Luigi R. Einaudi, et al., *Latin American Perspectives in Peru and Brazil* (Santa Monica, California: Rand Corporation, 1971), p. 2.

38. Jane S. Jaquette, *The Politics of Development in Peru* (Ithaca: Cornell University Dissertation Series, 1971), p. 154.

39. Einaudi, *Latin American Perspective*, p. 29.

40. Jaquette, *The Politics of Development* p. 202.

41. These various programs are also summarized in David Scott Palmer, *Revolution From Above: Military Government and Popular Participation in Peru, 1968-72*, (Ithaca: Cornell University Dissertation Series, 1973); and David Scott Palmer and Kevin J. Middlebrook, "Corporativist Participation Under Military Rule in Peru," unpublished manuscript, n.d., pp. 36.

42. By January 1971, only about 18 months after the Agrarian Reform law took effect, the government announced that 66,000 families had already benefitted from the law and that another three million hectares of land would be distributed to 112,000 families during the next two years.

43. Prior to 1969, on the Gini Index of Land Distribution Inequality, Peru ranked highest of the 54 countries scored, with a value of 93.3. Only 0.3 percent of the farms comprised 50 percent of the total land holdings. Peru then ranked seventh of the 52 countries scored on a Gini Index of Sectoral Income Distribution Inequality. About 21 percent of the population had about 50 percent of the income. See Charles Lewis Taylor and Michael N. Hudson, *World Handbook of Political and Social Indicators, Second Edition* (New Haven: Yale University Press, 1972), pp. 263 and 267.

44. Palmer, *Revolution from Above*, p. 3.

45. One wonders if President Velasco had read Karl W. Deutsch's article in the *American Political Science Review*, "Social Mobilization and Political Development"!

46. Palmer and Middlebrook, "Corporativist Participation Under Military Rule," pp. 5-8.

47. Republica Peruano, Presidencia de la Republica, Institute Nacional de Planificacion, *Plan Nacional Desarrollo para 1971-1975, Plan Global*, vol. I, July 1971, pp. 31-32; quoted in Palmer and Middlebrook, "Corporativist Participation Under Military Rule," p. 5.

48. Palmer and Middlebrook, "Corporativist Participation Under Military Rule," p. 3; and Palmer, *Revolution from Above*, p. 30. Citizens of Peru also have access to several escape mechanisms through which to bypass institutionalized channels of participation: protest marches, land invasions, strikes, presentation of petitions directly to the president or ministers, occupation of factories, and organized violence.

49. Palmer, *Revolution from Above*, p. 12; and Palmer and Middlebrook, "Corporativist Participation Under Military Rule," p. 29.

50. Palmer, *Revolution from Above*, p. 31. It is not difficult to imagine that the ultimate outcome of the April 25, 1974 military coup in Portugal will be a substantially more liberal and socialist regime than that of the two previous premiers, Marcell Caetano and A.O. Salazar. Although it is too early to be sure, initial signs are that the Spinola military regime has allowed Portuguese labor unions to form labor confederation; allowed communists to participate in the new provisional government cabinet; allowed the previously suppressed political parties to surface and organize for possible opposition; established some freedom of press and expression by acquitting two women accused of publishing a book offending public morals by attacking repression of women's rights in Portugal; destroyed former Premier Caetano's secret police and their methods; and called for release of all political prisoners, free elections within a year, freedom of the press, and a representative National Assembly. See "A Genteel Coup in Portugal," *Newsweek* (May 6, 1974): 32-34.

51. Palmer, *Revolution from Above.*

Index

Index

About the Author

Philip Coulter is Senior Political Scientist at the Center for Population Research and Services of the Research Triangle Institute in Research Triangle Park, North Carolina. Previously he was an associate professor of political science at the University of Massachusetts at Amherst and a visiting lecturer at the Institute of Social Studies in The Hague, the Netherlands. Dr. Coulter received the Ph.D. in political science in 1966 from the State University of New York in Albany. His main research interests include comparative politics, political development, and population policy. He has contributed articles to *Polity, International Journal of Comparative Sociology, Development and Change, Western Political Quarterly*, and other scholarly journals.